IN DEFENCE OF THEATI.＿

Aesthetic Practices and Social Interventions

Edited by
Kathleen Gallagher and Barry Freeman

Why theatre now? Reflecting on the mix of challenges and opportunities that face theatre in communities that are necessarily becoming global in scope and technologically driven, *In Defence of Theatre* offers a range of passionate reflections on this important question.

Kathleen Gallagher and Barry Freeman bring together nineteen playwrights, actors, directors, scholars, and educators who discuss the role that theatre can – and must – play in professional, community, and educational venues. Stepping back from their daily work, they offer scholarly research, artists' reflections, interviews, and creative texts that argue for theatre as a response to the political and cultural challenges emerging in the twenty-first century. Contributors address theatre's power as an antidote to various modern social ailments, its contribution to local and global politics of place, and its pursuit of social justice. Of equal concern are the systematic and practical challenges that confront those involved in realizing theatre's full potential.

KATHLEEN GALLAGHER is Distinguished Professor at the Ontario Institute for Studies in Education, University of Toronto.

BARRY FREEMAN is Assistant Professor and Program Director of Theatre and Performance Studies in the Department of Art, Culture, and Media at the University of Toronto Scarborough.

In Defence of Theatre

Aesthetic Practices and Social Interventions

EDITED BY KATHLEEN GALLAGHER
AND BARRY FREEMAN

To Joe —
Here we are, defending
as we do ... because
it matters, now more
than ever
In solidarity —
Kath

UNIVERSITY OF TORONTO PRESS
Toronto Buffalo London

© University of Toronto Press 2016
Toronto Buffalo London
www.utppublishing.com
Printed in Canada

ISBN 978-1-4426-3079-6 (cloth)   ISBN 978-1-4426-3080-2 (paper)

Library and Archives Canada Cataloguing in Publication

In defence of theatre : aesthetic practices and social interventions / edited by
Kathleen Gallagher and Barry Freeman.

Includes bibliographical references and index.
ISBN 978-1-4426-3079-6 (bound).   ISBN 978-1-4426-3080-2 (paperback)

1. Theater and society. 2. Theater – Political aspects. 3. Aesthetics.
I. Gallagher, Kathleen, 1965–, author, editor   II. Freeman, Barry, 1977–,
author, editor

PN2049.I54 2016   792   C2015-906627-1

University of Toronto Press acknowledges the financial assistance to its
publishing program of the Canada Council for the Arts and the Ontario Arts
Council, an Ontario government agency.

Canada Council   Conseil des Arts
for the Arts   du Canada

ONTARIO ARTS COUNCIL
CONSEIL DES ARTS DE L'ONTARIO
an Ontario government agency
un organisme du gouvernement de l'Ontario

Funded by the   Financé par le
Government   gouvernement
of Canada   du Canada | Canadä

Contents

Part V: Why Theatre Always

Acknowledgments

We would like to acknowledge the assistance of two graduate students, Dirk Rodericks and Meredeth Heyland, in helping us assemble the manuscript for this book. Our thanks as well to our generous contributors, and to the artists who work daily to make theatre matter for all of us.

IN DEFENCE OF THEATRE

Aesthetic Practices and Social Interventions

Introduction: Taking a Step Back

BARRY FREEMAN AND KATHLEEN GALLAGHER

Why theatre now? This is the question we put to the contributors of our book. It's an audacious question. In our daily struggles to meet the competing demands of life and work, the time it takes to ponder such deeper questions is often scarce. In particular, artists who make the theatre their vocation are often strapped for time: they have to finish that grant or self-publicize their latest project, and typically must balance multiple jobs to make ends meet. This book is our small attempt to create an opportunity for a group of artists, educators, and scholars to take a step back from the noise of everyday challenges and the exigencies of survival to ask not what they are doing but why they are doing it.

We challenged the contributors to this book to think about whether there is something special about theatre now. What are the virtues and values of theatre and performance that are, if not unique, at least especially important today? And our *why* question has a *where*, we have asked it of a set of accomplished and experienced individuals who mainly work in Canada. While many contributors speak of practices taking place in this country, we encouraged them not to think about what makes *Canadian* theatre matter, but what makes theatre itself matter, with Canada serving as a grounded site for analysis. For us, any totalizing idea of a "regional" or "national" framework for theatre is increasingly hard to articulate in our globalized and globalizing world, undermined by such trends as the touring of theatre through festival circuits, co-productions between differently located organizations, and artists whose work is taken up across the country and beyond. This complexity is illustrated by our contributors' many interregional and international connections in their theatre work and scholarship. This widening of scope is itself another reason for our contributors to "take a step back" to reflect on the "now," to philosophize rather than complain. We wanted contributors to paint portraits of lives in the theatre within the swirling, confusing, globalizing, technologizing, expanding, and shrinking world of twenty-first-century modernity.

The title of the book – *In Defence of Theatre* – seems to presume some kind of threat, some moment of "crisis" either in the theatre or in the wider conditions for cultural and artistic production in Canada. In a recent opinion piece for the *New York Times*, Gary Gutting notes that "crisis" and "decline" are the "words of the day in discussions of the Humanities," citing the startling statistic that only 8 per cent of undergraduates major in the humanities.[1] Terry Eagleton, writing in the *Guardian* with similar alarm, argues that "there is no university without humane inquiry, which means that universities and advanced capitalism are fundamentally incompatible," but he equally submits that a university without the humanities is a mere training facility or corporate research institute, as it would lose its most distinguishing feature:

> To preserve a set of values and ideas under siege, you needed among other things institutions known as universities set somewhat apart from everyday social life. This remoteness meant that humane study could be lamentably ineffectual. But it also allowed the humanities to launch a critique of conventional wisdom.[2]

Though the statistics are less bleak in Canada,[3] decreased funding and administrative slimming threatens the humanities, with the University of Alberta suspending admission to 20 of its humanities programs in 2013 because of cuts, which included one of its theatre programs.[4] In a 2015 address to a panel on the future of the humanities, University of Alberta English professor Stephen Slemon spoke even of a blossoming "Humanities Crisis Industry" and urged his audience not to let the "master narrative" of crisis become an unquestionable justification for radical cuts to the humanities.[5]

One of our observations from working with the authors of this book, deeply embedded as they are in the study of human culture, is that – with apologies to Terry Eagleton – their version of a reanimated humanities seems to be powerfully embedded in expressions of local culture, not at a remove, but launching their own critiques of conventional wisdom from inside the concerns of everyday social life. They have taken the speculative and critical stances of traditional humanities studies to make very local, and in some cases almost empirical, applications. Across chapters, the reader will see a clear emphasis on local companies, local artists, local venues, and local publics, rather than national or global preoccupations. One of the results, then, in inviting artists and scholars of theatre to consider the value of theatre in this moment has been our discovery of how critical perspectives available to them through an up-close, often documentary-like look at local manifestations of culture has reimagined an embedded, not a remote, form of humanities scholarship and artistic practice.

Nonetheless, the discourse of crisis in the humanities persists. It looms over the professional theatre as well; knives come out at any indication of setback or decline, such as when *Globe and Mail* theatre critic J. Kelly Nestruck recently interpreted falling audience numbers at the Stratford Festival a "serious existential crisis."[6] It is true that there are some indications that filling large venues has become more difficult (if, in fact, this was ever "easy" in Canada). In 2012 it was announced that the Vancouver Playhouse Theatre would close, threatening to shift to Canada the trend observed in the United States towards "right-sizing" theatres to better fit the actual demand. Also in 2012, the David Mirvish–Frank Gehry King Street West development in Toronto was set to replace the Princess of Wales Theatre with a condo development with 2,600 units in towers rising to 85 storeys, a new benchmark for the city and among the tallest in North America. After some pushback from the community, the designers capitulated and produced a revised design, scaling the project down and saving the Princess of Wales. Still, the episode illustrates that an old-fashioned theatre building is challenged to compete with this level of development energy and so-called "starchitecture." As Michael McKinnie's excellent study of theatrical and urban development in Toronto illustrates, cities in Canada and around the globe are in a new "now" in which the spaces of cultural production and reception are changing with as-yet-undetermined social and artistic practices and theatre landscapes.[7]

The question "Why theatre now" is also being asked in the many post-secondary drama and theatre-training programs across Canada, most of which have inadequate resources and faculty complements and which live a precarious existence in an era of cuts to public education. In May 2013, when Calgary's Mount Royal University decided to suspend its diploma-granting theatre program, a program that has produced many professional stage actors, the theatre community shivered, wondering whether it would be the first among others to face the axe.[8] While a string of closures has not followed, the constant threat has many educators, academics, and artists alike thinking about the most fundamental justifications for a theatre education today. For instance, a recent issue of *Canadian Theatre Review* on the theme of "Actor Training in a Changing Landscape" collected discussions among teachers and students about various problems with training: a lack of intellectual rigour, insufficient physical training, and a lack of cultural or aesthetic diversity of approaches, to name a few. But the issue's editors, David Fancy and Diana Belshaw, premised the whole exercise on a belief that "actors can – in the best of circumstances – serve an integral role in the imagining and execution of the stories we tell ourselves and by which we come to understand ourselves both individually and collectively."[9] Just as we are aspiring to do with our own volume, the discussions at points rise above the practical challenges to frame the problem in larger, philosophical terms. In a discussion about aesthetic diversity in actor training, for instance, the co-artistic director of Halifax's Zuppa Theatre Company Alex McLean asks, "What is it to be a performer or theatre company in 2014? What else is happening? ... How are people provoking or challenging each other and playing with the art form through training and new work, and what is your part in that?"[10] For McLean, as for us, theatre requires a vigilant and ongoing reckoning with urgent demands of the "now."

In that spirit, it is important for us to say at the outset that we conceived of this book as a positive and constructive reflection on the "now" of Canadian theatre. It is not that we are naive about the threats – there are political and ideological attacks to fend against, today as ever – but rather that we choose to see in this pressurized cultural moment an opportunity to reflect upon what it is that makes theatre exciting and worthwhile in this time and place. In many times and places in human history theatre has been a vital and popular place of celebration and debate. While the formal practices of the professional theatre arguably occupy a diminished role in public life in Canada today, this is partly owing to theatre's successful sublimation into other forms of performance throughout modern culture in an ever more crowded and high-quality field of activity of cultural production. Other mechanisms of consuming and producing culture are increasingly available in sophisticated forms without one having to leave the household. A 2011 Ontario Arts Council survey of public engagement in the arts found that while 99 per cent of respondents reported participating in some kind of activity related to music or visual arts at least once per year (activities that included listening to music or taking photographs "with artistic intentions"), the figure was only 64 per cent for live theatre (with only 8 per cent participating in theatre once per month).[11] Judith Thompson muses in this book at what a wonder it is that audiences go "out into the cold or the heat and [sit] in hard seats for up to three hours," and Ann-Marie MacDonald, similarly, that audiences have "carved out an evening" or "paid a babysitter." Of course, as several of our contributors argue from different perspectives, the need for presence in theatre, the need to *be there*, however inconvenient, may be among the things that make it so valuable.

And if changes in media and technology have made the landscape of cultural activities more competitive, they have at the same time injected new possibilities into the art form and enabled new forms of audience interaction. Dustin Harvey's descriptions in this volume of his work in Nova Scotia are a testament to the kinds of new theatrical and social relationships that may be forged with the help of technology and a roaming imagination about the possibilities for presence and connection. Any greater competition for resources in Canadian theatre can be read as the industry becoming a victim of its own success insofar as many new independent theatre companies have arisen all over the country – and not just in the large cities – which are creating exciting new work and are often collaborating with established theatres to bring in more diverse audiences. Theatre festivals, once considered "fringe," are now very well attended and have become important indicators of the burgeoning field, heralding new works and new partnerships. While government support remains crucial for the sector, companies are securing support through crowdsourcing and partnering with like-minded organizations in ways that can build community and enrich the work.

Another exciting dimension of theatre practice in Canada today is an expanded mandate for public education, well beyond the old-style education departments within theatre companies that mainly concerned themselves with marketing activities and sales. Now, in both small and larger projects, privileging the position of education as well as paying attention to the important ways in which theatre can engage in broader forms of public pedagogy are increasingly an essential part of the mandate of theatre artists and companies. While it may be true that college and university programs are also pressured, in such a climate, to take in and graduate more students than the professional industry can employ, the fact of there being strong interest in a theatre education is only a good indicator for the art, and those who don't go into the profession apply the skills they acquired elsewhere. If we take seriously Laura Levin's plea in this collection for an education in theatre that embraces an ever-wider conception of performance and its place in our social lives, this kind of stretch across disciplinary boundaries and silos of understanding, for all its disruptions, is also a clear sign of cultural and educational growth.

Taking a longer view, theatre has also been around for as long as human history and has endured its share of crises. It has continually changed form, popped up in new places, and found new air to breathe. In all times and places, it seems to have appealed to basic human needs: to gather and share, to laugh or cry, to argue or persuade, to honour or ridicule. For millennia, it has been an important ethical forum for us to rehearse our actions, to think about why we do what we do, to make concrete and available for public discussion those forces that move around and within us. Both Julie Salverson and Ann-Marie MacDonald talk in this book about the power of witnessing in theatre, and Judith Thompson seizes upon the concept of characters who "howl" in the theatre to be heard by a witnessing audience. This rich tradition didn't begin with the ancient Greeks or Egyptians, nor with the Indigenous peoples of North America or elsewhere; it dates back tens of thousands of years when we were spread thinly around the world in the few thawed areas of a glaciated globe. In his book *Palaeoperformance*, Yann-Pierre Montelle surveys the current anthropological and archaeological research and makes a convincing case that prehistoric humans enjoyed their own kind of social theatricality, some of it in caves. And these were not peripheral, incidental activities for ancient humans – subsistence was probably far too demanding for the purely frivolous – but essential components of the social life of the family and community. What we think of as "cave art," Montelle argues, was not really what we think of in the modern period as art – purely aesthetic – but was a mnemonic repository of experience, "information sharing."[12] Though interpreting Neolithic art involves much inference and speculation, there is evidence to suggest that these practices were not art for art's sake but "pedagogical and initiatory."[13]

Montelle's argument speaks to us for another reason as well. When we, as editors, had our own discussion about the question, a subject we kept returning to over and over was the so-called "social turn," a term which signals a special emphasis in theatrical practice, scholarship, and education on the social dynamics of how theatre is created and experienced. This broad movement, visible across artistic disciplines and arguably under way for decades, is the focus of Shannon Jackson's book *Social Works: Performing Art, Supporting Publics.*[14] In it, Jackson argues for a perspective that considers the social dynamics of art to be as important as its aesthetic qualities; "What if," she writes, "the formal parameters of the form include the audience relation, casting such inter-subjective exchange, not as the extraneous context that surrounds it, but as the material of performance itself?"[15] Montelle's *Palaeoperformance* would have us believe the social turn is a social *return* and that the social ends of art have never been far away from the aesthetic.

As explored in chapters in this volume by Dustin Scott Harvey, Nicholas Hanson, Edward Little, and Barry Freeman, the social turn is also becoming a way for theatre to shake free of a purely consumerist, transactional model of exchange and to experiment with grass-roots, community-based practices involving participatory engagements with audiences – if "audience" remains the right word at all. One term for this is "vernacular culture," which Clarke Mackey explains in his book *Random Acts of Culture* comprises four features: that to experience it, you "had to be there"; that it deals in ritualistic repetition but not economies of mass replication; that it shirks professional virtuosity and institutionalized divisions and norms of labour, engagement, and critique in favour of wide participation; and that it is not for sale.[16] Like us, Mackey does not advance a single theory with his book but explores what he sees as a broad shift in values that can breathe new life into mainstream arts practices. "Museums, arts councils, broadcasters, and universities must respond and evolve in response to an increase in vernacular practices," he writes. "Social resources will need to be committed to nourish the growth of grassroots culture."[17] When we invited artists and scholars to consider the place and the purpose of theatre at this historical moment in our increasingly globalized world, every contributor, without exception, turned to and drew from local stories, local places, our vernacular, and quotidian life.

Post-structuralism as a movement in literature and art has also urged a seeing of the performance of the everyday and the "spectatorship" of our normal experience, a subject explored in Laura Levin's chapter in this book on the value of performance as a mobile critical paradigm. While some have worried about the tendency to apply the language of theatre and performance to all kinds of cultural practices that may not have much to do with the discipline of theatre,[18] the explosion of forms of documentary theatre in recent years might, for instance, signal a modern interest in seeing social life in dramaturgical terms, and not simply satirizing social life through theatre as classical playwrights may have done. This interpenetration of performance and "real life" may point to a contemporary appetite for a poetics of theatre and public life. Such a sensibility may also explain the tendency we have noted in the theatre of the now – today's theatre – to eschew the universal in favour of saying something specific, in a site-specific place and time. For those of the view that globalization has a homogenizing effect on culture, theatre invested in localism and particularity may present an important antidote.

An additional realization of the intersection of performance and "real life" is the turn towards autobiographical narratives that are discussed in many of our chapters. In her recent book *Performing Autobiography: Contemporary Canadian Drama,* Jenn Stephenson argues that autobiography "is always a fictional construction, featuring an inescapable gap between the real-world referent and its fictional twin,"[19] later cleverly accounting for this gap by adopting the term "autofiction."[20] Another thread of Stephenson's argument is the evolution of our twenty-first-century cultural taste for consuming autobiography across the social sciences, humanities, and the arts, not to mention the Internet and all its permutations of self-documentation. The Canadian theatre pieces explored in this book clearly exemplify the interesting ways in which autobiographical performance "acts as a catalyst not only to revisit but also to revise and reinvent," whether these reinventions are made by actors, professional or amateur, depicting others' "real" lives (Kushnir, Maxwell, Harvey, Salverson, Keleta-Mae) or their own (Gallagher, Little, Thompson).[21]

We found several of these trends demonstrated in a June 2013 co-production in Toronto appreciated by both of us and co-created by, among others, several artists featured in this volume: Julie Tepperman, Aaron Willis, Alan Dilworth, and Andrew Kushnir. American playwright Sarah Ruhl's *Passion Play,* a three-act, nearly four-hour epic, was co-produced in a Toronto east-end park and at Eastminster United Church by Toronto independent companies Outside the March, Convergence Theatre, and Sheep No Wool along with the older Crow's Theatre, who together assembled a 35-member cast and crew (*Figure 0.1*). The play follows communities from Elizabethan England to 1930s Bavaria to mid-1980s South Dakota as they attempt to stage the story of Christ's crucifixion. In an interview with the *Globe and Mail,* director Alan Dilworth explains, "It's like slow food. In terms of our relationship with food now in North America, like, everyone's a foodie, and I want to create a world where everyone's into a slow kind of the theatre."[22]

The run of the show also included an afternoon talk with Sarah Ruhl, who came from New York to see the show and to have a public chat with Toronto playwright Julie Tepperman of Convergence Theatre before a packed audience at Toronto's Tarragon Theatre. With the fundraising events prior to the show, the near-sold-out run of the show, and the public education event staged mid-run, this is a fine example of contemporary co-productions and crowdsourcing. Staged in June between the end of the traditional theatre season and the start of the summer festival season, it was a border-crossing, global, and yet deeply local and

0.1 Julie Tepperman, Andrew Kushnir, and Mayko Nguyen in *Passion Play* by Sarah Ruhl (June 2013, Toronto). Photo by Keith Barker.

grass-roots event illustrating so much of what is "now" about theatre in Canada and why it is so very capable of competing with other emerging forms of culture. It was a piece that got people talking, about here and about other times and places, and about theatre as a meeting place for ideas and deliberation. Dilworth got what he hoped for: a slow theatre experience that had people longing for more.

One of the other pressures on the theatre of now, today's theatre, has been understood by many cultural critics as the neo-liberal imperative of utility, on what the arts can *do* for the economy, for social issues, for national narratives, and so on. Kathleen Gallagher, Julie Salverson, Judith Thompson, Julie Tepperman and Aaron Willis, and Andrew Kushnir all observe this trend in their chapters. This framework of unrelenting accountability, most pronounced in the arena of Applied Theatre, has made incursions into all kinds of theatre programming as the pressure to secure grants by illustrating the "effects" of theatre increases. Such a tendency has led to a renewed focus on the "affects" of theatre, as writers like James Thompson are concerned that this pervasive "concentration on social utility is in danger of abandoning the terrain of sensation."[23] Thompson's concerns are especially relevant to the study and research of theatre where, he argues, "people become clients, theatre workshops inputs, and performances are outcomes."[24] Sharing Thompson's defence of the often overlooked but significant qualities of affect in theatre is Erin Hurley, who summarizes straightforwardly in her recent work, "the affect-producing machine of theatre lets us know that we are (by letting us feel that we are here)."[25] The "affective turn," as it is commonly called – that is, theatre and forms of social life that privilege our senses, our emotions, and our social relations – has led to a burgeoning of new theoretical bodies of work now commonly applied to the scholarly study of theatre. The affective turn represents a demand for a different kind of engagement with theatre. Clough's understanding of affect calls out to the human capacity for action, an engagement that is alive and vital and embodied.[26] This movement, in the age of calibration and measureable outcomes, struggles to ensure that the sensory processes and feelings of theatre are not lost.

In our discussions about this particular quality of a push and pull between cognitive engagement and bodily/sensorial experience, we have found ourselves wondering whether yet another contemporary concern of theatre – a focus on the place of ethics and social justice – may in fact be driving this oscillation between meaning and affect. Of course these are not especially new categories; they were certainly evident in Brecht's "theatre for pleasure" and "theatre for instruction" dichotomy. But Thompson's project importantly rethinks this familiar and overplayed binary by insisting that "meaning culture" or the act of interpretation is itself a stratum of affect. According to Thompson, the word "affect" is designed to disturb the opposition suggested by the term's efficacy and entertainment.[27] It is certainly the case that occurrences of learning in the theatre are as much felt as they are cognitive experiences. This was likely always the case, but the affective turn in theatre, like the social turn, has usefully clouded such easy distinctions.

For most of the writers of our collection, "Why theatre now?" has been taken to point towards what *distinguishes* theatre now from theatre always, although some imagined a continuity between past and present. From discussions with our contributors, we identified five broad themes around which we have structured the book. The first, "A Politics of Place in a Global Age," finds in theatre a new politics of place, whether a local one rooted in communities and neighbourhoods, or whether expanded to address distant geographies and people. Barry Freeman enlists Bertolt Brecht as a guide in thinking through how theatre may work to defamiliarize the aggressive influence of twenty-first-century neo-liberal globalization. He finds in Debajehmujig Storytellers' *The Global Savages* project an example of how theatre is today not called just to represent the world, but to model alternative ways of living within it. In his chapter, Dustin Harvey discusses the motivations behind a series of shows produced by his company Secret Theatre, first in Halifax and later in locations across the country and internationally. For Harvey, working from a part of the country still beset by outmigration, theatre may be a means to further root us in place, building "an honest sense of intimacy, connection, and locality." In the final chapter of this section, Ted Little finds in his community-based work a number of opportunities arising from the local: the possibility to build consensus, to use local resources to "speak truth to power," and for individuals to commune or reckon with the larger society, and he considers both the rewards and the risks that obtain in the work. By discussing performance that operates at local and global levels simultaneously, the three authors of this section refute what Doreen Massey calls the "victimhood of globalization discourse" that sees local communities and individuals as helpless agents in an unchangeable, alienating world.[28]

Each of the pieces grouped together within the second theme, "Antidote for an Ailing Modernity," points to a different modern social or cultural malaise – for example, the ravages of disenfranchisement, the forces of distraction, or obsessions with consumption – and imagines how theatre provides an antidote. The first two chapters of this section both draw from the play *The Middle Place* by Andrew Kushnir, and in their different ways signal the power of metaphor and the central idea of a play's relationship to its audience. While Kathleen Gallagher is looking specifically at the binary of affect/effect in the theatre, Andrew Kushnir invites the reader into his play-making process and how he imagines a work's relationship to its audiences. Gallagher positions her ethnographic research with young people who engaged with *The Middle Place* against a wider "audit culture" insistent on immediately quantifiable results. She uses examples from her research to argue for the subtler ways that affect and presence work on theatre audiences, which serve to expand our understanding of what counts as "political" in the theatre. Kushnir deftly takes on the ubiquitous discourse of theatre as a "humanizing force" and offers fresh insights about what it is "we" may be craving by being together and what the theatre might be offering us through its rituals of stillness and silence. Alan Dilworth, in his chapter, makes the case for a rich, poetic language in today's theatre as a counter-discourse in "our age of the sound bite, partisan political campaigning, partisan policy making, and spectacle reportage." This section is rounded out by a short and foreboding original play by Catherine Banks, who shares with readers a playwriting process that relies on inspiration from the overheard conversations of strangers: "[W]e can take the measure of our humanity through the world of the play as we (safely) watch how the characters speak to and treat each other."

Our third section, "(En)Gendering Change," concerns gender in terms of the continuing challenge of achieving equal professional opportunity, but also in terms of how theatre might subvert limiting or harmful conceptions of gender. In a candid interview, Jackie Maxwell reflects on her role as the first woman to serve as artistic director of the Shaw Festival and what that company's enhanced mandate, and her own artistic choices, says to a contemporary audience interested in questions of gender. Maxwell's concrete examples from her experience at Shaw give the reader context for the values she puts forward as important in the "now"; in her own words, "here's a point of view about a time in the world." Naila Keleta-Mae takes a close look at Lorena Gale's play *Angelique* and asks us to consider how dominant epistemes and cherished national and historical narratives have influenced experiences of female blackness and how these are destabilized by a theatre that contests a past and reimagines a present. In her poignant chapter, Julie Salverson takes drama to men in military service and wonders what new thinking about gender becomes possible in such an unlikely encounter. Bringing Queen's University drama students and military men together for an exceptional experience of storytelling and performance, she concludes that "[t]heatre is vital in a profoundly damaged world in danger of disappearing itself."

The fourth section, "Breaking Down Barriers," takes a more prosaic approach by discussing the systematic and practical challenges that confront artists, educators, and academics alike in realizing theatre's full potential. Laura Levin suggests that we need to take more seriously the challenge posed to theatre by the idea of "performance." To do so would help break down disciplinary boundaries in schools and in the industry but also would take advantage of how ubiquitous the paradigm of "performance" has become in public life, including in social media and in politics. Nicholas Hanson confronts the oft-cited observation that theatre audiences are "aging" and considers which specific strategies in communication and programming will make theatre matter for the so-called millennial generation. From Julie Tepperman and Aaron Willis, the co-artistic directors of Toronto's Convergence Theatre company, we get the perspective on the value of theatre in the "now" from two busy working theatre artists. Offering their thoughts in the form of a dialogue, Tepperman and Willis enumerate some of the structural and institutional problems they encounter on a daily basis, in the face of which they have had to become "necessary producers" of their own work. In his chapter, James McKinnon discusses *Are We There Yet?*, a sexual education theatre project that he finds to be a model for how theatre can transcend its usual disciplinary modes to be of value in engaging publics beyond the arts. Rounding out the section is an interview with mathematician and playwright John Mighton, who makes the case for dissolving intellectual boundaries especially between the arts and sciences and who finds in theatre a way to creatively reveal new and unexpected truths.

In our final section, "Why Theatre Always," the authors wrestle with contemporary and historical understandings of, and desires for, theatre. Judith Thompson offers a profoundly personal glimpse into her career as a playwright, which she describes as her own "form of revolution." Through this eloquent account of how theatre has always "lurched [her] into life," she makes the simple case that "[m]aybe, sometimes, an act of theatre can show that human life matters." In a lively interview with Ann-Marie MacDonald, we learn of an almost sacred relationship with an audience and a drive to make stories that sequence an otherwise chaotic, alienating existence. In an era of mass communication, she insists that "sequencing and patterning are very, very deep within us and fractured images and accelerated image-making can't feed that, can't answer that hunger and that need." This final section is rounded out with an evocative poem and rumination by Daniel David Moses. The poem is a fitting conclusion to the collection for us because its micro examination of a moment of performance turns the perspective out to the audience, which in the poem has its own "hunger" for the stage, with "[m]ouths so alive in the darkness."

Taking this all together, it would seem that theatre is experiencing a reimagining for a new age. Whether the authors of these chapters found a purpose for theatre that is timeless or new, each of them invites you, the reader, into the expansive dreams and everyday concerns of working artists and scholars in Canada now. We have endeavoured to gather diverse voices for our collection with regard to scholars and artists, men and women, and regional representation across the country, though our priority was to solicit quality meditations on the significant matters that shape our contributors' projects in the theatre. While we have a larger number of contributions from Central and urban areas of the country reflecting on primarily Anglophone work, we would note that there is some "hidden diversity" among these voices that demonstrates the expansive and expanding profile of Canadian theatre artists beyond their "home" location. For example, a number of Ontario-based artists, such as Judith Thompson, Daniel David Moses, and Ann-Marie MacDonald, have their work produced across the country and themselves are engaged in collaborations that take them beyond their home context in keeping with the wider globalizing of Canadian theatre practices. James McKinnon did his graduate training in Ontario but is now a lecturer at the University of Victoria in Wellington, New Zealand, and his chapter discusses a project created in Alberta that toured across Canada. Our contributors' geographical diversity is matched by the diversity of forms and styles in which they chose to answer our question. The reader will find scholarly arguments, artist reflections, interviews, and creative contributions sitting side-by-side in this book. The diversity of styles reflects the vast diversity of experience among the writers but also our wish to let chapters about deeply rooted values and aims find expression in the appropriate genre. The variety, we feel, celebrates the creative, philosophical, and playful impulses that naturally emerge when asking a passionate group of educators and artists to take a step back and consider what most makes their work worthwhile. We hope that you find, as we have, some galvanizing sense of purpose in these pages, some new reasons to take the next steps forward.

NOTES

1 Gary Gutting, "The Real Humanities Crisis," *Opinionator: New York Times*, 20 November 2013, http://opinionator.blogs.nytimes.com/2013/11/30 /the-real-humanities-crisis.

2 Terry Eagleton, "The Death of Universities," *Guardian*, 17 December 2014, http://www.theguardian.com/commentisfree/2010/dec/17 /death-universities-malaise-tuition-fees.

3 "Trends in Higher Education Volume 1: Enrolment," Association of Universities and Colleges of Canada, http://www.aucc.ca/wp-content/uploads /2011/05/trends-2011-vol1-enrolment-e.pdf.

4 Geoffrey Rockwell, "U of Alberta Suspends 20 Programs," 4Humanities: Advocating for the Humanities, 19 August 2013, http://4humanities .org/2013/08/u-of-alberta-suspends-20-programs.

5 Stephen Slemon, "The Humanities Crisis Industry," ACCUTE: The Association of Canadian College and University Teachers of English, 10 March 2014, http://accute.ca/2014/03/10/the-humanities-crisis-industry.

6 Kelly J. Nestruck, "Now Showing at Stratford: Falling Numbers and a Bit of Stage Fright," *Globe and Mail*, 9 March 2013, http://www.theglobeandmail.com /arts/theatre-and-performance/now-showing-at-stratford-falling-numbers-and -a-bit-of-stage-fright/article9517866.

7 Michael McKinnie, *City Stages: Theatre and Urban Space in a Global City, Cultural Spaces* (Toronto: University of Toronto Press, 2007).

8 Stephen Hunt, "Alumni Lament End of Theatre Program; Mount Royal Board Reacts to Provincial Cuts," *Calgary Herald*, 25 May 2013, sec. Entertainment.

9 David Fancy and Diana Belshaw, "Introduction: Why Acting Training," *Canadian Theatre Review* 160 (Fall 2014): 5.

10 Barry Freeman et al., "Aesthetic Diversities in Acting Training," *Canadian Theatre Review* 160 (Fall 2014): 18–19.

11 OAC Arts Engagement Study, "Results of a 2011 Province Wide Study of the Arts Engagement Patterns of Ontario Adults" (Ontario Arts Council, 2011).

12 Yann-Pierre Montelle, *Palaeoperformance: The Emergence of Theatricality as Social Practice* (London: Seagull Books, 2009), 98.

13 Ibid., 56–7.

14 Shannon Jackson, *Social Works: Performing Art, Supporting Publics* (New York: Routledge, 2011).

15 Ibid., 15.

16 Clarke Mackey, *Random Acts of Culture: Reclaiming Art and Community in the 21st Century* (Toronto: Between the Lines, 2010), 18–23.

17 Ibid., 245.

18 See Tracy C. Davis and Thomas Postlewait, eds., *Theatricality* (Cambridge: Cambridge University Press, 2003).

19 Jenn Stephenson, *Performing Autobiography: Contemporary Canadian Drama* (Toronto: University of Toronto Press, 2014), 3.

20 Ibid., 8.

21 Ibid., 4.

22 Carly Maga, "Passion Play: A Slow-Food Version of Theatre," *Globe and Mail,* 7 June 2013.

23 James Thompson, *Performance Affects: Applied Theatre and the End of Effect* (Houndmills, UK: Palgrave Macmillan, 2009), 117.

24 Ibid., 118.

25 Erin Hurley, *Theatres of Affect: New Essays on Canadian Theatre* (Toronto: Playwrights Canada Press, 2014), 3.

26 Patricia Ticineto Clough with Jean O'Malley Halley, eds., *The Affective Turn: Theorizing the Social* (Durham, NC: Duke University Press, 2007).

27 Thompson, *Performance Affects*.

28 Doreen B. Massey, *World City* (Cambridge: Polity Press, 2007), 183.

PART I

A Politics of Place in a Global Age

1 Theatre for a Changeable World, or Making Room for a Fire

BARRY FREEMAN

For it is because we are kept in the dark about the nature of human society – as opposed to nature in general – that we are now faced (so the scientists concerned assure me) by the complete destructibility of the planet that has barely been made fit to live in.[1]

Though it sounds quite contemporary, this passage was written by Bertolt Brecht in 1955. It is taken from a piece he wrote as a response to the question "Can the present-day world be reproduced in the theatre?" which had been posed to him by the organizers of a theatre symposium in West Germany. Brecht's answer, that theatre should not "reproduce" the "present-day world" but show it as something *unnatural* that its audience had created and could therefore re-create, continues to be a compelling answer for anyone interested in theatre practices directed towards social change. No surprise then that in this book, Brecht is a touchstone: James McKinnon recalls Brecht's idea of a pedagogical theatre, Alan Dilworth refers back to the Brechtian "gestus," Jackie Maxwell notes the emotional impact of a production of *The Caucasian Chalk Circle*, Kathleen Gallagher admires Brecht's attempts to rewrite the relationship with the audience, and Edward Little observes how Brecht's "demonstrative" acting technique was an effective strategy in dealing with representations of trauma and violence. Clearly, Hans-Thies Lehmann is right when he notes that Brecht remains "a central reference point in considering newer theatre aesthetics."[2]

But as Lehmann also points out, constantly referencing Brecht can lead to "overly hasty agreement about what matters in 'modern' theatre."[3] Which of Brecht's views, we might ask, on either the nature of society or on theatrical representation, still have traction today? The targets of his social and political critique – injustice, corruption, and greed, for example – are wide and worthy targets today. But it may be more difficult to even know *where* these targets are today, which might account for the disconnect some feel between Brecht's plays and contemporary political aesthetics. Though the plays continue to appeal for their dramatic quality and playful theatricality, it isn't always easy to reconcile them with Brecht's earnest Marxist goals. There is a satisfying clarity to the archetypal evil figures of Brecht's fables: the persecuting church officials of *The Life of Galileo*, corrupt jailers of *The Threepenny Opera*, or the intellectually bankrupt gangsters of *The Resistible Rise of Arturo Ui*, but they may have lower cultural and political impact in a contemporary media landscape saturated with all manner of parody and satire. Still, whatever we think of the currency of his strategies today, Brecht's basic desire for theatre to present a changeable world offers a foundation for my answer to the question of "Why theatre now?": *because theatre cannot just imagine and represent the world differently; it can model new ways of living and relating to one another.*

I want to situate this argument in the context of twenty-first-century neo-liberal globalization, an evolving social, cultural, and economic climate that is changing the stories artists are telling, how they are telling them, and how audiences are invited to listen and participate. As J.P. Singh notes in *Globalized Arts*, "what is valued and how [all art] is being produced often now takes on global dimensions."[4] Trying to apply Brecht to this context, the specific example I will draw on will probably be unexpected: the Debajehmujig Storytellers (hereafter, "Debaj"), a professional Anishnaabeg theatre company based in Ontario, and more specifically their ongoing global performance project, *The Global Savages*. Equal parts storytelling, intercultural exchange, and community dialogue, *The Global Savages* is exemplary of what Jen Harvie speaks of as "socially turned art and performance"[5] practices that include participatory performance art, site-specific theatre, and community arts. Though the social and participatory elements of these practices vary widely, *The Global Savages* is an example of a project deeply oriented around a meaningful and sustained engagement with the communities with which it comes into contact. While on the surface of it, Debaj's practices are about as far as you can get from the poetics of mid-century Marxist political theatre, I see something Brechtian in them in that they defamiliarize the values that organize our relationships to time, place, and one another. *The Global Savages* project does this on two important levels:

first for its international collaborators and audiences, for whom the participatory experience of the project is exposure to an Indigenous world view, and second, on an administrative level, as the Indigenous values on which the work is based clash with the professional, consumerist logic of the professional arts world. In ways deliberate and inadvertent, *The Global Savages* exposes structures that organize time and space within contemporary Western modernity and helps imagine and model alternative modes of production and spectatorship. It breathes new air into Brecht's theatre for a changeable world and suggests a new way that theatre *matters* today.[6]

The Four Axes

Established 30 years ago on the Wikwemikong Unceded Indian Reserve on Manitoulin Island in Ontario, Debaj is the longest-running professional Indigenous theatre company in North America. Their work has evolved a great deal over their history. When Tomson Highway served as artistic director of the company in 1984–5, it was a collective of artists who had mostly relocated from Toronto and who invested most of their time workshopping new plays; Highway's own *Rez Sisters* was in part developed there. In those early days, the company also did a lot of children's theatre, but it refocused in the 1990s and 2000s on training young Indigenous artists in outreach projects in Northern Ontario, which it has expanded on in the last decade to include collaborations and exchanges across Canada and globally. Throughout its history, the group has staged original plays in the summer in its outdoor performance venue, the Holy Cross Ruins in Wikwemikong. Today, it runs a season year-round at its new indoor performance space, the Debajehmujig Creation Centre in Manitowaning, Ontario, just a few minutes' drive from Wikwemikong.

Though Debaj has historically produced plays addressing social and political issues affecting their community, plays such as Drew Hayden Taylor's *Toronto at Dreamer's Rock* in 1999 or the collective creation *New World Brave* in 2001, their work has for some years shifted away from that focus. Neither has their work of late been explicitly addressing globalization, although they are as implicated in its impact as anyone; its artists, for instance, did get involved in the recent Idle No More and anti-fracking protest movements. What has remained consistent over the group's long history is its loyal commitment to its home community on Manitoulin Island. Though the gravitational pull of a major arts centre like Toronto would sometimes make the company's choice to work in a rural area challenging, it has clung to Manitoulin because, as the company's artistic producer Ron Berti has framed it, it is in that community that the group's mandate to create healthy relationships, support and guide youth, maintain culture, language, and stories, and heal from the past is most meaningfully carried out.[7] Work conducted in Northern communities from 1997 onward extended this commitment to the local to other Indigenous communities in their region. While work in that spirit continues, I discovered on a visit in June 2013 that something was shifting again in their practice. Though it had always been important for the company that its productions represent Anishnaabeg values about resource sharing, sustainability, and responsible stewardship of nature, values that can be discordant with the orthodoxies of neo-liberal globalization, I found them in the midst of trying to determine how their creation and training practices wouldn't merely represent but also more fully enact their values for themselves, their collaborators, and their audiences.

Inspiration for this latest shift in their practice came from two sources. The first was a traditional Anishnaabeg teaching called "The Four Axes." This teaching, which can be found in iconographic form in ancient petroglyphs around the Great Lakes region (a spectacular example can be found near Peterborough, Ontario), suggests that there are four activities important to daily living and survival: building, planting, hunting, and harvesting. Given that Debaj's artists live on a reservation in a rural part of the country, these activities have always been at least some part of their lives, but they wondered what would it mean if they were actually integrated into the group's practice. The group was further inspired by a series of recent trips to Europe, on which they met like-minded artists committed to community dialogue and responsibility for environmental stewardship. In a June 2013 interview, Ron Berti put it to me this way:

Actually, we were doing all these things on the side here at home. We were interested in gardening and the environment. But we could never admit that this had anything to do with our arts practice. We didn't see it reflected anywhere else. After we saw what PeerGrouP [a community arts collective in the Netherlands] was doing, we said, "It's ok! It's ok to admit that the Earth means something to us! We don't have to keep that outside of the art!" Just like there was a time when you couldn't talk about the social benefits of the arts ... So we came back with energy and conviction that we were on the right path and could come out of the closet about it, and that there was a really clear connection between traditional teachings and the environmental movement.

Theatre offers a rich metaphoric space in which to publicly imagine and challenge any deleterious social consequences of globalization, but what Debaj is trying to do with this shift in their practices is something else. The way Ron recounts the history, there was a time when it wasn't important to argue that their work had a social impact; it was enough that it represented them. Now, they have moved beyond social impact as well to think about how they can actually live the values they profess to hold. This agrees with a wider movement in theatre and performance studies to hold social and ethical considerations to be as important as the aesthetic. Janelle Reinelt argues that theatre is served by unique "epistemological assets" in confronting globalization and builds her own bridge to Brecht:

> Performances can offer imaginative interventions at the very limits of intelligibility, i.e., performance can posit various possible conceptual and aesthetic schemas to provoke its spectators to seek their own finite relation to the enormous, sometimes over-whelming plurality of the new worldly context ... Theatrical events are subjunctive and symbolic imaginings of possible worlds that hypothesize the "what-if" worlds of imaginative alternatives ... or that old Brechtian stalwart subjunctive, "If history were to have been otherwise, what could have/would have changed the outcome?" Since we live in highly theatricalised times, performance becomes a means of testing the social imagination.[8]

Reinelt thus issues a utopian call for a poetics of alternative imagining, a call upon theatre's capacity to suggest that the world might be otherwise, perhaps the key driver behind what was Brecht's own call for theatre, renewed for the "now." Debaj's new practices are not only "symbolic imaginings" but tests of the "social imagination" in perhaps a richer sense than Reinelt intends, a way of threading their daily cultural and social rituals in and through their work in a way that is more fully responsible to their Indigenous world view. Debaj does not offer their practice as a Romantic prescription for how they or others may live in an alternative modernity beyond the influence of globalization, nor is it offered as a political provocation. It is instead a threading together of their artistic and lived practices in such a way that honours their traditions. On my visit in 2013 I saw professional artists working in a way that did not look like artists working elsewhere; in addition to their daily creative work, they were for example also out fishing together in the morning or tending to their multiple organic gardens (the seeds for which had been collected in Seed Swap events they organized for the community). Some were working in the shop experimenting with materials, others outside on a landscaping project. On a rotating schedule, artists had been made responsible for cooking a lunch or dinner they would eat together in the Creation Centre's spacious kitchen. The week after I was there, a group of women artists were going out to learn to hunt. The group is still finding the balance between these activities and the time they need to work on performances and events, but they are clearly well on their way to enacting the different vision Ron articulated in his epiphany.

These particular activities couldn't be adopted by any artistic collective anywhere; they are made possible by the circumstance of Debaj's artists living in the same rural community. They may also seem quotidian and outside a consideration of the meaning produced in their artistic projects. But these everyday practices of cooking, eating, or gardening together are small actions with large implications. They speak for me to a wider modern ethical dilemma that I find best articulated in the work of the 90-year-old Polish sociologist Zygmunt Bauman. In his dozens of books, Bauman dissects the social and ethical consequences of globalization and traces a broad transition from a "solid modernity" "bent on entrenching and fortifying the principle of territorial, exclusive and individual sovereignty" to "liquid modernity," "with its fuzzy and eminently permeable borderlines [and] unstoppable (even if bemoaned, resented and resisted) devaluation of spatial distances."[9] Bauman finds reason to critique both of these phase-states but reserves his deepest worry for the kind of powerlessness engendered by liquid modernity:

> No longer does the world appear amenable to kneading and holding; instead, it seems to tower above us – heavy, thick, and inert, opaque, impenetrable and impregnable, stubborn and insensitive to any of our intentions, resistant to our attempts to render it more hospitable to human coexistence. The face it shows us is mysterious and inscrutable, like faces of the most seasoned poker players.[10]

Brecht had worried about being "in the dark" as a state of ignorance, but Bauman worries about being "in the dark" as deep ethical paralysis, the human subject standing frozen before the edifice of an unknowable, inscrutable modernity. The danger to which Bauman's work alerts us is that of ethical disavowal, an overwhelming pressure, like that which Brecht had fought, to see the state of the world as natural and unchangeable. As Bauman writes, to such a world *"there seems to be no alternative.* No alternative, at any rate, that we the players, by our deliberate efforts, singly, severally, or all together, could put in its place."[11] The dilemma, then, is how to reconnect the individual sphere of influence to the complex, globally interconnected systems that criss-cross our lives, how to reimagine ourselves not merely as consumers sculpting out our identity from the available products on the market but as ethically engaged citizens who might question and change social and political structures. Debaj's choice to integrate rituals of building, planting, hunting, and harvesting is for me an answer to Bauman's rather bleak vision of contemporary ethical paralysis. It is a perfect illustration of what Gustavo Esteva and Madhu Suri Prakash call "grassroots post-modernism," the widespread consciousness that people needn't "think big" in order to oppose neoliberal globalization, that they can, in fact "free themselves in the same voluntary ways that they entered it."[12]

The Global Savages

So how do Debaj's different practices translate into a lesson for "why theatre now"? And what does this have to do with Brecht?

For Brecht, the political-poetic problem of the drama of his day was one of representation, leading to his tinkering with the mimetic practices of narrative, storytelling, symbolism (gestus), and so on. His interventions in these sign systems helped create self-conscious and reflexive theatre practices, but their success has probably also contributed to their depoliticization. Intervening in the sign systems of theatrical representation could after all only register as political if those systems were stable to begin with. The Western, Aristotelian system of theatrical representation Brecht was reacting to has become much more varied and hybridized in our own time, mixing "high" and "low" culture as well as cultural traditions from around the world, such that the capacity for representation to be politicized becomes highly contextual. Lehmann, no doubt overstating the problem, wonders if traditional, situationally based drama – the kind Brecht was trying to reject – is unable to represent the complexity of the modern world. What if, he asks, "the problems of the present exceed the representational capacity of the situational dramatic art?"[13]

If the political potential for theatre to confront and challenge neoliberal globalization, or to mitigate the "ethical paralysis" Bauman flags

1.1 Global Savages Josh Peltier, Joe Osawabine, and Jessica Wilde-Peltier (from left to right) explaining their map on the streets of Paris. Photo by Ron Berti.

as its most worrying outcome, is no longer contained in representation alone, perhaps Debaj demonstrates one way that, in a Brechtian spirit, theatre can model alternative ways of being and living in the "now." By attending to the social and experiential dimensions of the theatrical encounter, and not just to its formal, aesthetic objects – to what Laura Levin calls elsewhere in this book the "spatiality and 'eventness' of theatre" – we access a different way of thinking about why theatre matters today. In *Random Acts of Culture*, Clarke Mackey argues for a more expansive view of the arts that includes what he calls "vernacular culture," the everyday creative, expressive practices such as bedtime stories, community art making, or street art – practices that don't necessarily have a place in the world of the institutional fine arts.[14] Adopting a stark view of the "now" as one wracked by the "dire consequences of a two hundred year experiment in industrial capitalism," Mackey envisions a cultural landscape in which the sole aim is the production not of commodities for circulation and sale, but of art that occasions meaningful social encounter and relationship forming. Instead of seeing the art object as representation, Mackey turns to social aesthetics, the representative and significant capacity of the social exchange happening in and through theatre itself. "If it is possible," he writes, "to think of artistic practices as metaphors for other kinds of human collaborations, the metaphors of the Hollywood celebrity or the televised soccer game provide different models than do nighttime storytelling or neighbourhood pageants."[15] What kind of a metaphor is theatre for the world? What relationships does it propose to time, space, and social relations?

I find the answers in Debaj's ongoing project *The Global Savages*, a multifaceted performance and community engagement project that has to date toured to a number of places across Canada and, in Europe, to Scotland (twice), France, Belgium, and the Netherlands. The more formal theatrical performance component of the project is a story told by four traditional Anishnaabeg characters – the "Global Savages" of the title – who tell, as Ron Berti put it in my interview with him, "the 18,000-year animated oral history of the indigenous peoples of North America aka Turtle Island in 90 minutes or less" (*Figure 1.1*). The performance shares a number of traditional stories and teachings, rooted in Anishnaabeg values around community, respectful stewardship of the land, and a commitment, to cite a phrase Debaj frequently uses these days, "to the preservation of humanity" (which is another teaching illustrated in the ancient petroglyphs).

The ethic of community and ecological sustainability on which the stories of the performance are based already models an alternative ethic to neo-liberal capitalism, but so too does the performance's spatial and temporal reorganizing. The dramatic conceit of the performance is that the four storytellers have been travelling for 18,000 years to tell their story and that they aren't just artists visiting a city or festival with their performance but nomadic storytellers who come to live in their new context for a short time, learn from it, and share something of their own traditions. They request that their performance take place not in a traditional theatre space but outdoors, "beside a fire, and under an open sky," and the group spends time "preparing" the performance space after they arrive by securing the necessities of survival: water, shelter, and a space for a fire, around which the audience will ultimately gather to hear their story (*Figure 1.2*). To devote this kind of care to each of the new contexts that the Global Savages travel to, they spend at least a week just getting to know both the environment and the people. A number of activities unfold in parallel during these informal periods of exchange. When the company first arrives at a new location, they do a ritual "sunrise walk" through the community along a "locally significant route." This serves to remind the Global Savages that they are guests in a new territory but that they are ambassadors for their people as well. As well, during their time in situ, members of the company explore the community and engage

1.2 *The Global Savages* in performance on Terschelling Island in the North Sea at the Oerol Festival. Photo by Ron Berti.

in spontaneous interactions with strangers in public in "costume" – actually traditional Anishnaabeg leather clothing – as the Global Savages. One prop they use in their interactions is a map the Global Savages made, an 18- by 12-foot canvas map of the entire world with no names, no borders, just the landforms, and which has North America in the centre, specifically Manitoulin Island. (The first time they used the map, a 12-year-old boy pointed at it and said, "Oh, you're in the middle," to which they responded, "Well yeah we're in the middle, it's our map!") In addition to such social rituals and guerrilla street theatre, Debaj also reserves plenty of time for talking and eating with people with whom they work, as well as for volunteering with local organizations, which they cite as one of the quickest routes to understanding what is on the minds of people in an unfamiliar place. The sum of all the formal and informal exchange is a sense that *The Global Savages* does not just represent or imagine the world differently, but uses theatre to model a more sensitive and sustained intercultural exchange that is formative of new relationships.

The Global Savages' multiple extra-theatrical engagements mean that the alternative spaces it creates don't only operate during the space and time of the performance encounter but also within the social encounters around the work, as well as on the administrative levels of their collaborations with professional organizations and theatre festivals around the world. An anecdote from Debaj's experience with *The Global Savages* illustrates that the kinds of "vernacular" exchange they want are not always an easy fit with this world. When Debaj "pitches" *The Global Savages* to potential collaborators, the only practical demand they make is the requirement mentioned earlier that the performance itself – the oral history of the Anishnaabe people – take place "beside a fire under an open sky." As Debaj artistic director Joe Osawabine puts it, "if we can figure out the fire, everything else will work itself out."[16] The company was not prepared for the difficulty they would face in getting this one request fulfilled. Their first attempts to do the performance around a fire in Halifax, Vancouver, and in Rotterdam, Netherlands, all fell through on account of misunderstandings with organizers or prohibitive municipal regulations. Next, at an outdoor site-specific festival in Derendte, Netherlands, the organizers put them outside but on top of a concrete pad, which felt wrong for the piece given its argument for a rootedness in the earth. In Paris they were performing at a theatre complex shared by a number of companies, and getting permission from all of them proved impossible in the end. Finally, they succeeded on Terschelling Island in the North Sea with a fire outside on the land, but it poured rain, causing them to stop the show and find shelter, rebuild the fire, and start again (the same thing happened when I saw the performance in June 2014 on Manitoulin Island).

Fire regulations exist for good reasons; for centuries, theatres frequently burned down for the lack of them. At the same time, it is remarkable that a simple fire – which for tens of thousands of years of human history was the likely venue of much "theatre" – is nearly impossible to re-create in the usual contexts of professional performance. For me, this illustrates the denaturalization Brecht was seeking, on the level not of representation but within the professional systems surrounding artistic production and presentation. Necessary safety regulations not thought to be ideological in nature turn out to be at odds with an Indigenous world view. Debaj's determination in the face of this specific obstacle is not a failure of the project but one of its great successes: accidentally, they find themselves exposing the material conditions surrounding each context they enter. The request for a fire, along with the whole social, semiformal, duration-based structuring of *The Global Savages*, enacts a different system of value that makes visible the default rules of engagement in globalized artistic practices. The figurative throwing water on their literal fire is one illustration of the fact that the global circuits of artistic production and presentation into which they project themselves reveal themselves at points to be rooted in values antithetical to what they do. I rediscover this whenever I try to write about Debaj, and my attention is drawn to fact that the rhetorical vocabulary used to describe performance practices – project, work, company, touring, performance, emerging, initiatives, etc. – are borrowed from a discourse of industrial commodity production that inadequately describes the way they conceptualize their practice. But in spite of clashes of value and ever-present potential for misunderstanding, Debaj perseveres in looking for like-minded partners to collaborate with, taking the chance to speak out of their community, which is, after all, the reason they leave their supportive home community at all.

Making Room for a Fire

The continued, though waning, predominance in Canada of a "poetic realist" style of dramaturgy leaves much room for artists to experiment with modes and styles that propose alternative relationships to audiences. Among the lessons to take from Debaj's work, and from this exercise of thinking it through in parallel with Brecht, is that what Lehmann calls the "ethico-political" in the theatre may well depend on differently imagined forms, environments, and engagements with audiences.[17] The creation of different spaces is an act of political imagining that can expose the normative modes and networks of cultural production and permit unstructured and unexpected outcomes. *The Global Savages* is an example of the sort of politicized performance practice that Shannon Jackson says doesn't just adopt "an anti-institutional stance" but also "help[s] us to imagine sustainable social institutions."[18]

Debaj demonstrated this for me in a completely different way in June 2014 by inviting me to participate in a week-long discussion they had organized called "The Many Day Talk." What was remarkable about the Many Day Talk (and a welcome change after the three academic conferences I had attended immediately before it) was its radical openness: its discussions began with no agenda and no expectation of an outcome – they were simply an opportunity to talk among a small group of artists and academics Debaj had worked with over the years. And so we talked, for many hours and about many things. We spoke about the conflicts of value they were experiencing between their own culture and those they were encountering. We spoke of the foreignness of academic culture itself because they had recently been invited into an academic discussion and asked questions posed within a scholarly discourse with which they weren't familiar, and they were embarrassed by not being able to decipher or understand what was being asked. We spoke of all the gaps, between contexts, values, and languages, and we thought through ways to interact and engage that were not oppositional, but graceful and grateful. That week had all the qualities they – and anyone else – might want for the theatre: it was careful and thoughtful, patient and honest, a differently ordered space and time that they could open in their own home, on their own terms. And we lit several fires.

Silvija Jestrovic writes of Brecht that his approach to theatre has two utopian agendas: "belief in the possibility of breaking the manipulative structure of representation, and belief in the capacity of theatre to seriously alter the course of history and politics."[19] If, as I have argued, we tweak the first of these agendas to be not just about representation but also about the nature of the social engagements surrounding theatrical encounter, then we refresh the second agenda, that is, at least if we adopt a more prosaic and reachable "utopia."

The Global Savages reveals for me that the answer to "Why theatre now?" is not so much that it creates a new utopia fashioned to our own age, but that it creates a space where different values and practices can be shared and experienced and, in so doing, where one can imagine in the first place that such is possible. In *Does Ethics Have a Chance in a World of Consumers?* (a book posing its own audacious question of the "now"), Bauman considers the problem of feeling disempowered in modernity and laments the fact that many of the democratic political and social institutions of our time were the product of a bygone phase of "solid modernity" that have not found "effective substitutes."[20] Skirting along the edge of a resigned cynicism through the book, Bauman at one point quotes a passage from Italian author Italo Calvino that seems at first to be despairing, but which may actually offer a more measured ethics for our time. Calvino puts the following words in the voice of a fictionalized Marco Polo:

> The hell of the living is not something that will be: if there is one, it is what is already here, the hell where we live every day, that we form by being together. There are two ways to escape suffering it. The first is easy for many: accept the hell and become such a part of it that you can no longer see it. The second is risky and demands constant vigilance and apprehension: seek and learn to recognize who and what, in the midst of hell, is not hell, then make them endure, give them space.[21]

The passage supplies an eloquent declaration of what we can hope for in the theatre: that by doing hard work balanced by constant doubt, we find what it is we deem valuable and make a space for it to live and endure.

34   Barry Freeman

NOTES

1 Bertolt Brecht, *Brecht on Theatre: The Development of an Aesthetic*, ed. and trans. John Willet (London: Methuen, 1964), 275.
2 Hans-Thies Lehmann, *Postdramatic Theatre*, trans. Karen Jürs-Munby (Abingdon, UK: Routledge, 2006), 29.
3 Ibid.
4 J.P. Singh, *Globalized Arts: The Entertainment Economy and Cultural Identity* (New York: Columbia University Press, 2011), 23.
5 Jen Harvie, *Fair Play: Art, Performance and Neoliberalism*, Performance Interventions Series (Houndmills, UK: Palgrave Macmillan, 2013), 5.
6 Tragically, Josh Peltier, one of the artists in Debaj's *Global Savages* project, passed away in spring 2014. Josh was a kind person and brilliant artist, and I hope this chapter serves as a testament to the value of what he created.
7 Shannon Hengen, *Where Stories Meet: An Oral History of De-Ba-Jeh-Mu-Jig Theatre* (Toronto: Playwrights Canada Press, 2007), 65.
8 Janelle Reinelt, "Three Thoughts toward a Global Poetics," *Contemporary Theatre Review* 16, no. 1 (2006): 152.
9 Zygmunt Bauman, *Does Ethics Have a Chance in a World of Consumers?* Vienna Lecture Series (Cambridge, MA: Harvard University Press, 2008), 8.
10 Ibid., 110.
11 Ibid., 111 (emphasis in original).
12 Gustavo Esteva and Madhu Suri Prakash, *Grassroots Post-Modernism: Remaking the Soil of Cultures* (London: Zed Books, 1998), 25.
13 Lehmann, *Postdramatic Theatre*, 12.
14 Mackey, *Random Acts of Culture*.
15 Ibid., 243.
16 "The Global Savages Pitch," YouTube video, 7:36, posted by Deba-jehmujig Storytellers, 8 January 2013, http://www.youtube.com/watch?v=SMOpZfyII6w.
17 Lehmann, *Postdramatic Theatre*, 186.
18 Shannon Jackson, *Social Works: Performing Art, Supporting Publics* (New York: Routledge, 2011), 11.
19 Silvija Jestrovic, *Theatre of Estrangement Theory, Practice, Ideology* (Toronto: University of Toronto Press, 2006), 117.
20 Bauman, *Ethics*, 74.
21 Ibid., 77.

2 Make What You Need

DUSTIN SCOTT HARVEY

I am standing in the middle of a disused storefront, chunks of plaster lying on the floor pushing against my bare feet. I am shirtless. I am pant-less. I am wearing a long red curly wig, and yellow swimming trunks two sizes too small. I look a bit like a Viking at a beach party. I am sweaty. I can hear the sound of some people shifting in their seats, a few quiet whispers, some late-night revellers walking by the window. I am wondering if the tension is going to break. I am reminding myself that I've been here before – in Aarhus, in Montreal, in Cardiff, in Halifax. I am thinking I should end the awkwardness. Then, a person rises from the audience sitting around me. Her voice is tender. She speaks with a slight quiver. "If all the people stayed," she begins, "my family would be here with me, and I'd get to see my three grandchildren that live in America." A man approaches the microphone. He's holding an open can of Beamish stout. He speaks, "We'd see our friends all the time so we'd be all sitting around the pub with nothing to talk about." And another, "Cork would be the culture capital of Ireland. People from Dublin would move here." It continued like this for a few more minutes. For me, it was a perfect way to say goodbye to this city, along with this group of people I just met.

The principle underlying my work and guiding my curiosity is the beauty found in the connections between strangers. It is found in the way the theatre brings us together, creates a platform for sharing, draws attention to relationships, and humanizes a space. It proposes for a moment that beauty is something real, something to be encountered.

Intersections between the theatre and beauty gave me insight into a true purpose for art: to change the way you relate to other people, to alter how you go about doing things in the place you live. Theatre created the feeling in me that there is something more, something bigger than myself. More importantly, it matters as it does to me because the connections we share in those moments help dissolve the boundaries and isolation of the human condition, and have the ability to make us feel less alone. If what we are longing for is the need to relate to another human being, then theatre promises to be a vehicle for this to happen. It also has the potential to meaningfully reflect on the forces that separate us. In contrast, the process of commodification and privatization of social space has created a behaviour in our contemporary society that tends to erode authentic human contact and values of public space. Although modern progress has instantly made the world feel smaller, careful observation reveals that contemporary society produces in us, more than anything else, barriers to authentic human connection. In spite of this, contemporary theatre can still provide a space for shared closeness and intimacy. The context of shared space forms the way to building communities.

Public relationships to place can be transformed by making the connection theatrical, by playing on perceptions of social space. We can see our audiences as co-conspirators and think of theatre as an event and as a temporary community. In Nova Scotia, the interrelationships connected to site are meaningful because they encompass a myriad of people and places come, gone, and soon to be. The dilemma Nova Scotians encounter most is having to go where the work is, either leaving loved ones behind or staying behind despite the consequences. Emotional connections to home, and nostalgic narratives about isolation and loneliness, are something particular to my experience here and, as I've discovered, are narratives commonly found in other parts of the world as well. As a Nova Scotia–born theatre-maker, the son of a stock car driver and an aesthetician, I grew up in a small village near the Halifax airport when the province was undergoing a lot of outward migration to Ontario, though that movement was rapidly shifting to Alberta. As far as the arts were concerned, it was a period in which the province saw a great number of artists who felt unsupported leave for larger centres. Against this backdrop, I chose to stay in Halifax. But, as I saw more of my friends and collaborators leave the city, I found myself working alone, rebuilding my circles of friends and asking myself questions about this place and my relationship to it. This feeling forged in me a powerful sense of connection to place.

As a theatre-maker, I have been intent on making the shared experience the point of the theatrical encounter, not just a by-product. It is perhaps not surprising that the characteristics I use to describe

theatre illustrate intimate connections to home. For example, my reason for making theatre in Halifax emerged out of the desire to make
people care more about their home, in ways that make them want to
stay. By asking what such connection to place means to our lives, and
how it might transform the present moment, I work towards creating
an environment that performers can weave through, to build an honest
sense of intimacy, connection, and locality. These theatre practices can
heighten participation, make collaborators out of spectators, and give
human depth to the moment. I would argue that the success of theatre
now comes from its ability to overcome barriers to authentic human
connection.

Secret Theatre

In these circumstances, and with the intentions just stated, I have developed theatre work that explores the boundaries of theatre and site, and
re-appropriated media into new theatre experiences. In 2003, I created
the Secret Theatre company as a vehicle to help generate and tour my
work. The company operates through flexible, project-based partnerships that further creation and production, and many of its projects in
art and performance have been collaborative. Since its inception, Secret
Theatre has created eight full projects in Nova Scotia. These projects
include theatrical walks in the Halifax Common with the help of iPods,
live film experiences, site-responsive performances, participatory audio events, video installation, networking talks, and a project oriented
around letter-writing to our younger selves. Disused storefronts, train
stations, cafes, public parks, street corners, dance studios – these all become spaces for Secret Theatre encounters. Each production is about
creating meaningful, shared experiences that are thoughtful, intimate,
and temporary. Recently, the group has developed an international touring profile and presented at internationally recognized festivals and
venues, for example, the Aarhus Festuge (Denmark), Cork Midsummer
Festival (Ireland), Chapter Arts Centre (Wales), OFFTA (Montreal), and
Winterlab (Victoria), among others.
    Secret Theatre's use of rough sites and intimate sizes playfully chal-
lenges audiences and evokes notions of theatricality over drama. For
example, these experiences are not play driven but rather depend on
the combination of text, music, sound, and action for their dramatic
potential. I approach this with a raw, lo-fi aesthetic and a DIY mentality.

In spite of technology's role in my practice, I am interested in its limitations, which is why I often use analogue and obsolete technology rather than digital. Devices and systems such as Hi-8 cameras, raw video feeds, overhead projectors, and visual presenters – with their imperfections and shortcomings – illustrate this preoccupation I have with how the image is created and sustained and how it relates to the live theatrical dynamic. The success of this approach comes from understated formal and theatrical references to performer and spectator relationships. For example, roles of actor and spectator sometimes shift, putting the audience in the position of performer.

As a theatre-maker, I have been preoccupied with approaches that combine two or more artistic disciplines in such a way that none of them dominates. In other words, installation, media art, and film languages also serve as design approaches to making content. For instance, the shape or flow of a performance might be taken from one discipline, and the elements that exist in that structure – a combination of light, text, and sound – may be related by a framing device of another. The place where the two coexist emerges as something new and unique. More importantly, an aesthetic logic, or the principles by which the piece is assembled, opens up a space for risk-taking and reduces theatre to a basic expression: an experience that depends upon a suspension of disbelief on the part of the viewer. Accordingly, and for this reason, the presence of the viewer is essential in the fulfilment of the work, which changes because it is being viewed. Technology is something we engage with every day, and incorporating it into the theatre gives us an opportunity to subvert or challenge the role it has in our lives. Theatre gives us the opportunity to explore how technology both assists and interferes with our need for human connection.

Influential to my developing notion of intimacy, locality, and connection were the writings of the Situationists, a group of young students, artists, scholars, architects, and philosophers that emerged in Paris in the late 1960s, who practised a kind of ideology that to me was part art, part performance. They resisted formal organization and sought to create public interventions called "situations" that drew attention to social behaviours. These situations interrupted the regular experience of a place and focused on creating a new encounter with it. The intention was to reawaken perception, to confront usual relationships, to deepen a citizen's involvement and participation, to re-humanize. In addition, the Situationists tend to be associated with the concept of psycho-geography, which emphasizes a playfulness and drifting around urban environments. Psychogeography was defined in 1955 by Guy Debord as "the study of the precise laws and specific effects of the geographical environment, consciously organized or not, on the emotions and behaviour of individuals."[1] Concepts such as psychogeography emerged for the Situationists as an aesthetic practice and a social game. Another way to put it is that they employed "a whole toy box full of playful, inventive strategies for exploring cities ..., just about anything that takes pedestrians off their predictable paths and jolts them into a new awareness of the urban landscape."[2] The Situationists were also attuned to how commodities create a social context within which *having* is given higher priority than *being*. Most important for my purposes, the privatization of public space engenders a state of passiveness and obeisance to the spectacle. In other words, our lives are not an expression of our innermost desires, but rather a preoccupation with control and ownership. Situationism matters to theatre at this moment in time because it suggests a vital function of theatre today: to awaken us to our need for other people, to create particular environments for intimate connection, and to arouse a common unity within people.

THE COMMON: For as Long As You Have So Far

THE COMMON was a project created by Robert Plowman and me in the spring of 2009. This experience was made for one person in a public space. Using the urban landscape that makes up Halifax's largest urban green space, *THE COMMON* was a 45-minute theatrical walk beginning at Halifax's North Common and ending at Victoria Park, during which the participants navigated their path with the help of a headset (*Figure 2.1*). In the performance, a vast 240-acre plot of land, the mysterious natural creek buried underground, the immense gardens, and the dominating buildings erected around them all become a captivating backdrop for an intimate adventure that only existed between their ears.

The Halifax Common tends to be a place associated with controversy. If asked what portion or percentage of that space is reserved for public use in the city, many residents of the city would suggest it is only a small section known as the North Common, the skate park, and the Public Gardens. In fact, "approximately 20%–25% of the original 240 acres remain as public green space. Much of the South Common is now occupied by public and private buildings. The Central Common and the North Common are primarily designated recreation sites."[3] The Common has evolved over the years, from 1750, when it was established by

2.1 Audience participant looking at past/present view of *THE COMMON* from the perspective of the show's guidebook. Photo by Dustin Harvey.

the British colonial government as 240 acres for gathering firewood and grazing livestock, to today, when it has diminished to 80 acres. Public safety in and around the space has been in the news in recent years, due to a number of "swarming" incidents of youth assaulting or mugging people in the park. I saw in the Common an opportunity for theatre to be used to reanimate a space, to provide a sense of connectivity and engagement, to reinforce the relationship between the past and present, and to stimulate a metaphor that altered the way people engaged with the city. I wanted to provide a physical way of relating to place by putting spectators at the centre of the experience, to awaken their relationship to place and to transform their understandings.

My collaborator Robert Plowman and I mapped out ideas about performance and geography that would become *THE COMMON* in a series of meetings at the very beginning of the process. We established a dramatic structure in which to explore the ideas: Act 1, "The time before you showed up"; Act 2, "You and me"; and Act 3, "Leaving something behind." These corresponded to three main psychogeographical shifts in the landscape: the North Common was very open and public like a meeting place; the section through the Public Gardens was much more intimate and mysterious; and the area leading up to the ending in Victoria Park had lots of monuments with names of people written into stones, on bricks, and on plaques. Next, we created a series of initial story sketches and arranged them in a running order that fit with the structure. In almost every case we used the objects and spaces to inform the story. In addition, starting at the fountain in the North Common, audiences followed the path of a natural creek that once flowed openly throughout the city, arriving at a fountain in Victoria Park. The timings of sequences were adjusted to the pre-set walk so that it could be played as one long track. The experience was scored with a series of musical themes composed by Brian Riley. We recorded and edited vocal and field recordings, putting them into a format suitable for an ordinary MP3 player.

The combination of fiction and fact used was to create a theatrical sense of disbelief and reanimate the space. For example, along the way, audiences encountered descriptions in the audio that transported them through decades in time: they drifted by the skate park when it was an Egg Pond and the Citadel as it was being surveyed by Charles Morris; they sat at the bench in the Public Gardens where Sanford Fleming devised time zones, where Samuel Cunard won a shipping contract, and where Joseph Howe fought a duel. Interwoven into the history were a handful of myths and urban legends, for example, a window of a house that turned black each time it was replaced, moose grazing on Citadel Hill, and a ghost ship in the harbour, among others. In addition, the guide endowed the listener with a fictional backstory about a grandmother, a great-great-grandmother, and a relationship that started as a chance meeting with a stranger. At the fountain in Victoria Park near the end of the experience, the participant was asked to write a note to the stranger, a message for their imagined scene partner. Upon leaving the piece of paper at a marked location, they also found a note, left behind by the person ahead of them. In spite of the headset, the story was so effective in playing on participants' imagination that some felt they experienced a number of coincidences in which uninvolved bystanders appeared to be in on the experience. In other words, some people thought we had staged or physicalized the story at moments for them, while others thought they were themselves the ones being watched as if they were the performers in the play. The success of *THE COMMON*'s experience comes from the subtle and theatrical references to the audiences' connection to place in ways that are intimate and surprising.

Neither the use of the headsets nor the placing of people in public space explains the undeniable craving audiences had for this kind of theatre experience. Feedback I received from surveys, the demographic of the attendees, and audience reviews, however, revealed a broader desire for different kinds of theatre events represented by *THE COMMON*. In other words, audiences seemed to crave intimate experiences that connected them to place. The use of the headsets and the situation of putting people in public spaces for creative intervention struck a chord. I remember audiences wanting to linger at the end of the experience, telling me it felt as if they had come out of a drug-induced trip and needed some time to re-enter the regular world. The favourable outcome of *THE COMMON* was a result of deliberate formal and informal uses of place, memory, and drifting. For me, this is what makes theatre transformative today. The audiences could have a surprising, intimate, and memorable connection with the city – a place they pass through every day.

FAREWELL: A Goodbye Party Made for a City

A city's "personality" should contribute to the "personality" of the performances that happen within it, just as a city's best restaurants should source local ingredients and elements from the local experience. This is what can make "place" into something more, something extraordinary. But this is usually not the case. Most touring theatre companies, if you ask them, will tell you their goal is to maintain the same production look and values no matter what city you are in. Among the qualities considered distinctive to touring are repeatability, predictability, and consistency. According to this approach, theatre work has little connection to people or place. Like the use of site in *THE COMMON*, a city-specific project I created with Chad Dembski in 2010 called *FAREWELL* played on notions of locality, intimacy, and connection, creating performances that attempted, again, to forge connections between people and places.

When *FAREWELL* was produced in a new location, the first step was to discern the characteristics of the new community from the moment of arrival.[4] It was also our intention to examine questions of utopia and propose a vision of theatre as a temporary community or imagined place built on the connections between strangers in the performance venue. We sourced a number of local elements to put into the performance, including audio recordings of different city ambiences, photographs of neighbourhoods, and food that evoked a memory of place. These elements supported the city-specific idea but also established a sense of place familiar to audiences watching the show. The success of the strategy comes from gently and playfully evoking personal relationships to the past and future of the city. In other words, it was a going-away party for the city in which catharsis was the goal.

My need to establish a sense of place specifically comes from my Halifax community changing with outward migration. For example, Chad and I drew on something very specific to Halifax, that people are always leaving for larger cities, by placing questions in the performance such as "Why do you live where you live?," "What does it mean to live in a community?," "Who or what do you want to say goodbye to?," and "Who or what would make you stay?" In other words, the stakes of needing to establish a sense of place created a platform for the audience to question the intimate connections they had to their city. Throughout the performance, the audience was gradually encouraged to participate and share with one another. At one moment in the performance, the audience was invited to the microphone to tell us what this place would be like if all the people who had left had stayed instead.

The interest in using urban space as opposed to rural communities came from subtle references to development issues in Halifax specifically. For example, urban sprawl is a problem that continues to expand the populations of suburbs and spread out the city while the downtown stagnates. This idea was exemplified in Halifax by all the empty storefronts and lack of foot traffic. If you asked what people thought of the downtown, many would tell you it did not feel vibrant or vital. In spite of this, the downtown emerged as a metaphor for a sustainable future of the city, a provocation to stay. The strategy of relating the performance to the specific city throughout the piece comes from all sorts of references to location. For example, we performed the piece in raw spaces including disused storefronts, train stations, abandoned buildings, and studios. Although the site itself awakened audiences' senses, it also highlighted parts of the city they usually ignored or looked past. In addition, using a camera and some really long cords, we captured a view of an ordinary street corner and projected it like a scenic flat or virtual mirror. Throughout the performance, Chad and I acted inside and outside, performing in front of the image for the audience and, in contrast, performing slow-motion goodbyes out in the street for the camera. Sometimes, unsuspecting passers-by would stop and look into the camera. Sometimes they would join in on our "farewell."

The opportunity to share, connect with strangers, and humanize the city can be closely linked with the intimate relationships that were discovered during the performance. For example, strangers talked openly during the performance about their loved ones who moved away or a life

that would be different if all the people who left had stayed. Like the anecdote from the opening of the chapter involving an elderly woman and
her grandchildren, very personal feelings were discussed. In devoting a
moment for audiences to open up and share their vision of what the city
would be like, the roles of audience and performer were less defined,
with audiences sometimes assuming both the performer and spectator
positions. By using roles of performer and audience that are mutually
assumed and exchanged, this activity had one important function: to
bring performer and spectator closer together. For me, this constructed
a temporary environment that demonstrated how people are connected
on a much larger scale and when given the opportunity will form intimate bonds even with strangers. Moreover, this demonstrates to me how
two places can connect over great distances.

Theatre has been rightly praised for creating emotive experiences that
are cathartic, though some presenters believe that intimacy is killing the
theatre because these experiences involve smaller audiences that do not
produce enough income for theatre projects or festivals to be profitable.
For theatre to be vital now, artists are encouraged to assess the physical, conceptual, and contextual opportunities of their environments and propose
work that responds specifically to them. For that reason, theatre now needs
to place emphasis on being present at this moment, at this place, at this
time, with this group of people. It needs to establish a sense of belonging.

LANDLINE: Slow Dancing with Their Arms Around the Nation

Connection, intimacy, and locality are essential principles of the shared
experience of theatre. In my more recent work, I have explored these
principles not just in the exchange between strangers but also through
participation strategies that place the viewer inside the work. This represents a shift in my practice towards forms that allow for audiences to be
in direct contact with each other and without a performer. For theatre
today, participation matters because it brings an aspect of liveness to the
experience and endows spectators with a certain amount of creative risk-
taking necessary for discovering new things.

I met Adrienne Wong from Neworld Theatre in 2011. Adrienne was
showing her PODPLAYS as part of the PuSh Festival in Vancouver. POD-
PLAYS were audio tours that took audiences through Vancouver streets
using headsets and MP3 players. The work shared a lot of similarities
with the work I was doing in THE COMMON. In a statement that describes her interest in the piece, Adrienne writes,

I'm a theatre artist frustrated with conventional theatre practice where the professionals DO and the audience WATCHES. My projects emerge out of my own desire as an audience member to engage directly with the action, to participate. Looking at this list of projects alongside those listed by Dustin and Secret Theatre, it's hard not to notice the similarities. I was pleased to find another artist working on these preoccupations – if only to have someone to chat with about the potentials and challenges of working in an audio format as well as our desires to challenge ourselves ... and the form itself. An idea for a new project emerged quite easily and naturally out of these conversations. The only thing keeping us apart was the vast geography of the nation.[5]

I was immediately struck by the coincidence of another person on the other side of the country doing similar work. I remember meeting Adrienne at the end of the experience. We talked about the possibility of working on a new piece together that pushed beyond the headset formats we had been working on and played on notions of serendipity.

Six months later we began working on *LANDLINE*, a shared experience for two strangers on opposite sides of the country.[6] The piece uses city streets, cell phone technology, and poetic suggestion to engage audience members in an unlikely game of rendezvous. The way the piece worked was simple. Audience-participants were guided via text message to a well-chosen location for a possible meeting. They arrived and were given an iPod and a headset. Two audience members each had an iPod that Adrienne and I synced through a countdown in real time using a video chat. Once synced, the audio was in essence playing simultaneously over both headsets. The audio track contained a set of directions urging the participants to drift through the city and conjured a place thousands of miles away. The audio guide asked them to scout locations to become the backdrop for scenes and prompted them to use their own mobile phone to text stories and memories to a number they were given at the beginning. When it came time for interaction, for sharing text messaging, the audio track prompted the listeners to engage with their phone and accommodated for the time to respond. Because participants were instructed to scout their own locations for scenes, it alleviated the need for us to develop a guide or map to follow. An incoming text message completed the exchange, and two strangers were in dialogue with each other. The spectators were then guided to an interior space in their own cities where they encountered a table set for two. They would sit and discover the face of the other via a video chat.

LANDLINE's final moment made the city disappear, leaving two individuals – at once the performer and audience for the other – in a simple moment of theatrical intimacy. The success of this last moment, Adrienne suggests, depends on the participants' ability to overcome the distance, to humanize the other, to use technology for the purposes of bringing them closer together in the here and now:

> [D]istance itself is part of my interest in this project. We now live with the technology to share sound files, images and words cheaply, easily and almost simultaneously ... I want to entangle listeners on opposite sides of the country, to create a situation where one's actions is linked to the other ... With *LANDLINE* I want to engage audience in an event that can only happen now, that extends their imagination to hold the entirety of the country and one other individual at the same time.[7]

By establishing a carefully choreographed sequence of events, the project encouraged people to become performers in an imaginary play while creating an atmosphere of quiet contemplation. *LANDLINE* offers individuals an opportunity to be part of a parallel experience in a distant city. Over great distances, two strangers, through doing something at the same time, act as scene partners, making the places around them come alive through simultaneous engagement (*Figure 2.2*). *LANDLINE* is a coast-to-coast performance for two, slow dancing with their arms around the nation.

LANDLINE takes a Situationist game of possible rendezvous, an accidental meeting in a public place, as an elaborate metaphor by asserting that a far-reaching yet intimate connection is, on some point of comparison, the same as the theatrical event. We intended *LANDLINE* to challenge the idea of the shared experience, to put people in relationship with one another, to discover similarities and differences, and to see participation as a crucial part of theatricality in which roles of performer and audience are mutually assumed and exchanged. We were inspired by the playful idea of drifting around urban environments and wanted to make the city come alive through audience interaction. In doing so, we experimented with strategies to allow the audience to assume roles of both viewer and performer. This is particularly important for theatre today because it reflects an audience that requires a certain amount of accessibility, and inclusion, if theatre is going to matter to them personally.

2.2 *LANDLINE*, 2013. Photos by Millefiore Clarkes (onethousandflowers.tv) and Peter Carlone.

Epilogue

I remember reading some comments in an online preview article about *FAREWELL* in 2011. The anonymous post said what we were doing was a waste of tax money, and that maybe they should apply for money to buy a fancy car and drive around calling that an art project. A local television broadcaster had also just released a piece calling out other artists' projects as examples of misused taxpayers' money, lining up people on camera to vent their opinions about the waste that was the art. As much as one should always avoid reading such comment sections, I do feel that our society's relationship to art and art-makers is conflicted. In my subsequent projects, I started making efforts to put my face to my work. I want the public to know who I am and who my collaborators are. I want them to understand where we are coming from, what our passions and interests and curiosities are. I want them to see us in our homes, in our kitchens. At performances, I want them to always be in direct contact with us, talk to us, interact with us. Now I make a point of asking, "Are you comfortable? Do you have any questions about the piece or the work I can answer?" I try to be a better host. For me, it is all about making it personal, making the public-artist relationship more human. And it is also about trust. What is important is that we all participate. We come together to experience something, together. It is about human connections to each other and the activities that give life meaning.

NOTES

Rae Brown, Adrienne Wong, Chad Dembski, Erika Hennebury, Brian Riley, Elling Lien, Robert Plowman, Kirsty Munro, Jamie MacLellan, the City of Halifax, the Province of Nova Scotia, James Tyson, Jens Folmer Jespen, Norman Armour, Sherrie Johnson, Kris Nelson, Bea and Cy Harvey, and Gus Harvey: thank you.

1 Guy-Ernest Debord, "Introduction to a Critique of Urban Geography," trans. Ken Knabb, *Les Lèvres Nues* 6 (1955): 1, http://library.nothingness .org/articles/SI/en/display/2.
2 Joseph Hart, "A New Way of Walking," *UTNE Reader* (July/August 2004): 1, http://www.utne.com/community/a-new-way-of-walking.aspx.
3 Friends of the Common, "Appendix 1: Overview: Halifax Common" (public invitation for artist proposals, Halifax, 2013), 3.
4 As of spring 2014, we have presented it as *FAREWELL CORK* in Ireland, *FAREWELL MONTREAL* in Quebec, *FAREWELL CARDIFF* in Wales, *FARE-WELL AARHUS* in Denmark, *FAREWELL VICTORIA* in British Columbia, and *FAREWELL HALIFAX* in Nova Scotia.
5 Adrienne Wong, "Artist Statement" (unpublished grant proposal, Canada, 2012).
6 *LANDLINE* was created by Adrienne Wong and me. Music was composed by Brian Riley. It was produced by Neworld Theatre in Vancouver and Secret Theatre in Halifax.
7 Wong, "Artist Statement."

3 When You're Up to Your Ass in Alligators

EDWARD LITTLE

Swamped

My father was an auto mechanic who struggled to make ends meet as the owner/operator of a full-service garage in Cumberland, British Columbia – a small town on Vancouver Island that owed its existence to coal mining. By the 1960s most of the mines had closed, business was suffering, and money was tight. Survival was day-to-day. Most of the time Dad had to go it alone – fix the cars, pump the gas, do the books, collect bad debts, cope with increasing vandalism, and, something he continued to enjoy, *manage* public relations. For this he kept a ready store of jokes and aphorisms. "When you're up to your ass in alligators," he would quip, "it can be hard to remember that your original intention was to drain the swamp."

This was how I came to understand the idea of *the bigger picture*. But by the time I entered grade six in the mid-1960s, I was more concerned with escaping the swamp than draining it. That's when the theatre came to town. My first experience – a travelling show – transformed the stage of our school gymnasium into Aladdin's cave. Later, we created our own piece, guided by an inspiring young teacher who would soon abandon the classroom for a career on stage. I remember these events as among my earliest experiences of wonderment and awe – the kind of awe that opens "people to new possibilities, ideas, and directions in life," that makes "people forget themselves and their petty concerns," and that creates a feeling of simply being "a part of a whole."[1] Years later, I came to understand that for me, theatre was a pretty direct route to what psychologist Jonathan Haidt describes as "the hive switch" – an autonomic neurobiological response that enables us "(under certain conditions) to transcend self-interest and lose ourselves (temporarily and ecstatically) in something larger than ourselves."[2]

For me, the question "Why theatre now?" has more or less the same answer as "Why theatre then?" Then, it triggered my imagination and flipped my hive switch in ways that celebrating Halloween by trashing fences and cars in Cumberland did not. Now, it supports my faith that our hope rests in "the uniquely human ability to share intentions and other mental representations" – that is, a *shared intentionality* that represents, again in Haidt's words, the evolutionary "Rubicon crossing that let our ancestors function so well in their groups."[3] Somewhere between then and now, my experience of creating and performing theatre reified Raymond Williams's idea of "community as the necessary mediating element between the individual and the larger society."[4] Not unexpectedly, the kinds of community-engaged, swamp-draining, radical, and interventionist theatre that I am drawn to now embraces a vision of collaboration, a desire to combine art with utility, an intention that Alan Filewod describes as the "instrumentality of theatre as a social practice ... conditioned by a cultural tradition that has its sources in the utilitarianism of British working-class culture."[5]

It Takes a Village

"Why theatre now?" It's also a question about the kinds of theatre emerging, thriving, surviving, or adapting in our current ecology and why. Instrumentality and utilitarianism, for example, are the roots of applied forms of theatre and the work of many who work as "artists-in-residence" within communities, neighbourhoods, institutions, or organizations. A growing number of these theatre workers might be more accurately described as "resident artists" – artists who have made a conscious decision that their inspiration, their "canvas," their venue, their process, and their artist output will be a holistic part of their neighbourhood's life. This work is nourished by widespread public participation and routinely draws on oral history, storytelling, and documentary and verbatim forms. Angèle Séguin with Théâtre des Petites Lanternes in Sherbrooke, Quebec; Ruth Howard with Jumblies Theatre in Toronto; Don Bouzek with Ground Zero in Edmonton; David Diamond with Headlines Theatre in Vancouver; Savannah Walling and Terry Hunter with Vancouver Moving Theatre,' Cathy Stubington with Runaway Moon Theatre in Enderby, BC; and Lina de Guevara and now Mercedes Bátiz-Benét with Puente Theatre in Victoria are but a few working in this way in Canada. Each of these operates at a deeply grass-roots level to respond to local conditions and speak truth to power; to advocate for community autonomy in an age of globalization; to offer consensus building in response to a persistent "crisis of legitimacy";[6] to pick up the social detritus scattered in the aftermath of what William Golding has characterized as "the most violent century in human history";[7] or simply to help build and sustain healthier communities. As Cathy Stubington once explained to me, "my approach to politics in the community play is oblique. I bring people together to make puppets out of *papier mâché*, and the talk just naturally turns to politics."[8]

Why *this* theatre now? In part, it's about the documentary impulse. Writing about collectively created documentary drama in the 1970s, Alan Filewod observed that

> at the core of the documentary impulse is an implicit critical statement that the conventional dramatic forms of the culture in question no longer express the truth of the society, usually because those conventional forms cannot accommodate rapid social change. The documentary approach provides a way for artists to realign the theatre to these changes.[9]

Plus ça change. Jenny Hughes cites Mark Espiner to argue that the recent "prominence of verbatim theatre can be explained as an attempt to establish authentic or reliable frames of reference for thought, feeling and action in a highly mediatised society," that in an era of theatricality, theatre is rediscovering "its true role" – to expose the truth.[10] David Hare asserted that verbatim theatre was stepping in to do what "journalism isn't doing" in the post-9/11 war on terror.[11] In 2010, Derek Paget observed that documentary forms tend to come to the fore in troubled times.[12] Certainly our present times qualify. We have got endless wars, violence, and human rights abuses; escalating corporate corruption and governmental collusion; a vertically organized mainstream media characterized by "celebrity worship and corporate fawning";[13] and mounting anxiety over rapidly increasing social and economic inequity.

Beyond the documentary impulse, these troubled times are a catalyst for artists interested in developing community as a "mediating element between the individual and the larger society." This is fertile ground for those seeking to work in alliance across sectors to counter the privileging of the personal, for those hoping to challenge an ubiquitous "confessional mode" that at its most profane gives rise to narrow self-interest and a narcissistic state where an "ethics of autonomy" exerts hegemony over an "ethics of community."[14] For many, participatory community engagement is a way to draw out the more altruistic aspects of the confessional mode – to open spaces where marginalized people might assert themselves politically in the public sphere;[15] to support shifts towards self-reflexivity, personal scholarship, and auto-ethnography; to advocate for the evidentiary inclusion of oral history and survivor testimony in trials, First Nations land claims, and truth and reconciliation commissions.

Montreal Life Stories

It was the heady promise of instrumentality, utility, and the opportunity to assemble a team of resident artists that drew me, in 2007, to the five-year, Community-University Research Alliance (CURA) project Life Stories of Montrealers Displaced by War, Genocide, and Other Human Rights Violations. We set out to raise awareness about the long-term repercussions of crimes against humanity. To this end, four of our project's working groups – Cambodian, Rwandan, Haitian, and Holocaust – partnered with community-based organizations to conduct hundreds of interviews within their respective communities. From its inception, however, we also aspired to reach *beyond the archive* and engage the broader public in deeper social and political engagement concerning mass violence. For this, three additional research clusters – Education, Refugee Youth, and Performance – worked across the project with additional community partners to generate education materials, to engage youth, and to bridge generational, cultural, social, and perhaps even ideological divides. The performance working group was licensed to use theatre to work with source material that included interviews as well as the experience of those interviewing, or being interviewed, or otherwise working with the Life Stories project.

The question of *why* theatre and performance in what was essentially an oral history project was clear to us from the start. We would offer parallel, arts-based methodological alternatives to the oral history interview. We would attempt to inspire cross-fertilization between our various research clusters. We would work to generate critical and analytical perspectives on the Life Stories project and experience as a whole. I saw the project as an exciting but daunting opportunity to create a framework for resident artists to work together over a sustained period of time on what we considered to be some of today's most pressing issues. We set out to discover, test, and grow the limits of arts-based inquiry and research creation directed towards a consensual shared intentionality capable of

entering the contested terrain of social memory, truth, justice, and reconciliation. Between 2006 and 2012, the Life Stories project, including affili-
ates, interns, students, faculty research members, artists, and community
participants, grew to a total of 305 people – a veritable village. Theatre's
creative and collaborative impulse flowed through our project like life's
blood – a carrier of community spirit. Our approach was decentralized,
experimental, and emergent: performance group members formed
smaller project teams around issues, questions, or projects they wished
to explore. Often, these involved participants from other working groups
or the general public. In these ways we sought to connect to the broadest
possible range of participants and ideas. We conducted interviews with
local artists whose work resonated with our own, hosted workshops and
demonstrations, developed a playback theatre ensemble, and generated
nine performance research-creation pieces with public outcomes.

In many ways, the performance group functioned along the lines of
most community-engaged theatre projects. Our authenticity and our legitimacy were born of shared experience and personal connections to
stories and source materials. Our aesthetic fabric consisted of an *artistic
weave* of creative interpretation – and a *social weft* of local knowledge,
shared experience, utility, and accountability. Many of our *villagers* attended each and every production, and in this way, our performances
tended to build upon each other to produce a sustained discourse and
a cumulative effect. Our art reflected our environment. Our collaborative and emergent processes, for example, embraced and affirmed the
increasing movement towards hybridity in genocide studies, which we
experienced early on in 2009 at an international conference hosted by
the Life Stories project.[16]

The research phase of the Montreal Life Stories project ended in
March 2012 with *Rencontres* – a month-long series of 47 public events.
Looking back, I consider that a key accomplishment of our work as resident artists was the effective creation of a project-wide *training ground* for
shared intentionality – a space of embodied exploration and learning
where theatre's unique combination of emotional affect and cognitive
reasoning could challenge our perspectives, enhance our transparency
and accountability, shape the stories we wished to tell, and – in Augusto
Boal's[17] sense of the word – "rehearse" the messages we sought to communicate. In these ways, Montreal Life Stories adds its weight to Bill
Cleveland's argument for "Why theatre now?" – because "for society to
achieve maximum social health, every Government Ministry needs a cultural policy, and every organization needs an artist in residence."[18]

Bring on the Elephants

A closer look at Montreal Life Stories offers insight into some of the factors at play in arts-based approaches to consensual shared intentionality. Moral foundation theory argues that "intuitions come first" and "strategic reasoning second," that the strategic function of moral reasoning is more akin to "a politician searching for votes than a scientist searching for truth."[19] Haidt illustrates their relationship using the analogy of a rider (controlled processes) on an elephant (automatic processes).[20] In the beginning, according to Haidt, was the elephant. Riders evolved later to serve in capacities akin to press secretaries or lawyers: "Under normal circumstances, the rider takes its cue from the elephant, just as a lawyer takes instructions from a client."[21] But it seems that our elephants value reputation over "truth." We are "obsessively concerned about what others think of us, although much of the concern is unconscious and invisible to us."[22]

One upshot of this is that when it comes to feelings, affect, and emotion, we tend to privilege "*confirmatory thought* – the one-sided attempt to rationalize a particular point of view" – over *exploratory thought*, the "evenhanded consideration of alternative points of view."[23] To counter this, our resident artists had the advantage of operating in something akin to a controlled laboratory situation adhering to what Haidt cites as three conditions that stimulate *exploratory thought*: first, "that decision [or theatre]-makers learn before forming an opinion that they will be accountable to an audience"; second, that "the audience's views [responses] are unknown"; and third, that they "believe that the audience is well-informed and interested in accuracy."[24]

Haidt's challenge that "if you want to change someone's mind about a moral or political issue" you must "*talk to the elephant first*" throws down a gauntlet that theatre is well positioned to take up.[25] Fortunately, intuition can be shaped by reasoning, particularly when reasons "are embedded in a friendly conversation or an emotionally compelling novel, movie, or news stories."[26] What Erin Hurley characterizes as "the affective turn in theatre criticism" sheds light on *how* theatre gets elephants and riders to sit down and talk to each other.[27] For Hurley, "feeling" in spectatorship consists of affect, emotion, and mood.[28] Affect is the autonomic, intuitive physiological response that in turn generates the emotions that "name our sensate, bodily experience in a way that at once organizes it and makes it legible to ourselves and consonant with others' experiences or emotional lives."[29] "Mood" relates to the various ways that the theatrical experience creates "a disposition or background state that orients us to certain kinds of emotional responses and reactions."[30]

In community-engaged projects such as ours, "mood" is not only generated during and immediately prior to performances, it is also imbedded in a "gathering phase" shaped by extended time together, the research and experiences of other project teams, *and* previous performances.[31] The receptive "mood" for our work had its genesis in a project-wide conviction that arts-based inquiry was legitimate. This was further validated early on by the two keynote speakers at our 2009 conference. Playwright and educator Lorne Shirinian voiced his deep conviction that difficult stories must be told, that pain and grief can be tolerated and made meaningful as stories, and that such stories play a crucial role in "converting private history into public knowledge."[32] Psychologist and playwright Henry Greenspan argued that, in order to move forward, society must respond to an urgent need to dismantle ritualized roles of teller and listener so that we become "partners in conversation."[33]

Intentions and Values

In *Popular Theatre in Political Culture*, Tim Prentki and Jan Selman argue that the efficacy of community-engaged theatre rests on the clear communication of the *intentions* and the *values* that inform the creation of artistic work and that are inherent in aesthetic choices.[34] I would further argue that this is also key to becoming "partners in conversation" and mediating "feeling" and emotional affect. Our intentions in Montreal Life Stories were clearly bound up with shared values predicated on harm reduction, social justice, and "care for the victims of oppression" – values rooted in what moral foundation theory describes as "a liberal moral matrix."[35] All working groups in Montreal Life Stories subscribed to three principles of ethical engagement: (1) "*shared authority*"[36] extending to all aspects of the project's conceptualization, administration, realization, and dissemination; (2) *ongoing project-wide reflection* through blogs, collaborative projects, workshops, annual meetings, conferences, and publications; and (3) – as the project's title suggests – a fundamental commitment to *the life story* within a larger sociopolitical context.

The life story approach asks fundamental questions about when, where, why, and by whom stories are told. To this, the performance group added questions intimately connected to consensual shared intentionality. How might our two core disciplines collaborate to tell stories about mass violence? How would we negotiate inter- and intra-community politics? How should we balance the need and desire to commemorate against factors such as "compassion fatigue," distrust of outsider intervention, and the physical and psychological risks associated with premature promotion of reconciliation or forgiveness? How could we approach staging stories of violence or survival without, in Julie Salverson's words, contributing to "an erotics of injury"[37] or succumbing to "the lie of the literal"?[38]

Conceptual Blending

We tackled these challenges from various perspectives. A basic consideration of the interplay between *conceptual blending*, intentions, values, and "feelings" in community-engaged work sheds some light on the efficacy of our work. Bruce McConachie departs from theorists who position performance as "the willing suspension of disbelief," instead championing *conceptual blending* "as the cognitive basis of spectating."[39] McConachie contends that spectators engaged in the performance of a play "usually experience 'actor/character' as a blend, not as separate entities."[40] This has profound implications for participatory community-engaged performance, where factors such as the actors' personal history and affiliations, the ownership and context of the stories they tell, and their reasons for telling hold and generate deep affective significance for the community.

Lisa Ndejuru's one-person, deeply personal autobiographical play *Le Petit Coin Intact*, for example, publicly affirmed the artist's, and by extension our own, sense of empathy with the emotional risks and exposure that many of our research creators had experienced personally – and which in all cases we were asking of interviewees.[41] The visceral impact of the piece stemmed from its nature as "self-revelatory performance"[42] experienced through conceptual blending. Ndejuru described her approach in the *Rencontres* section of the Life Stories website:

> I have been struggling for decades with what it means to be Rwandan-Canadian – what Rwanda's tortured narrative of colonialism, war, genocide, dislocation and poverty has meant and could mean for my family, my community, my country, my world. I have some ideas. But before I can ask others to move towards the understanding I long for, I must grab the talking stick, step into the story circle and explore those risks myself. This is a one-woman dramatic reflection about holding on tightly to the things worth holding onto and shedding everything else.[43]

Lisa was well known to our Life Stories audiences in her roles as co-leader of the Rwandan working group, community counsellor, activist, and member of our playback theatre ensemble. Many also knew of her personal experience of an event that stood for a number of us as a sobering reminder of the dangers of the premature promotion of reconciliation. In 2007, Lisa was part of a group working to establish a Rwandan youth community centre that could be shared by all – Hutu and Tutsi alike. Immediately preceding the opening ceremonies, a violent argument resulted in the stabbing death of a young man. The centre never opened. For Life Stories audiences *Le Petit Coin Intact* offers an artistic compression of key themes relating to self-reflection, personal courage and the risks inherent in Shirinian's call to convert private history into public knowledge.

Our playback theatre group, the Living Histories Ensemble (LHE), also drew on self-revelatory performance and conceptual blending to develop an innovative "Bridge" technique that effectively modelled shared authority and reified Greenspan's idea of "partners in conversation."[44] Led by dramatherapist Nisha Sajnani, the LHE spent time with all seven working groups and organized public playback events within the Rwandan, Haitian, Cambodian, and Jewish communities. All sessions combined collective interviewing/story-gathering with debriefing for interviewers and interviewees – thus also providing space for individual and community healing. Playback involves audience members sharing stories that are then "played back" by actors improvising under the direction of a "conductor." The original storyteller is then asked to comment. Normally performers work to shut down "self-talk" – to put aside their personal "feelings" in order to concentrate on listening deeply to the story and playing it back "objectively." The LHE's "Bridge" technique requires that performers first respond with performances of resonant moments of experience or empathy drawn from their own lives *before* they attempt to represent the recounted story.[45] This foregrounds shared risk and demands a complex approach to deep listening to both self and the other. Here, conceptual blending can bring into play both positive and negative implications proceeding from personal subject positions relating to bias, assumption, judgment, and cognitive dissonance – moments of contact or collision between positive and negative emotional systems connected to moral reasoning. In this way, the LHE positions itself at the intersection of oral history, performance, trauma, emergent inquiry, and shared intentionality as a place from which to first draw out "feelings" and then to engage both tellers and witnesses in a cathartic public working through of affective response.

Shahrzad Arshadi's performance piece *It Is Only Sound That Remains* combined conceptual blending and "mood" to explore the affective qualities and politics of sound and deep listening in a piece advocating for the "larger" life story. Billed as "sound theatre," the work was an expression of what Shahrzad experienced as a deep "post-mortem" sense of friendship with Ziba Kazemi – the Montreal photojournalist executed by Iranian authorities in 2003. The project's impetus was an invitation at the time of Kazemi's death to provide French-Farsi interpretation and translation between Kazemi's son and his grandmother in Iran. Shahrzad subsequently spent considerable time reading Kazemi's personal writing and correspondence and listening to the extensive collection of audio recordings that Kazemi had made of her personal life – recordings of a mother talking to her infant son, conversations with the sounds of meal preparation in the background, moments of time together as her son grew through childhood. In performance, audiences were invited not to *see* but rather to *listen* to a richly textured layering of Persian music and poetry, archival sound, journal entries read aloud, and narrative by Shahrzad.[46] The piece eschewed mention of the violent end to Kazemi's life – the story that propelled her into the public eye. Yet, for Life Stories audiences, recognition of this unspoken context and Shahrzad's personal connection was an essential component of the overall mood, reception, and experience of the performance.

A final example of conceptual blending further illustrates its role in fostering mutual trust, transparency, and accountability. *Stories Scorched from the Desert Sun* by Hourig Attarian and Rachael Van Fossen explored "testimony as process" in a dialogic approach to research creation, focusing on ethical concerns and practical approaches to curating and mediating the emotional affect of depicted, recounted, or simulated violence on spectators.[47] The piece was created from oral history interviews conducted by Hourig, as well as her own autobiographical writing, reflections, and direct experience of war.[48] To this Hourig and Rachael added an overarching narrative frame composed of a "present-time" dialogic exchange between themselves as performance creators. Hourig described her intentions as "all about memory against forgetting, public truth-telling, knowing and understanding our past, doing justice to the stories and to the people involved, but at the same time, it is also crucially about healing and creating awareness."[49] Rachael and Hourig were particularly concerned that addressing instances of graphic violence and trauma through the power and immediacy of theatre not trap audiences in a counterproductive experience of sensationalized or eroticized violence. To counteract this, in addition to their theatrical context as narrators, the actors in the piece adopted a Brechtian "reporting" style aimed at performing a "more muted," less emotional approach to the more graphic elements.[50] One verbatim account involved the memory of a woman who, as a child of barely six in 1915 Turkey, alone and unable to comprehend her loss, slept for several nights in a field beside the body of her murdered Armenian mother. Transposed into performance, the actor played the role "as a curious young girl simply reporting the facts of the discovery of her mother's body. Her playable action became 'I am trying to figure this out as I am speaking,' with an absence of sentiment."[51] As Hourig expressed it, "what is essential for me is that the story does not get bogged down in the violence and the trauma, because *that* is not the message, that is not where I want the story to stagnate. I also do not want us, as an audience, as readers, listeners to be caught in that voyeuristic and grotesque trapping."[52] Many in the Life Stories audience were aware not only of Hourig's personal connection to the stories, but also that these performances marked the first time that she was sharing her own story in public. As she reflected,

> On the night of the performance I was engaged in an act of "multiple watching." I was watching the actors, I was watching parts of my life story, I was watching the audience, and a part of me internally was watching me watch the actors and my story … I realized that it was much more difficult hearing my story out aloud, than hearing [the others].[53]

Affirmation and Intervention

As the previous examples suggest, the affective power of much of our work stemmed from the way in which its *affirmation* of intentions and values was enhanced by conceptual blending.[54] In keeping with the core principles of community-engaged art, however, we also knew that to effect meaningful change within, as well as outside of, our project, we would need to strike a productive balance along a continuum delineated by *affirmation* (i.e., the strategic reinforcement or reiteration of commonly held traditions, beliefs, or values) and *intervention* (i.e., a cathartic rite of passage wherein identity, representation, and ways of thinking and living as sanctioned by state, religion, culture, and/or community might be questioned or subjected to change).[55] We needed, in other words, to create theatre capable of challenging our own confirmatory thinking and arresting our own "habitual thought."[56] How, in an oral history project heavily invested in fidelity to life stories and testimony, could we develop a shared intentionality accommodating the "iconoclastic imperative"[57] of the artist to challenge orthodoxies and pose difficult questions? How could we draw attention to what is *not* being said, to that which is contained in a glance, a gesture, or a sound? How would we productively engage with the implications of life narratives that are "saturated with morality" and circulate within neurobiological parameters that privilege intuitive feeling and emotion over moral reasoning?[58]

Sandeep Bhagwati's "Lamentations: Gesturing within a Realm of Shadows" moved us decidedly into the realm of intervention with his unorthodox engagement with Life Stories video-interviews.[59] Sandeep's project involved viewing interviews with the sound turned off in order to study moments of social and cultural rupture and displacement in the gestures, facial expressions, and body language of the interviewees. These moments – embodied by actors working through a process of "imitation, analysis, and synthesis" – became the basis of a performance text that, as Sandeep explains, focuses on the visceral "essence of displacement" where "a body, displaced into a new social and cultural environment, does not remain the same body."[60] Here gestures are "taken over by the will to survive, re-modelled to conform, fit in, even basically communicate in this strange new world."[61] Sandeep chose to avoid incorporating words or language from the interviews so as to eschew what Richard Sennett characterizes as the "tyrannies of intimacy" – the shutting down of dialogue that can occur as a result of the invocation of experiential authority.[62] The *Lamentations* project challenged assumptions that an emotional truth makes a social and political point more valid and pertinent, and it insisted that we – as artists and audience – consider what is lost when the personal comes to dominate the political. *Lamentations* essentially staged a self-reflexive, affective critique of the risks Sandeep perceived in North American culture (and our project) of an unexamined privileging of the "confessional mode."[63]

Back to the Swamp

Why theatre now? At least some of the answers will be found in the emergence of new intersectoral collaborations and alliances predicated on theatre's efficacy as a facilitator of shared intentionality. Neuroscience, cognitive linguistics, and moral psychology are confirming what practitioners and participants of community-engaged arts have long known: that the theatrical impulse is an essential part of human expression; that it is an effective intuitive strategy for individual and social organization; that it can be applied to trigger the "hive switch"; and that it is intimately tied up with empathy – the "*camino real* linking the emotional entanglements of actor/characters to mirror neurons and chemical changes in the brains of audiences."[64]

Yet, as Jenny Hughes points out, war and terrorism also seize the public imagination through "theatrical acts,"[65] and as history demonstrates, the hive switch – particularly when aligned with political ideology, religion, faith, or morality – is often deployed to create shared intentionality that both "binds and blinds."[66] The recent insights of science and psychology into *how* theatre works have not escaped the attention of the military-industrial complex. Natalie Alvarez's current work includes tracking the Canadian, American, and British military's use of simulated combat situations that apply theatrical *affect* to condition soldiers to maintain physiological response and associated chemical changes in the brain in an optimal "force multiplier" zone.[67] Here stress is maintained at levels high enough to trigger extreme alertness while overriding individual moral reasoning. The zone produces an autonomous default to military training – to obey a chain of command, to attack, to shoot, to kill. The conditioning attempts to prevent soldiers from crossing beyond the upper limits of the zone where they become mentally or physically incapacitated by fear or panic. Notably, the military is exploring these avenues through participation in theatricalized simulation, not through less expensive options such as films or training videos.

Community-engaged resident artists are "playing" at something akin to a team sport where the goal is democratized shared intentionality and social efficacy. Here basic training serves to condition players to keep an eye on the bigger picture – a common good. Why this theatre now? Because, otherwise, when you're up to your ass in alligators, it can be hard to remember …

NOTES

1 Jonathan Haidt, *The Righteous Mind: Why Good People are Divided by Politics and Religion* (New York: Pantheon, 2012), 244.
2 Ibid., 245.
3 Ibid., 219.
4 Raymond Williams, *The Long Revolution* (Harmondsworth, UK: Penguin, 1965), 65.
5 Alan Filewod, *Committing Theatre: Theatre Radicalism and Political Intervention in Canada* (Toronto: Between the Lines, 2011), 1.
6 Jurgen Habermas, *Legitimation Crisis*, trans. Thomas McCarthy (Boston: Beacon Press, 1975).

7 William Golding quoted in Eric Hobsbawm, *The Age of Extremes: The Short Twentieth Century, 1914–1991* (London: Michael Joseph, 1994), 1.

8 Cathy Stubington, personal communication to author.

9 Alan Filewod, *Collective Encounters: Documentary Theatre in English Canada* (Toronto: University of Toronto Press, 1987), 14.

10 Jenny Hughes, "Theatre, Performance, and the 'War on Terror,'" *Contemporary Theatre Review* 17, no. 2 (2007): 149–64.

11 David Hare quoted in Will Hammond and Dan Steward, eds., *Verbatim Verbatim: Techniques in Contemporary Documentary Theatre* (London: Oberon, 2008), 63.

12 Derek Paget, "Acts of Commitment: Activist Arts, the Rehearsed Reading, and Documentary Theatre," *New Theatre Quarterly* 26, no. 2 (2010): 173–93.

13 Linda McQuaig, "CCPA Connections Newsletter," *Canadian Counseling and Psychotherapy Association*, February 2011, 1.

14 Haidt, *Righteous Mind*, 105–6.

15 Kay Schaffer and Sidonie Smith, *Human Rights and Narrated Lives: The Ethics of Recognition* (New York: Palgrave Macmillan, 2004).

16 For information about the 2009 conference "Remembering War, Genocide and Other Human Rights Violations: Oral History, New Media, and the Arts" (2009), or about other conferences, people, research, working groups, projects, resources, and interviews connected with Montreal Life Stories, visit http://www.lifestoriesmontreal.ca.

17 Augusto Boal, *Theater of the Oppressed* (New York: Urizen Books, 1979).

18 Bill Cleveland quoted in Edward Little, "Cultural Mediation," *alt.theatre: cultural diversity and the stage* 6, no. 2 (2008): 7.

19 Haidt, *Righteous Mind*, 91.

20 Ibid.

21 Ibid., 70.

22 Ibid., 91.

23 Phillip Tetlock quoted in Haidt, *Righteous Mind*, 76.

24 Haidt, *Righteous Mind*, 76.

25 Ibid., 50 (emphasis in original).

26 Ibid., 71.

27 Erin Hurley, *Theatre and Feeling* (Houndmills, UK: Palgrave Macmillan, 2010).

28 Ibid.

29 Ibid., 23.

30 Ibid., 21–2.

31 In "traditional" theatre, the gathering phase is the period immediately preceding the show – promotions, dinner, lobby displays, etc. See Susan

Bennett, *Theatre Audiences: A Theory of Production and Reception* (New York: Routledge, 1990).

32 Lorne Shirinian, "So Far From Home," in *Remembering Mass Violence: Oral History, New Media, and Performance*, ed. Steven High, Edward Little, and Thi Ry Duong (Toronto: University of Toronto Press, 2013), 53.

33 Henry Greenspan, "Voices, Places, Spaces," in High, Little, and Duong, *Remembering Mass Violence*, 40.

34 Tim Prentki and Jan Selman, *Popular Theatre in Political Culture: Britain and Canada in Focus* (Bristol, UK: Intellect, 2000).

35 Haidt, *Righteous Mind*, 297.

36 Michael Frisch, "Sharing Authority: Oral History and the Collaborative Process," *Oral History Review* 30, no. 1 (2003): 111–13; emphasis added.

37 Julie Salverson, "Change on Whose Terms? Testimony and an Erotics of Injury," *Theatre* 31, no. 3 (2001): 119.

38 Julie Salverson, "Imagination and Art in Community Arts," in *Community Engaged Theatre and Performance*, ed. Julie Salverson, vol. 19 of *Critical Perspectives on Canadian Theatre in English* (Toronto: Playwrights Canada Press, 2011), 125.

39 Bruce McConachie, *Engaging Audiences: A Cognitive Approach to Spectating in the Field* (New York: Palgrave Macmillan, 2008), 18.

40 Ibid., 50.

41 Lisa Ndejuru, "Le Petite Coin Intact" (*Montreal Life Stories,* 21 March 2012), http://www.lifestoriesmontreal.ca/en/montréal-life-stories-rencontres-events.

42 Renee Emunah, *Acting for Real: Drama Therapy Process, Technique, and Performance* (New York: Brunner/Masel, 1994).

43 Ndejuru, "Le Petite Coin Intact."

44 Greenspan, "Voices, Places, Spaces."

45 Nisha Sajnani et al., "Turning Together: Playback Theatre, Oral History, Trauma, and Arts-based Research in the Montreal Life Stories Project," in High, Little, and Duong, *Remembering Mass Violence*, 104.

46 Caroline Künzle, "Ssh! Listen …," *alt.theatre: cultural diversity and the stage* 9, no. 1 (2011): 33.

47 Hourig Attarian and Rachael Van Fossen, "Stories Scorched from the Desert Sun: Testimony as Process," in High, Little, and Duong, *Remembering Mass Violence*, 111–27.

48 Hourig Attarian and Hermig Yogurtian, "Survivor Stories, Surviving Narratives: Autobiography, Memory, and Trauma across Generations," in *Girlhood: Redefining the Limits,* ed. Yasmin Jiwani, Candis Steenbergen, and Claudia Mitchell (Montreal: Black Rose Books, 2006), 13–34.

49 Attarian and Van Fossen, "Stories Scorched from the Desert Sun," 119.

50 Ibid., 121.

51 Ibid., 121.

52 Ibid., 119.

53 Ibid., 117.

54 For a more detailed discussion of these and other Life Stories performance projects see High, Little, and Duong, *Remembering Mass Violence*, as well as the special double issue of *alt.theatre* (9, nos. 1 and 2) focusing on oral history and performance: http://teesridtheatre.weebly.com.

55 Edward Little and Richard Paul Knowles, "The Spirit of Shivaree and the Community Play in Canada; Or The Unity in Community," in Salverson, *Community Engaged Theatre and Performance*, 20–34.

56 John Dewey, *How We Think: A Restatement of the Relation of Reflective Thinking to the Educative Process* (Chicago: Regnery, 1971).

57 Edward Little, "The Iconoclastic Imperative," *alt.theatre: cultural diversity and the stage* 6, no. 3 (2009): 4–7.

58 Haidt, *Righteous Mind*, 282.

59 Sandeep Bhagwati, "Lamentations: A Gestural Theatre in the Realm of Shadows," in High, Little, and Duong, *Remembering Mass Violence*, 77–90.

60 Ibid., 81.

61 Ibid.

62 Richard Sennett, *The Fall of Public Man* (Cambridge: Cambridge University Press, 1977), 337.

63 A video excerpt of this project is available at http://www.histoiresdevie montreal.ca/en/oral-history-and-performance.

64 McConachie, *Engaging Audiences*, 95.

65 Hughes, "Theatre, Performance, and the 'War on Terror,'" 149.

66 Haidt, *Righteous Mind*, 187.

67 Natalie Alvarez, "Empathy, Doubt, and the Simulated Encounter," *Performance Studies (Canada) Project* (April 2012), http://performancecanada .com/?post_type=portfolio&p=545.

PART II

Antidote for an Ailing Modernity

4 Politics and Presence: A Theatre of Affective Encounters

Introduction

The fact that, in and of itself, affect has no point is its critical point of departure, and if the fact that there "is no point to it" offends those who seek clear prescriptions, end goals or fixed visions the response must be that no change is possible without enthusiasm, commitment and a passionate sense of the possibility of a better life.[1]

The world, our world, is depleted, impoverished enough. Away with all duplicates of it, until we again experience more immediately what we have.[2]

As I mine understandings I have collected over the last decade at least, understandings about theatre, about young people, and about the political and cultural climate of early twenty-first-century social life, I continue to wonder why I persist in encumbering theatre with such a load to carry. Alan Read subtitled his last book about theatre, "The Last Human Venue."[3] Is that what I think too, I wonder? I have also been wrestling with a vague sense that to draw theatre into the political arena, to be persuaded by its intellectual, social, and political capacities, requires a much cooler head and a detachment from the realm of feeling if theatre is to stand a fighting chance against the ideological forces of neoliberalism and globalization. Those already swayed by the beauty, the aesthetic power, the *affect* of the theatre will see no defence necessary. But "political theatre" across cultures and over time has been celebrated more for its cool, distanced detachment than for its alluring or affecting qualities. In recent years, however, the most compelling examples of political theatre I've encountered have also been among the most

moving. Perhaps there is no surprise here, but the ages-old division between political theatre – theatre that critiques the status quo and heralds
change – and more aesthetically attuned theatre seems still to reinforce
an enduring gulf in the field. To be sure, there is no perfect example
of theatre that neatly fits in one or the other of these two camps, for
theatre often refutes such easy categorizations. And theatre, after all,
or the appraisal of theatre, is such a profoundly subjective experience
that one can hardly imagine consensus on what is or is not political, is
or is not aesthetic. Nonetheless, I will attempt, in this chapter, to use my
own recently completed research project as a case study to try to unravel
this tension between the two poles, not simply for my own edification
but because I think the strength of theatre *now* and in the days to come
depends on it. I am increasingly convinced that seeing beyond these historic divisions between political and affective theatre is key to harnessing
the potential of theatre as a political, counter-discursive, and embodied
way of seeing and learning in the face of the hegemony of globalization
and its pull to sameness.

To this case study of an ethnographic project examining the theatre-
making practices and performances of diverse young people across the
dissimilar cities of Toronto, Taipei, Boston, and Lucknow, I will bring
the recent work in Applied Theatre of James Thompson[4] and the relevant cultural critique of Richard Sennett.[5] These two thinkers, along
with some others, will be invited into this melee of conflicting theatre
histories and desires. I hope it is not ahistorical narcissism that makes
me believe that this particular tension between the cool, sharp edges of
intellectual and political theatre and the soft, warm contours of "affective" theatre is a dilemma of "our times." Such a debate between differ-
ing forms and aspirations of theatre is certainly not new. But shaking up
older ideas about such divisions seems somehow especially important
"in the now" if theatre is to make something of its moniker as "the last
human venue."

The Case: The Theatre as a Meeting Place for the Social Sciences and Humanities

The last five years have kept me very engaged with a research project that
has allowed space and time to glimpse the cares, the concerns, the passions, and the resistances of young people living at the edges of accept-
ability, barely making it to school because of the basic, daily challenges
that life presents. At their schools, we – my research team and I – have

joined them in drama classrooms, seeing their processes of working and the performances they have created as a window onto their engagement with life, its trials and pleasures. Watching them work with theatre forms has opened up a way for us, as researchers, to better understand the things that these young people care about, what they want from life, and how they imagine a compassionate and engaged community. Using theatre, as we have done, and spending time trying to understand how they communicate uniquely through the theatre, has made it possible for us to appreciate, to some extent, the everydayness of life as a teenager in some fantastically different places in the world. Making theatre with young people, and appreciating their efforts to communicate through theatre, has also helped me grasp how theatre is aspirational at its very core. Theatre teaches us unequivocally about people's hopes and for what and whom they care and, consequently, also about those things that encumber dreams and beset imaginaries. Because of this particular set of experiences I have had with young people, over the last 15 years, I now cannot help but see theatre as a way of being in the world, a way to kindle collaboration, an unapologetic tactic for exercising creative impulses and desires *with others*.

Because our work was ethnographic, it meant that over five years in these particular spaces, we were open to the everyday features of these different classroom and theatre-making cultures. We got caught up in the comings and goings, the highs and the lows of the spaces we visited. We were interlopers, watching and thinking and listening to others. Although this was a multi-sited ethnography, for the purposes of this chapter I will focus exclusively on one of our sites, a large public school in downtown Toronto. An especially fortuitous part of being in the everydayness of this site in Toronto meant that we became acquainted with a particular theatre company, Project: Humanity, as they had come to the school to work with the students and to ultimately share their play *The Middle Place* with them. And because the play was in the style of verbatim theatre – built, as it was, from their previous work with young people in a shelter for homeless youth – some of the company's artists came to carry out workshops with the students, both so they would better understand the genre of verbatim and so they would have some idea about how the company had used theatre to work with the young people whose stories were at the centre of their play.

Written by Andrew Kushnir and directed by Alan Dilworth, the documentary play has 5 actors portraying 16 youth, 3 caseworkers, and 1 playwright, Kushnir himself. *The Middle Place* was "the piece of theatre inspired by the interface between youth and theatre practitioners,"[6] as Project: Humanity describes it. The play was crafted from over 500 pages of transcribed interview texts sharing stories about the young people's relationships, their survival tactics, and their tenacious hope.

Cultural anthropologist and social theorist Richard Sennett, in his latest book, *Together: The Rituals, Pleasures and Politics of Cooperation*, illustrates the power of cooperation to countervail the social dangers of what he calls "The Uncooperative Self."[7] He argues that there are models of working – an architecture of cooperation – that may establish political togetherness in the wider public sphere. Using the historical model of the Renaissance workshop, he asserts that the nub of cooperation is active participation rather than passive presence. Sennett also warns that the distance between the elite and the masses is increasing, as inequality grows more pronounced in neo-liberal regimes in the global north and south. Strangers, then, across great gulfs, have more and more a fate in common.

At the heart of this rather unremarkable idea of "cooperation" is the notion of "the workshop," the very thing we were watching unfold with the students and the actors from Project: Humanity. "As a cultural site, workshops from ancient times onwards developed elaborate social rituals," writes Sennett.[8] Though Sennett is often speaking of labour and artisans and workshops as ways to make meaningful the secular rituals of life or to see through conflicts and difference to hear another's perspective, what I was struck by in watching Project: Humanity creators Andrew Kushnir and Antonio Cayonne work with the young students of our study site was the way in which they took them as complete human beings, not people-in-the-making as so many are apt to do when working with adolescents, and that they took as a given a diverse group's desire to create work together. In Sennett's book, he is lamenting the ways in which modern life and neo-liberalism have created an "us-against-them" view that has distorted our capacity to live together, although he is convinced that people are capable of cooperating more deeply than the existing social order envisions. It was this belief in *action through theatre making* that helped me understand the work of Kushnir and Cayonne as profoundly political and pedagogically sophisticated. It did not simply presume a "togetherness" with the group of students but *earned it* through an important process of allowing difference to bubble up, while still clearly making the case that we were better off together than apart, acknowledging in their own way, perhaps, Victor Turner's reading that we are "programmed for cooperation, but prepared for conflict."[9] Their theatre performance of *The Middle Place* in so many ways echoed this very theme, now reverberating in the hearts and minds of the young people with whom we had worked.

Susan Bennett's theorizations of "audience," as it is construed as a cultural practice, are also relevant here. She observes that as an audience, what matters is "our willingness to engage with performances in ways that speak to the most intimate detail of our experience."[10] The young people working with the actors were not merely an audience to their work but were co-constructors of ideas and creations. While they were an audience to *The Middle Place* production, they also created their own theatre pieces following the show, inspired as they were by the genre and by the stories of the lives they had heard about in the play. Bennett's historical readings of theatre's audiences helps to explain how the workshop with the students and the play itself became *meeting places* as well as how this unfolding relationship rewrites, as Brecht's work once did, the terms of that meeting. Bennett examines Brecht's desire to search for a new audience, to "establish an oppositional cultural practice"[11] to make obvious the ways in which theatre audiences had previously affirmed dominant ideologies. Bennett goes on to examine those who had influenced Brecht – Meyerhold, Eisenstein, Piscator – and their challenges to mainstream conceptions of audience, finally pointing to contemporary forms of feminist and queer performances that also attempt to rewrite the relationships at the core of the production-reception contract. As I watched the students and facilitators work, it seemed to me as though Project: Humanity had created a new form of "naturalism," not like that rejected by Brecht and others, but a naturalism that invited a reflexivity and an interrogation of one's own assumptions.

As the production moved from touring schools to mainstream stages (Theatre Passe Muraille in 2010 and Canadian Stage in 2011), the company continued to extend their ideas of theatre as a "meeting place" by curating the lobbies of the theatres and extending the experience of the performance well beyond the curtain call through various forms of audience interaction. Their call to engagement, if not action, remained central. "Culturally overcoded," as Bennett calls it,[12] two very different theatres in Toronto began to create meaning long before the performances began, even though most of the audience's experiences of meaning take place at the time of the performance, she writes. But one of the greatest contributions of her study of theatre audiences is how we might come to view the theatrical event beyond its immediate conditions and as a social composition.

Though our research team did conduct about 75 post-performance interviews with youth and adult audience members at both Theatre Passe Muraille and Canadian Stage, an interview with four of the actors from the play, and further interviews at our Toronto school research site with the youth who had seen the play both in their school auditorium and at the theatre, it was our ethnographic experience over time with the youth, and our burgeoning relationship with the theatre company, that really brought into sharp focus the place of affect theory in the reception and production of theatre and its important relationship to socially engaged and political theatre.

The Affective Register: "He Thinks Its Thoughts? No. He Feels His Feelings."

In the 1982 film *E.T.*, the US military, trying to understand the relationship between two beings – the young boy Elliot and E.T., the extraterrestrial from outer space – mistakes their relationship as cerebral only but is corrected by Elliott's older brother, who tries to explain the special bond that has been formed between the two. Elliot has a bodily, sensorial response to the feelings projected by E.T. They have a meeting place between them, imbued with thought *and* feeling. Creating a relationship beyond sentiment, they come to share a perspective on the universe.

The insight about human connection made in the film *E.T.* sits nicely alongside James Thompson's meditation on what is happening in the experience of performance. What is especially important for this chapter, from Thompson's 2009 book, *Performance Affects*, is his argument that what reaches us through the senses, in theatre, is foundational to the politics of theatre and performance, eschewing entirely the notion that the affective realm repudiates political awareness and action.[13] His work therefore sits squarely in what has been described by many as the *affective turn* in social research.[14] His book is, in one sense, an argument that positions the affective register in theatre as key to both the aesthetic and the political force of theatre. The work Thompson cites, like the work of Project: Humanity that I observed, paid careful attention to the affective register of theatre but also generated radical intentions on the political register. How does that work?

While empathy is a concept often invoked in discussions of theatre's affective power, it is one I have tended to avoid because of the many pitfalls associated with mistaking an imagined scenario for a real one, or taking the momentary "feelings" of an experience to stand in for those felt by others in real material circumstances. Tomes have been written on empathy and its limits that I won't rehearse here. But Richard Sennett approached the concept in ways that I have found very useful for understanding its place in the theatre. Sennett insists that curiosity figures more strongly in empathy than in sympathy: "Both sympathy and empathy convey recognition, and both forge a bond, but one is an embrace, the other an encounter."[15] He argues that empathy, or efforts to *practise* empathy, have a particular political application. While sympathy can be understood as one emotional reward for the "thesis-antithesis-synthesis play of dialectic," empathy is linked to dialogic exchange, driven by curiosity but entirely lacking the satisfaction of closure that sympathy invokes. In his view, sympathy allows us to remain focused inside ourselves while empathy forces us outside. For a politically engaged theatre, this might mean that we cannot assume a shared existence, more and more the chorus of globalism, but must earn one.

In our post-performance interviews at Theatre Passe Muraille and at Canadian Stage, there were several young people who identified with the experience of shelter life and therefore with many of the experiences shared in the play. They had an easy way in. For each of these youth, the terrain of sensation was pronounced. One young man we interviewed was the eldest of seven children in Kenya but came to Canada for an education and to send money back home to his family. He lived in a youth shelter:

ASAD: Actually, the play's real 'cause, as I was saying I've experienced since I came to Canada. I stayed in Horizon shelter for youth for three months. So I've seen a lot of people who've been stay at the shelter. I've been living, I've eating, I've been sleeping there. So I've seen people have dreams. People who doesn't have dreams, they are just there for nothing ... they are there to ... hmm ... what can I say? ... for the sake of the day to pass. So I know how it was in the play. I know how it was. And it was the true thing what they were saying on the play ... I got a lot of hard time when I was in the Horizon 'cause sometimes I come from school, I'm tired, I want to read – I can't read. So I have to wait till 11 [when] people go to beds. I have to come out through the beds. Come and read. I have to wake up early to go to school. I can't go to sleep, I have to wait till 11. And come out when the lights are down in the rooms. I like the place where they are talking about their dreams. And also, I like the place where someone is ready to help his or her parents 'cause they have the value of her parents. It's good to have the value of your parents, even if you're in a bad condition ... That's what I am ... I am in that situation. I'm in a bad situation. I live all alone. I know how my parents are and how they survive. But I have to think about them. Because I come from a big family, family of seven. I'm the first one. I'm responsible of all my sisters and brothers there. So you see ... how ... I mean ... I'm in student shelter, you know, I'm all alone. I know how my parents are in a hard situation. So I have to do something to help them. They can't survive with a little money. They have six children back home ... My grandma too. So I have [to] support my family.[16]

Because the company negotiated that a certain number of tickets were always reserved for shelter youth, we were able to interview several of them:

INTERVIEWER: If you had to tell Project: Humanity something about this play, what would you say? What would you want them to know?

INTERVIEWEE: Honestly, I'm really happy that something like this ... It was me. I'm really happy that they actually went out and took the time for free. They didn't have to do it. They did it and it took their time to learn about people like us, because we get shut down all the time. If you walk by Covenant House, someone in a suit walks by and you say hi, they don't look at you. They won't even look at your face. You are like, "Hi, have a good day." I say that to everybody. I just like that. I say, "Have a good day, sir." He won't even turn around. Nothing. He won't even step towards me. It's because I'm a shelter kid. No matter how nice I look, they know I still live there. I think it [this play] definitely changes people's views, because it makes us seem like ... Yes, we have problems too. We are still people; we still have intelligence ... I'm really happy that I took my time to go. I'm really satisfied with the play. I think it was really great. I think it gave a really good perspective of us. We are still people, regardless. The things she said about, like the ten thousand dollars giving it to her mom. If I have ten thousand dollars, I'd give all my money to my mom. All my money. My mom has a nice place, whatever. But my dad ... They are going through divorce right now. My dad is basically leaving the country because he doesn't want to pay support. So my mom doesn't have the money for her house. She doesn't know if she can pay her rent. I would give all my money to my mom. It wouldn't last long because it's like $1600 per month. But I would still do it because it's something.[17]

Having a powerful affective response to the play didn't always mean having a positive response:

INTERVIEWEE: I'm gonna say one thing that killed me in that play. When the actress said, "My dad used to hit me." I was like, "Fuck, I can't deal with this." I turned my head and closed my ears. Last time I saw my dad before I went to CAS [Children's Aid Society] he tried to strangle me, because I cleaned up my bathroom in New Years. He was like, "Get the fuck out of here!" He was screaming at me, choking me. I literally kicked him and ran into the bathroom and locked the door. And then Covenant House ... Because I hate to bring stuff like that up. My dad always beat the shit out of me. We always had that problem. I had to go to the hospital a bunch of times for that. I cannot sit here and listen. When it happens, I tried to cover my ears. I started crying, and the girl beside me started to cry. It made me cry even more. I really have bad problems with situations like this. It's not something that's easy for me to do. I have really bad flashback problems. Hearing something like that triggers me so hard. I don't know what to do. I literally almost left the play, but then she stopped talking. So I calmed down.[18]

Another young man who saw the play also found its affective register almost too difficult to handle:

INTERVIEWEE: This was right on point. It was right on point. Uh, at one point, I ... uh ... I actually couldn't take it. I couldn't take it in a sense where, um, I felt it, like everything they were saying, everything that was being acted out, down to the very teeth, was [pause] exactly how it is. It was becoming a little bit too much for my heart to handle. I was like, um, "ok I can't do this. I can't do this." But I thought through it, and I watched, and um ... really, in a sense, it wakes you up. It wakes you to a reality that isn't pushed to the forefront ... And me being in the shelter right now, seeing the drama every day, every day, every day, it hit a cord, like [snapping fingers three times]. Yeah. I would love for more people to come here and see this, because honestly, after seeing this, I don't even feel like I want to go back to the shelter. I'm gonna be working twice as hard to get out, after seeing this ... And living in the shelter that I've seen it, living in a shelter, you get people telling you you are dumb every day. You get people telling you maybe you should aim a little bit lower. Maybe you should try something a little bit easier. So after a while, you ... it's true what they just said, it wears you out. After a while, it eats away at your personality, eats away at your self-esteem. It just eats away at you. And you stop believing in yourself. You stop believing you can do anything. It's just [pause] period. Not a place you want to be ... I was thinking to myself maybe I shouldn't be seeing this right now. And it's a good thing because ... I was gonna take my girlfriend to see this play, and she couldn't come. And, to be honest with you, in a sense, I kind of wish she did see it, because these are the things that everyone needs to know. And in another sense I'm kinda happy that she didn't see it, because I'm not sure her heart could have handled it. So really it's like mixed feelings. It's really, really heart-felt, really emotional. I was getting emotional up there. At one point, I turned my head away, and I was looking at the opposite direction, I just couldn't [pause]. Yeah, it was deep.[19]

The surprise that these young people express about their feelings and responses to the play lends credence to Julie Salverson's observation in this volume: "we live in a time where the ability to feel – ourselves, others, the world we live in – is disappearing. Without this essential faculty, so central to the language of theatre, we lose our ability to know who we are and what matters."[20] An irony, from my vantage point, with the affective responses here is that they were inspired by the theatrical aesthetics of the piece, the form of the piece. It is a mistake to assume that proximity to the content, its "real-life" qualities alone, are what made this piece speak, as it did, to so many young people. Because the show was not over-produced, as so many forms of "entertainment" are in the cultural landscape of young people, there was a sharpness to this sensory experience. The surfaces of the lives were baldly presented, without an overlaying of didactic or interpreted meanings. While the young people did not always have the vocabulary to talk about form, it was clear to me that the playwright had cut back on content (mining, as he did, from 500 pages of transcribed text down to a 60-page, 70-minute performance) so we could see the thing, in all its starkness. Affects and effects in tuneful tandem.

As did Bennett, Thompson draws on Brecht, though not to rehearse the familiar poles of "theatre for pleasure" and "theatre for instruction." Instead, he likens Brecht's familiar description of epic theatre – "what is natural must have the force of what is startling"[21] – with Benjamin's reading of Brecht's work producing "astonishment" rather than "empathy"[22] and Brian Massumi's interpretation of Deleuze's work as a "shock to thought."[23] In collecting all of these readings of the apparent gulf between effects and affects, Thompson is inviting the reader to consider affect as a stratum of meaning rather than its opposite. "Affect might produce a shock to thought," he writes, "but that thought cannot be simplistically detached from the affective realm."[24] Political engagement then must not be banished to that part of the body called the mind or divorced from its genesis in affective response.

I would argue that the responses of the students I have cited demonstrate deep affect and that they are also political in the sense of confronting social stigma and marginalization. But one might wonder whether they are political in the Brechtian sense; do they demonstrate the uncovering of a wider ideology of power? Perhaps longitudinal empirical research might help us argue this latter point more convincingly, but I remain satisfied that when people wake up even a smidgen with a "shock to thought," action may follow, or it may not. It may take several more astonishing, shocking, affective experiences to galvanize a resolute response. But without the awakening in the first instance, much less is thinkable. After a "shock to thought," it will take some energy not to act.

Side Affects: The Political Comes into Play

What I am proposing here is that one of the possible outcomes of theatre that works affectively on its audience is political. If we take Clough's premise that affect is related to the augmentation or diminution of the body's capacity to act, engage, and connect, or what she describes as its sense of aliveness, we are seeing the political as a question of capacity or intensity rather than of knowledge alone.[25] Erin Hurley, along with the literary theorists she draws from, considers the affective work of theatre as an opportunity to move the "personal or intimate terrains of feeling into public forums to test the political and social resonance of the personal and to sense the ideological contours of lived experience."[26] Like Hurley, Thompson believes theatre affects can be read as an experiment in reverberation between personal feeling and sociopolitical timbre. Affect, then, is an expansive term, not simply the opposite of cognition. Extending Clough's work, Thompson uses Gumbrecht's notion of "nonhermeneutics" to argue that the affective realm expands the contemplation of arts' processes and engagements beyond that "thin band of consciousness we now call cognition."[27] What is innovative about Thompson's work is that he uses Gumbrecht's positioning of a "presence culture" against a "meaning culture," in which Gumbrecht is reacting against the institutional dominance of the hermeneutic dimension, and gives this "presence culture" a fresh political reading. In other words, where Gumbrecht is resisting the dominance of interpretation in scholarly methods, an interpretation which is incapable of reading the complexity of experience, Thompson is suggesting that that very arousal of sensation through theatre "might loosen the icy grip of certain oppressive visions of how we should be in the world"[28] and lead to forms of political focus.

With some irony, Thompson is effectively using Gumbrecht's work to support a political reading of affect, while Gumbrecht himself would disavow any such interpretation of the utility of what he calls "presence culture" and what others more readily refer to as affect. In affect, Thompson finds a criticality well worth examining further; for me, it is a powerful assessment of theatre performance that inspires political arousal by drawing productively on the senses. While such utopic notions of beauty, joy, and peace may seem to be at odds with the material world and therefore offer *an escape* from it, Thompson is simply suggesting that the affective experience of such aesthetic states of being may, equally, *initiate* a radical process of critical engagement with the world.

> INTERVIEWER: Is there anything else you would like to say? Anything beyond the questions I've asked you?
>
> INTERVIEWEE: It's made me wanna get involved, like, I mean I've wanted to get involved for a while but it's kinda like, it's kinda like the last shot. Like, "come on do something already" you know – it just made me wanna ...
>
> INTERVIEWER: Do you have any ideas about how you would want to get involved?
>
> INTERVIEWEE: Well, I would wanna like, umm talk to Antonio (I think that's what his name was) and, like, try to get involved with the shelter just maybe just going there and being a friend if anyone wants me to be their friend. Like, I don't know what I could do, but I'm just willing to do something.[29]

The almost inarticulacy of this interviewee's response would support Thompson's insistence that the "decisive moment of transformation is found in an abandonment of 'solutions' and 'interpretations' and a location of consciousness in gesture and sounds."[30] Yet, in the audit culture in which we now live, when we cannot easily enumerate the specific benefits of having engaged in or witnessed a piece of theatre, when we cannot list its positive effects, it potentially loses its sway or power in the world.

There is one other aspect of encountering a beautiful or powerful or affective performance that bears examination. The young man just quoted who wants to "do something" and the earlier interview with the young man who wished his girlfriend had seen the show with him both suggest the communitarian and relational aspects of affect. In Elaine Scarry's account of beauty and justice, there often develops in the beholder a sense of urgency and "a desire to bring new things into the world."[31] In Thompson's reading of this, rather than an exclusive and private response, this response to the affect of art is a stimulus to collaborative work, an invitation to participate, or an engagement with others, to offer other people the same sense of pleasure, whether that be the jolt of painful awareness that new consciousness brings or the poetry of struggle revealed through *The Middle Place* to youth audience members. In Thompson's reworking of the "expansiveness of beauty" – suggesting that such affective experiences cannot be contained in one person but rather compel a sharing with others, a forward-moving momentum – such experiences reveal "a desire to maintain and share a heightened sense of presence."[32]

Part of the critique of forms of theatre that exploit suffering and pain centres on what is sometimes referred to as the "aesthetics of injury."[33] Some argue that this kind of theatre, especially in Applied Theatre projects with marginalized communities, has potentially profound ethical problems, as the risk of re-violation is ever present. *The Middle Place* may indeed have such a claim levelled against it, with its exploration of terribly difficult and painful lives of homeless young people with so few prospects for realizing their dreams. No matter what ethical guidelines one adheres to or how good theatre-makers' intensions might be, the possibility of exploitation is always present. The human relations underscoring the artistic choices must remain in the foreground. And as with beauty, the same set of powerful possibilities is also possible for the representation of pain on stage to instigate a political, communal response.

Presence

> INTERVIEWEE: When you sit at home and watch TV, there're so many things happening around you. You are distracted by your phone. You are distracted by your parents telling you to do something. Whereas a play, you are just sitting there. It feels like it's just you and the people in the play. It didn't feel like there was an audience. It was just you and the actors ... That's a difference between TV, because you actually feel it. You are actually in the moment.

"There's something you have to know about my family ... they always show up," explained my brother once to his son in recounting the propensity in our family to come when we're invited. My brother was right. We do show up. What does it mean to show up? Is this simply an old-fashioned courtesy? A sense of obligation? No. It is fundamentally about knowing that being there is what counts, whatever the outcome. Today, we can be "present" in a thousand different and often terribly impressive ways. Digital platforms for communication are astonishing. But the felt presence of sharing a physical space, watching bodies encounter one another, feeling the breath of the stranger behind you on the back of your neck – it matters.

What makes theatre "the last human venue," if it is indeed that, is the possibility of community and co-presence. Andrew Kushnir, in this volume, persuasively argues that we go to the theatre to congregate and that this is a deeply humanizing experience. When we congregate, all manner of responses, affective or otherwise, to a performance and to each other remain open. But Kushnir says we also desire the work that the theatre demands of us:

> [O]ne of the attractive differences between storytelling in film and theatre is that theatre can feel much more like work. The illusion is more tenuous and demands more audience involvement and reinvestment. There is intense rejuvenation when the work pays off; when you feel, as an audience, you have helped hold up the metaphor; when you feel like you have been in silent but communal dialogue with the play; when you have situated yourself and your spectator-peers in a dilemma, dialectic, or investigation. It is a distinctive feeling ... The act of sitting still with that particular focus, in communion with others doing the same, can be entirely revivifying.[34]

I am inclined to think that theatre is the last human venue because being together in the way that theatre demands, in silent communion for a stolen moment in time, engages us affectively and opens the possibility for critical thought and political engagement precisely because of the suppleness of metaphor. Metaphor affords multiple entry points, invites strangers in, provokes analogous and critical thinking, and can command formidable affects. Again, I encumber theatre with an enormous burden. But, in my experience, there are few venues in which the "shock of thought" and its attendant affective responses are jointly summoned. We segregate these responses at our own peril. "We" have accepted a muted social life detached from the full potential of our human power to engage, affectively and critically, Sontag protests at the opening of this chapter.

The theatre is one place of experimentation where this ubiquitous condition might be confronted.

Theatre cannot promise the world; it may simply open a door. Sometimes that is the best that theatre can accomplish. And it is enough.

NOTES

1 James Thompson, *Performance Affects: Applied Theatre and the End of Effect* (Houndmills, UK: Palgrave Macmillan, 2009), 128.

2 Susan Sontag, *Against Interpretation* (London: Vintage, 2001), 7.

3 Alan Read, *Theatre, Intimacy and Engagement: The Last Human Venue* (Houndmills, UK: Palgrave Macmillan, 2009).

4 Thompson, *Performance Affects*.

5 Richard Sennett, *Together: The Rituals, Pleasures and Politics of Cooperation* (New Haven, CT: Yale University Press, 2012).

6 Project: Humanity, "About," http://www.projecthumanity.ca/past-events/#/the-middle-place-2009-2011/ (accessed 15 July 2015).

7 Sennett, *Together*, 179.

8 Ibid., 57.

9 Victor Turner, *From Ritual to Theater* (New York: Performing Arts Journal Publications, 1982), 11.

10 Susan Bennett, *Theatre Audiences: A Theory of Production and Reception* (Abingdon, UK: Routledge, 1997), vii.

11 Ibid., 24.

12 Bennett, *Theatre Audiences*.

13 Thompson, *Performance Affects*.

14 Patricia Ticineto Clough with Jean O'Malley Halley, eds., *The Affective Turn: Theorizing the Social* (Durham, NC: Duke University Press, 2007).

15 Sennett, *Together*, 21.

16 Theatre Passe Muraille Youth Interview, 9 November 2010.

17 Theatre Passe Muraille Youth Interview, 29 October 2010.

18 Ibid.

19 Ibid.

20 Chapter 10.

21 Thompson, *Performance Affects*, 129.

22 Ibid., 129.

23 Ibid.

24 Ibid., 130.

25 Clough and Halley, *Affective Turn*.

26 Erin Hurley, *Theatres of Affect: New Essays on Canadian Theatre* (Toronto: Playwrights Canada Press, 2014), 5.
27 Hans Ulrich Gumbrecht, *Production of Presence: What Meaning Cannot Convey* (Stanford, CA: Stanford University Press, 2004), 236, as quoted in Thompson, *Performance Affects*, 120.
28 Ibid., 125.
29 Theatre Passe Muraille Youth Interview, 3 November 2010.
30 Thompson, *Performance Affects*, 131.
31 Elaine Scarry, *On Beauty and Being Just* (London: Duckbacks, 1999), 46.
32 Thompson, *Performance Affects*, 145.
33 See Julie Salverson, "Transgressive Storytelling or an Aesthetic of Injury: Performance, Pedagogy and Ethics," 2nd ed., *Theatre Research in Canada* 20, no. 1 (1999): 35–51, http://journals.hil.unb.ca/index.php/TRIC.
34 Chapter 5.

5 If You Mingle: Thoughts on How Theatre Humanizes the Audience

ANDREW KUSHNIR

I was approached by the artist-led non-profit Project: Humanity in 2007 to write a play about youth shelter residents, to be performed for youth in shelters and high schools. Though completely uninitiated in the form, I got it into my head that I should employ verbatim theatre techniques; I was convinced the specificity of these young people's words, experiences, and perspectives would trump any and all poetry I could dream up on their behalf. And what's more, I felt my encounters with residents of Youth Without Shelter, as they happened, were the vivid stuff of theatre. Directed by Alan Dilworth, the piece had 5 actors enact my selected interactions with 16 shelter youth and 3 of their caseworkers. I played myself – a well-intentioned Outsider/Interviewer. And what was originally envisioned as a play for young people would go on to have a much more expansive life: productions for general audiences at Theatre Passe Muraille and Canadian Stage and a national tour to Great Canadian Theatre Company (GCTC) in Ottawa and the Belfry in Victoria.

When we performed *The Middle Place*, we frequently held talkbacks after performances (*Figure 5.1*).[1] The portraits of so-called at-risk youth in the play are complicated and untidy. The nature of hope and despair in the play makes for a disquieting tension. And these complexities, coupled with the show's unusual aesthetic, meant that these Q&As with audiences tended to be quite vibrant. I took great pleasure in this addendum to the piece and, along with the cast, was more than happy to shed whatever light I could on the play's creative process, our company's particular (and newly developed) verbatim theatre techniques, and the youth who had generously permitted me to share their words. In February 2011, following one of the evening shows at Canadian Stage, a man put up his hand and said, "Up until tonight, I would have crossed the

5.1 Akosua Amo-Adem, Antonio Cayonne, Jessica Greenberg, and Kevin Walker in *The Middle Place* (from left to right). Design by Jung-Hye Kim. Photo by Aviva Armour Ostroff.

street to avoid any of these kids. Having seen this play and heard their stories, I will think twice about doing that. And at the very least, if I still decide to cross the street, I'll know it has likely more to do with me than it does with them."

Theatre's imperative can certainly be *to entertain* or *to educate*, but I am most compelled by its capacity *to humanize* the members of an audience. This plays out in the physical ritual of theatre-going, the imaginative encounter supplied by a strong piece of theatre, and the subsequent "denoising" that can happen within ourselves and between one another as we engage with timely and compelling work. To me, a successful theatrical experience bears a likeness to travelling alone in a foreign country. It has you meeting new people, discovering unfamiliar flavours, sounds, landscapes, and customs – but it is as if through encountering that which seems alien, you are brought closer to yourself and your own narratives. In our "information age" – one teeming with news, facts, and opinions – have we succumbed to an illusion of seeing more of the world while in fact growing inadvertently more sedentary in our thinking and feeling? Are we moving towards or away from being citizens that question, for instance, why we might cross that street to avoid certain youth? The gentleman at Canadian Stage was aware of homeless youth – enough to conceive of them as something worth crossing the street to avoid. He had likely encountered at one time or another an online petition, an ad, a newspaper or magazine article, news of a fundraiser, some bit of outreach coaxing him towards an empathetic leap. Doubtless he had seen a homeless youth depicted on film or television. What was it about his experience in the theatre that inspired him not only to rethink his way of being in the world but to announce it to a room full of strangers? I'm not sure reading *The Middle Place* at home would have elicited his particular response. Had the content of the play been represented as a documentary film or a sizeable article in the *Toronto Star*, I am not confident this man would have been affected in quite the same way.

In literature, in journalism, in theatre we often hear about "humanizing the 'other.'" To me, this concept has the ring of "the 'other' has been changed" or even, "the other's humanity is more evident because I recognize it." I have tried to pay attention to the way people use the word "humanize" (even my own usage), particularly following pieces of theatre asking questions of social justice – that is to say, pieces of political theatre that both bring the issues of the day into the room for consideration and look to implicate the spectator. During the various runs of *The Middle Place*, I most often encountered two different takes on the expression "to humanize." Some audience members – typically people working with homeless youth – would say, "You have humanized *youth homelessness* with this play." As a playwright, I understood "to humanize" in this case as giving an issue time, space, and theatrical metaphor. I could see why some front-line workers would respond with this. To *humanize*, in this way, is to put a human face/voice to something that may be predominantly represented through statistics, commonly held belief, or conjecture. To *humanize* is to necessarily deepen our understanding of something and to complicate or challenge preconceptions; it is to remind us that something perceived as a "social problem" or "issue" is in fact human beings in trying circumstances typically deserving of our empathy.

That said, on a number of occasions, an audience member would comment to me, "You have humanized *those kids*." It's possible that these audience members were trying to communicate something very similar to "you have humanized *youth homelessness*," but the phrasing is noteworthy and, for me, both tricky and exciting. I liken it to when people have

told me (and it has happened often), "You've given those kids a voice."
This sort of comment always makes me uncomfortable because I balk
at the idea that artists are giving their subjects a voice through verbatim
theatre work. In fact, I think verbatim theatre, which employs interview
transcripts to fashion dialogue and dialectics, does something wholly different than giving voice; it *transfers* voice – from an originator through an
interpreter to an audience. The human subjects I engage with, record,
transcribe, and theatrically contextualize have voices well before I meet
them. I have gravitated to them for that very quality, the voices they possess in the world. What certain individuals and groups lack are not voices,
but listeners – the focused and active variety – which is precisely what the
theatre can supply. As a theatre artist, I can bring people together in a
room and we can coexist with stories, ideologies, and conflicts that may
be elusive, challenging, or even unpleasant. I can do my very best to
carefully structure a theatrical encounter that keeps listeners engaged
with voices, viewpoints, crises, and at times irreconcilable questions of
justice. And so when an audience member offers such a comment about
humanizing shelter kids or giving them a voice, my sense is that they are
betraying something quite different. They are in fact saying, "The play
helped me listen to those kids' voices" or "As an audience member, *I*
have been humanized."

It is by no means revelatory to suggest that we are culturally starving
for humanizing activities. Today, we find ourselves working very hard to
stay in the loop, to maintain our roles as nodes in various networks. We
are constantly passing messages along, often at the expense of having
any in-depth encounters – with either the messages or the people we
are passing them off to. We have become increasingly accustomed to
"skimming" through human stories, and so "skimming" through how we
feel and think about them. We have been encouraged to become high-
efficiency consumers on all fronts. And we engage more and more with
entertainment that offers respite from our networks, rather than undergoing experiences that acknowledge our presence, the power of our
imaginations (individual and collective), and our own capacity for transformation. In his "Anti-Web 2.0 Manifesto" featured on ChangeThis.
com, Andrew Keen offers, "The cultural consequence of uncontrolled
digital development will be social vertigo. Culture will be spinning and
in continual flux. Everything will be in motion; everything will be opinion."[2] Successful theatrical experiences have the potential to provide a
therapeutic cocktail that is in short supply: stillness, a singular focus, and
something that could be referred to as "slow time."

When reporter and biographer Robert Caro was asked by *Time* magazine about the speed and brevity of the information age, he responded
with, "To me, time equals truth. There is no one truth ... It's very important to have time to ask all your questions."[3] The amount of time
that theatre takes is significant, as is the character of that time. Theatre
requires us to spend more time with certain ideas and feelings, in the
company of others doing the same. There is a quality to this time. American academic James Billington invokes Keats's "silence and slow time" in
a 2001 speech given at the Library of Congress entitled "Humanizing the
Information Revolution."[4] He was speaking of libraries, but his invocation is at the heart of what theatre can be in our current social climate.

> The library ... still takes us out of our noisy hurry-up present-minded world
> into that Keatsian world of silence and slow time ... which favors active
> minds over spectator passivity, putting things together rather than just tak-
> ing them apart – and leads us on into the ongoing pursuit of truth, which
> helps to keep us from the pursuit of each other.[5]

Theatre is of vital importance today because it slows our pace – it requires us to take the time to actively piece together another's narrative.
Theatre *publicly* invites us to be listeners, thinkers, and feelers within a
general social climate that tends to dissuade (if not sabotage) reflection,
breath, and critical thinking. That Keatsian silence can very much be
theatre's capacity to serve as a refuge from the cacophony that is so-
called expertise, popular opinion, trending stories, the disguised and
not-so-disguised forces of consumerism. It can often feel as though the
world has us seeing much but witnessing little. Theatre can achieve quite
the opposite. Director and professor David Ian Rabey says of Howard
Barker's aesthetic, "The sense of having witnessed too much is crucial. It
leads not to a drunkenness or a reeling exhaustion but a roaring sense
of possibility and a rinsing out of accumulated expectations."[6] Theatre
gives us the time to witness too much.

What is it about the time in the theatre that humanizes us? I believe it
has something to do with congregating in service of metaphors – metaphors that cannot live without a communal effort to attend to them. In
his collection of essays and speeches *Obedience, Struggle & Revolt*, David
Hare provides the following as a caution to theatre artists:

> A play is not actors, a play is not a text; a play is what happens between
> the stage and the audience. A play is a performance. So if a play is to be a

weapon in the class struggle, then that weapon is not going to be the things
you are saying; it is the interaction of what you are saying and what the audience is thinking. The play is in the air.[7]

Why is it heaven when you sit down in a near-empty movie theatre to
catch a film, and why is it hell to be one of six people in the audience
of a fringe festival show? It has something to do with theatre's pressure
of participation and the relief that comes with sharing the undertaking. People need to "show up" to the theatre – both literally and figu-
ratively. It's a demanding form, and I would argue that one of the
attractive differences between storytelling in film and theatre is that
theatre can feel much more like work. The illusion is more tenuous
and demands more audience involvement and reinvestment. There
is intense rejuvenation when the work pays off; when you feel, as an
audience, you have helped hold up the metaphor; when you feel like
you have been in silent but communal dialogue with the play; when
you have situated yourself and your spectator-peers in a dilemma, dialectic, or investigation. It is a distinctive feeling when you're making
meaning of something. The act of sitting still with that particular focus, in communion with others doing the same, can be entirely revivi-
fying. As Hare says, there is something being held "in the air" between
artists and audience – a tacit job, a human collaboration – that makes
it a uniquely humanizing experience.[8]

Everything in theatre is metaphor, whether it be the set that is not a
real place or the dialogue that is not real people talking (even in verbatim theatre). In a recent article in the *Guardian*, British playwright
Tim Crouch quotes Austrian writer Peter Handke on metaphor and the
stage: "Light is brightness pretending to be other brightness; a chair is a
chair pretending to be another chair."[9] Crouch adds, "Art's power is its
ability to contain the idea of one thing inside something else." In terms
of theatre that overtly asks questions of social justice, metaphor is that
fundamentally inclusive thing that elevates the experience of information, fosters a sense of democracy, and helps personalize (and emotional-
ize) social awareness. Metaphor resists our progressively literal thinking/
feeling in the "real" world – it can provide an alternative to the binaries
of good/evil, stylish/lame, leftist/rightist. At its finest, metaphor allows
for the possibility of multiple-truths-at-once, and as human beings, we
crave that kind of imaginative freedom. Whether we are conscious of it
or not, we come to the theatre for this sense of community in the joint
task of imagining things that are not really there in order to have very

real feelings about them. We come together to bring that metaphor to life, and the collaboration – when it is going well – has us intimately intermingling with the subject matter in question and the group of people questioning it. By virtue of participating, we are inexorably implicated in a communal truth-seeking mission.

Theatre's capacity to create "slow time," a focus, a stillness, and a community fashioned around metaphor are all fine and good, but what is the best use of this synergy and in what way does contemporary life call for it? Edward Bond, on a recent visit to Toronto, claimed that the stage is an outward extension of our psyche – that the stage and drama were born out of a human need to see dilemmas represented and played out.[10] As beings, we conceived of a house because we needed somewhere to live. We conceived of the stage because we needed somewhere to feel, to question, to safely witness the consequences of human impulses. I would add to this: we conceived of the stage so as to have encounters that may otherwise be impossible. Yes, theatre lets us share space with gods and ghosts, with Julius Caesar, Joan of Arc, and Mark Rothko. It lets us relocate to czarist Russia, medieval Denmark, 1940s New Orleans. It can also afford us an encounter with the most marginalized factions and members of our own society – people we may otherwise be too afraid or ashamed to engage with. And this for me is theatre's unrivalled niche and imperative: its capacity to ask questions of justice through encounters *on a human scale*. We are humanized by our proximity – our sharing of space (physical and psychic) – to things that can challenge and disrupt our own narratives. Theatre is such a sensible way of engaging with dangerous and clashing politics, with people we disagree with, with people we dislike or even despise. If we eschew that sort of encounter in the "real" world, then how else can it happen? And without that encounter, how do we judge, as a society, what is important? It is no wonder to me that the gentleman at *The Middle Place* announced his personal epiphany to a room of strangers – it was the room of strangers that helped him get there and he was likely hoping to find others who had undergone a similar shift in thinking. Theatre is a personal and public action at once. Not unlike church or a yoga class, it is simultaneously social and introspective, and it can be that rare practice that activates both the imagination and conscience simultaneously.

Our social awareness can be spotty, often disserved by our journalism and media. Our government can be chronically opaque; our increasingly polarized political landscape, unwelcoming. It's all creating a need for a theatre that can give us more information and the opportunity to better discover where we stand with it. Howard Barker says,

> In a society disciplined by moral imperatives of gross simplicity, complexity itself, ambiguity itself, is a political posture of profound strength. The play, which makes demands of its audience, both of an emotional and interpretive nature, becomes a source of freedom, necessarily hard won. The play which refuses the message, the lecture, the conscience-ridden exposé, but which insists on the inventive and imaginative at every point, creates new tensions in a blandly entertainment-led culture.[11]

And so, for me, the question of "Why theatre now?" is twinned with "What kind of theatre now?" Playwright David Hare makes this point:

> Audiences, at this time of global unease, urgently feel the need for a place where things can be put under sustained and serious scrutiny. They want the facts, but also they want the chance to look at the facts together, and in some depth.[12]

He adds, "Our lives must be refreshed with images which are not official, not approved; that break what George Orwell called 'the Geneva Conventions of the mind' ... They may come in this unique arena of judgment, the theatre."[13] When we developed *The Middle Place*, my director/ collaborator Alan Dilworth shared with me a quote from photographer Edward Burtynsky. Speaking of his own industrial landscapes, Burtynsky said, "For me, these images function as reflecting pools of our time."[14] Alan likened verbatim theatre to these raw images of the human world as if to say, "This is what's happening. Now, how do you feel about it?"

I think, however, that the socially minded theatre I'm referring to (and will further reference) can stand some ethical examining with regard to its humanizing effect. An interesting component of what the man at Canadian Stage communicated is that *The Middle Place* made him feel more self-aware but that he could not guarantee a change in behaviour. Were he to run into a group of youth on the street and decide to cross the street, knowing full well that it was his irrational fear or prejudice that was motivating that action, he was not likely to announce, "Hey guys, it's me. Not you!" while doing it. It raises the question, "what do the youth get out of it?" Does a humanizing of the audience benefit the audience exclusively? With *The Middle Place*, were shelter youth objectified in service of another's humanization? Do we become active listeners of their experience or simply consumers of their stories for our enlightenment alone? Though a full-blown examination of these complex questions would pull us too far from the central concerns of this book, it would be remiss of me to not flag them and reflect further on humanizing theatre practices.

In her *Looking White People in the Eye*, Sherene Razack writes,

> I recall trying clumsily to explain to a colleague that *we* (people of colour) are always being asked to tell our stories for *your* (white people's) edification, which you cannot *hear* because of the benefit you derive from hearing them.[15]

Storytellers should be critical of their storytelling and in the verbatim form, which transparently employs words provided by others to be arranged by a playwright, must pay particular attention to Razack's warning "Those whose stories are believed have the power to create fact."[16] The storyteller is privileged – my experience of whittling down 500 pages of transcripts into a 60-page dramatic text has reinforced for me that I am only providing a version of the truth. Essentially, my version. Whether or not this privilege can ever be fully reconciled, the creative team on *The Middle Place* made a host of decisions around process and production as a result of our engagement with the question of objectification. This included decisions about casting the play (professional actors instead of shelter youth), play development (bringing shelter youth and caseworkers into rehearsal, performing the play to the shelter for community feedback), and finding a tangible return to the community of origin (fundraising for youth shelters across Canada through benefit performances). Free tickets to any of our productions were offered to youth shelter residents, as was transportation to and from the theatre. It was important for us to create access to the work, to create a structure for critical response, and most importantly, to let that feedback inform the evolution of both our methodology and the work itself. *The Middle Place* was absolutely influenced by the youth and caseworkers who engaged with it.

As a footnote to this question of whether humanizing the audience benefits those depicted, I should mention that Project: Humanity toured *The Middle Place* to many high schools (attended by students living in shelters), we played the piece in youth and adult shelters across the GTA, and thanks to voluntary exit interviews at Theatre Passe Muraille and Canadian Stage (conducted by Kathleen Gallagher and her research team and about which she writes in this book), we know that many shelter youth ended up seeing the show with general audiences. Admittedly, the response from a few youth was "I know this story already. I'm living this story." But the emphatic pattern in our research is that many youth expressed a feeling of being humanized by their time in the theatre – that is to say, they not only felt a room of strangers awaken to the three-dimensionality of young people, but they themselves felt more attuned to their own courage, anxieties, hopes, and aspirations. Returning, then, to those initial audience comments about who is being humanized by a piece of theatre, I concede that we did in fact strive to "humanize those kids" – but specifically youth in contact with our development process or the eventual production *as audience members*.

As far as the gentleman at Canadian Stage goes, there is no way to foretell the extent of his transformation. I can certainly attest to moments in the theatre that have radically changed my thinking and consequently my being in the world. Theatre's capacity to alter consciousness can plausibly alter action some time after the curtain goes down. It is my belief that unless people become more aware and alive to the realities of others – in a caring, informed, and authentic way – personal (let alone social) change remains very difficult. I have endeavoured to "pay attention to the interpretive structures that underpin how we hear and how we take up the stories of oppressed groups."[17] I have at times misstepped, revisited practices, and tried to keep creating space for a healthy critique of both the art and how it is being made.

This is not necessarily intended as a call for more verbatim theatre, but there is something in the form that masterfully takes advantage of theatre's capacity to humanize the audience. I find the documentary play such a fine way to awaken people to the world and its myriad complexities. Though it shares some qualities with journalism, verbatim theatre is a form that can transcend snappy sound bites. It is often a less impulsive conduit for information, with many verbatim plays taking years to take shape (Robert Caro's adage comes back to mind: "Time equals truth"). The form provides lots of space for a wide range of voices and perspectives. Through proxies (the actors) it allows audiences at large to hear from people who may otherwise not want, or are unable, to address us directly. It can immerse audiences in important contemporary topics of debate and underline the urgency of social and political awareness. When it's done well, it can engage us, make us feel something, and leave us with something to work on or work through. It can implicate us. In the case of

The Middle Place, how does the welfare and well-being of one of society's most disadvantaged groups speak to the state of our own priorities, our values, and even our democracy?

Howard Barker is not a fan of the form.[18] I believe he would say that *The Middle Place* is a failure of the playwright's imagination, and in a way, he would be right. Perhaps I was not creatively brave enough by avoiding writer-generated dialogue. But I kept coming back to the fact that my personal engagement, my encounters with these young people in Rexdale, had shifted my thinking and feeling about so-called at-risk youth. If I were to transfer these encounters, word for word, to the stage, would I not be able to afford the very same opportunity to those who cannot access (or choose not to access) the lives of these young people? I intuited that bringing these words into spaces that do not typically play host to these youth or their stories would inspire the requisite metaphor and that the ensuing theatre could stretch those interacting with it.

If there is hope for the audience in *The Middle Place*, it is hard-won. One of the caseworker characters in the play – when asked by the interviewer, "How do you hang on to hope?" – provides one of my favourite lines from the play: "Practice it. Like *wanna* have hope." When the Interviewer (who could be read as a chorus or surrogate for the audience) asks to be unburdened of his despair and doubt, to be reassured that these young people with very complicated lives will all turn out all right, he is granted not respite but rather a further action: he is given more work. If we want relief after 70 minutes of encountering young people with very adult-sized problems, the play does not give it to us. In this regard, I think Howard Barker would give me a break. "Theatre is a place that makes demands on an audience, in order to lead them into moral and emotional conflict and, through this conflict, to encounter a 'hard won' freedom."[19]

The form is most often likened to documentary film – one blogger-critic of *The Middle Place* went so far as to say, "If Kushnir had done a documentary movie instead of a play it would look and sound and feel very similar, just with more faces."[20] I have to respectfully disagree. *The Middle Place*, like most of the verbatim theatre I have encountered, is not providing an experience that other mediums can sufficiently replicate. The audience's relationship to metaphor, space, and time makes for an experience and encounter that bears little resemblance to a documentary film. The play is demanding. It asks us to hold in our psyches what is happening in the room, what that happening represents, and how we feel about it. As Tim Crouch put it, "the idea of one thing inside something else."[21] And this means we are embroiled in the theatre, we *undergo*.

I could deconstruct and defend the verbatim form at length, but I will focus on one example and its singularity. Consider what I call "Kaaliyah's Aria," which comes in the final quarter of the play.[22]

> KAALI: This is not my place ... this is not my home, this is not my bed, this is ... not my walls.
>
> TYLER: So I'm screwed *[laughs]*.
>
> KAALI: I'm, it's like, I come here, I came here with a mission, to come here for like a month, and leave an' find my own place, and everyone tells you, you can ask anybody. But after a while, this side will drain you or make you feel like "Ok, yeah, I'm busting my ass, I'm tryin' to do this, tryin' to do that" but then you see everyone else not doing anything and then ... like everything is coming to them but then you're working so hard and nothing is coming to you. And you can just lay back a while, and you can lay back to the point that You. Drop. Everything. You stop going to school. You stop working. *[emphatic]* And you become a big bum.
>
> BARBARA: I wouldn't say I have family or friends. Like especially ending up in a place like this, you seem to wonder, like, there's really no one there for you.
>
> KAALI: Y'see the thing. Sometimes I wake up and I feel so unfocused, like, feel like I'm here and I'm not doing anything, but really, yeah, like I'm in school, right, I'm registered for nursing. And I'm doing nursing. But it's just. Like nursing is so hard and then like I have to come back here, and it's not even my home and I have to come here and do chores and have people telling me stuff that I really don't wanna have to hear, have to put up with orders and people's bad hygiene problems and stuff. And I'm like ... and I'm willing to work really hard for my edication but it's just right now I come to a halt ... in my life, where like, the shelter thing is wearing me down and tearing me down and a lot of people who will not come on this little taping thing will tell you the truth, won't tell you, but the truth that this place wears you and will tear you down to the dirt if you don't leave and step up. *[pause]* Don't come here think it's gonna be easy, cause it's not. S'gonna hit you when you wake up one morning, you'll say, "Fuck, I'm here."

Verbatim theatre allows us to encounter Kaali's profoundly complex psychology with minimal artist intervention (*Figure 5.2*). There are no camera tricks, she is not projected on a massive screen, her ideas and

5.2 Akosua Amo-Adem as Kaali in *The Middle Place*. Photo by Aviva Armour Ostroff.

expressions are at times difficult to follow because a writer has not tidied them. Over the course of her aria – which plays out in about four minutes – Kaali shifts from a feeling of being dislocated and adrift to a kind of frustration and defeat, followed by a plea to be understood, an articulation of despair, a lashing out, a further deflation. Underneath this is a raging need to survive, to stand out, to excel. And the strata of her being does not end there – many truths operate at once. Actor Akosua Amo-Adem, who could not have been more formidable and selfless in her portrayal of Kaali, stood relatively still and delivered this cri de coeur in Alan Dilworth's delicate and essential production. The fact that we hear these words at all is the result of anonymity (which I offer to anyone and everyone I interview in my work). But let's imagine for the sake of argument that she was willing to do a documentary film. No matter how dynamic her confession, we would likely tire of the optics. Without inter-cutting images, pulling in for a close-up – or even some underscoring – it would be immensely difficult to communicate this kind of moment on film. In the theatre, it not only transpires with no question or disengagement from the audience, it draws you to the edge of your seat. We spend "slow time" with Kaali in a way that no magazine article, news story, or documentary film could achieve.

Perhaps more significant is the transfer of voice that I alluded to earlier. One of the benefits of a proxy (the actor, the metaphor) is that it can free the audience to hear what is said rather than fixating alone on who is saying it. Moreover, I am compelled by the overall gesture of transferring a voice from the world onto the stage. Is it possible that by witnessing and engaging an actor embodying Kaali's words, we are closer to imagining ourselves embodying those words? If we can participate in an actor's practice of empathy and help support the metaphor that enshrouds it, are we perhaps closer to being empathetic ourselves? Theatre serves Kaali's story in an inimitable way. Perhaps it is only in the theatre that we can most acutely hear how her tendency to bully her peers is rooted in a very personal pain and sense of failure and that this struggle is as complex as any of our own lives. She has not been humanized (though had the real-life Kaali come to see the show, I believe she might have been); rather we as listeners have become more human and humane to her. Theatre has facilitated the empathetic leap.

I have had the great pleasure of collaborating with Dr Kathleen Gallagher on a new verbatim theatre project inspired by fieldwork and research she did in two Toronto drama classrooms between 2008 and 2013. We have had many conversations about theatre and its social imperative, and she once shared the following anecdote. Years ago, she taught at an all-girls high school and on the first day of classes, the principal (in my retelling, a severe nun in grey) addressed the newly admitted students. This nun took her place behind the podium and a sweeping hush fell over the room; eyes widened. The principal looked at this gathering of young women and said, "You are not a random sampling."[23]

Kathleen's anecdote evokes for me theatre's capacity to situate and celebrate audience members as both special individuals and members of a community, coalesced for a joint undertaking. To riff on that nun's opening line: "You are not a random sampling. It is no accident that you find yourself here. You are of consequence. You belong. And were it not for you being here, none of this would be the same." And of course: "Were it not for you being here, you certainly wouldn't be the same." I seek out theatrical experiences that markedly pull me from my human isolation in this precise way, that bring me into myself and so into the world. Whether or not we are as acutely aware as the ancient Greeks about what role the theatre plays in our humanity, we still gravitate towards this form of communal acupuncture.

Today, audience members have to be conceived of as more than consumers of theatre. Programming strategies (or worse yet, play-making strategies) around getting "bums in seats" succeed at doing just that – reducing people to a fatty body part that wants, above all, to be comfortable. The upshot is the dehumanization of the theatregoer, the underestimating of her intelligence, the delivery of formulaic narratives, and the affirming of platitudes and simplistic politics. A playwright once broke down for me the recipe for a hit Broadway play: one set, a dysfunctional family, and a big secret revealed within the last 15 minutes. There have been some exquisite pieces of writing that follow this arc, but is this storytelling model the full extent of theatre's capacity to beguile us, rouse us, make us more aware? What about "travelling"? What about engaging with unfamiliar feelings?

Many spiritual leaders argue that awareness is the healer of separation. To what extent is theatre *the* creative form in which we can become less separated from ourselves and from one another? And can theatre now aspire to be more than a kind of painkiller or sedative, but instead a practice and preventative therapy? In Tony Kushner's *Angels In America, Part Two: Perestroika*, the Angel implores the human race to stop migrating, to stop changing, so as to avoid pain and suffering.[24] She cries out, "*If you do not MINGLE you will Cease to Progress*" – but Kushner wants us to defy her. To mingle is to progress, to transform, to become more aware and active within ourselves and as a society. If we make full use of its virtues, theatre will remain the act of much mingling; it will endure as that magnificent invention through which we can and do whet our humanness.

NOTES

1 Andrew Kushnir, *The Middle Place* (unpublished script, 2011).
2 Andrew Keen, "Against You: A Manifesto in Favor of Audience," *ChangeThis*, 2007, http://changethis.com/manifesto/show/35.03.AgainstYou.
3 Belinda Luscombe, "10 Questions for Robert Caro," Time.com, 21 May 2012, http://content.time.com/time/magazine/article/0,9171,2114437,00.html.
4 James H. Billington, "Humanizing the Information Revolution," Library of Congress, 2001, http://www.loc.gov/loc/lcib/0110/digital.html.
5 Ibid.
6 David Ian Rabey, *Howard Barker: Politics and Desire: An Expository Study of His Drama and Poetry, 1969–87* (Houndmills, UK: Palgrave Macmillan, 1989). Also see Howard Barker, *Arguments for a Theatre* (Manchester: Manchester University Press, 1997), 48.

7 David Hare, *Obedience, Struggle & Revolt* (London: Faber, 2005), 118.
8 Ibid.
9 Tim Crouch, "The Theatre of Reality … and Avoiding the Stage's Kiss of Death," *The Guardian*, 18 June 2014, http://www.theguardian.com/stage /2014/jun/18/theatre-reality-adler-and-gibb-tim-crouch-playwright. Also see Peter Handke, *Kaspar and Other Plays*, trans. Michael Roloff (New York: Farrar, Straus, and Giroux, 1969), 10.
10 Edward Bond, "Symposium – Edward Bond Festival" (symposium, Toronto, ON, 17 June 2012).
11 Barker, *Arguments for a Theatre*, 48.
12 Hare, *Obedience, Struggle & Revolt*, 28.
13 Ibid., 128.
14 Edward Burtynsky, "Artist Statement," EdwardBurtynsky.com, 2013, http:// www.edwardburtynsky.com/site_contents/About/introAbout.html.
15 Sherene H. Razack, *Looking White People in the Eye: Gender, Race, and Culture in Courtrooms and Classrooms* (Toronto: University of Toronto Press, 1998), 48.
16 Ibid., 37.
17 Ibid.
18 For Barker's contempt of a "theatre of journalism," see Alison Croggon, "The Irresponsible Mr. Barker," *Theatre Notes*, 2004, http://theatrenotes .blogspot.ca/2004/06/irresponsible-mr-barker.html.
19 Barker, *Arguments for a Theatre*, 48.
20 The Panic Manual, "SummerWorks Review: The Middle Place (Project: Humanity)," *Panic Manual*, 13 August 2009, http://www.panicmanual.com /2009/08/13/summerworks-review-the-middle-place-project-humanity.
21 Crouch, "Theatre of Reality."
22 Kushnir, *The Middle Place*, act IV.
23 Kathleen Gallagher, conversation with author, 2008.
24 Tony Kushner, *Angels In America, Part Two: Perestroika* (New York: Theatre Communications Group, 1994), 52.

6 Towards a Theatre of Rich, Poetic Language: David Latham's Image Work as a Way Forward to Creating Critically Essential Theatre for Our Time

ALAN DILWORTH

For me, the value of theatre in our time is a given. My interest is rather in *what kind* of theatre and how meaning is made with the artists and audience. In this chapter, I argue for the need for a theatre of rich, poetic language and consider one particular theatre practice as a promising way forward for creating such an essential theatre: David Latham's text-based image work. Latham's image work is a balancing force in our age of the sound bite, partisan political campaigning, partisan policymaking, and spectacle reportage. It is nourishing, slow food language theatre in a fast-food world. The chapter shall proceed as follows: an introduction to David Latham, his image work, an exploration of what is at stake for this work in "the now," and a brief conclusion. To build this essay, and create the case for why a theatre of rich, poetic language is critically essential for our time, I have relied heavily on an in-person conversation I had with David Latham to make the case I wish to make unequivocally here: David Latham's image work is one compelling approach in the quest to discover a theatre of rich, poetic language in our times.

The Man and His Work

David Latham is a director, actor, and teacher. He has worked in Canada, Australia, New Zealand, the United Kingdom, and the United States. He was director of the Playhouse Acting School (Vancouver), dean of the School of Drama at the Victorian College of the Arts (Melbourne, Australia), and director of the Birmingham Conservatory and Theatre Training at the Stratford Shakespeare Festival, where he is now a training consultant and the coordinator of the Michael Langham Workshop for

Classical Direction. David is a master teacher and has been at the fore-front of the development of actor pedagogy for many years.

> *Image was a name given to this process by a student I worked with. When we say "image" we mean an actor's response or experience of a specific word or series of words in a text.*

A two-dimensional description of a fundamentally three-dimensional process is a difficult task and a poor substitute for experiencing the work itself, but the importance of this work demands an attempt. It is imperative to understand that Latham's image work is not a rigid methodology; what is described below is an umbrella process, a fluid approach to working with the power of images in language plays. It is not a literal step-by-step how-to.

> *We are not simply dealing with words on the page. The words on the page are a kind of map, or surface story. To me that's what the text is about. It's about the actors and director seeing that surface story, and then seeing deeper and deeper into what is below the story.*

Image work is a process whereby Latham has an actor "experience" the word or words that compose an image in a text, then has the actor attempt to communicate (to a fellow actor or to Latham himself) the fullness of their experience of that image using only the word that composes the image.

> *Each word has its own image. And we are connected to these words. I remember once Kristin Linklater saying we look at the word "moon," and know that man has walked on the moon and the story of it is completely different.*

The process is shaped in such a way that the actor has a sensory image experience rather than a processed intellectual response to the image.

> *In rehearsal I'll say speak from the image, but often what actors want to do is "fashion" it. "Oh, I have this image of the moon, the sea" so that it becomes "Oh, what would the sea sound like ... hmm ... " But that is not what is being asked, what is asked is to speak from your experience of the image. That is something different. It is often surprising, and it can feel strange, unknown and vulnerable.*

Latham's "imaging" results in a layering of the written "image" (the writer's creation) with the fullness of the actor's personal sensory image experience (what is in effect the actor's experiential embodiment of the image).

Glenn Gould had this interaction with another pianist. They were discussing performing Bach. In reference to Gould's creative liberties with Bach's music the other pianist said, "Well you play what you play, but I will play what Bach wrote." Gould responded, "You may play what Bach knows that he wrote, but I play what Bach didn't know he wrote."

The result is that the receivers (fellow actors and audience) of the actor's image communication have their own personal sensory image experience, rather than a more processed intellectual response. The outcome is a much more complex, experiential, and meaningful theatre experience for everyone involved.

We take the map the writer has written, the text, and we bring our experience to it, and open it up. We make discoveries in the text – not necessarily intellectually – that the writer didn't deliberately write in. The words and images become a key for us, a key to release something within us. You want the actors to be within the story; that means the audience will be within the story.

Latham's imaging forms the foundation of the rehearsal process from which the acting company works through the play with various points of focus (space, verse lines, transitions, etc.), thereby shaping the image work layer after layer into an experience that is shared with audiences.

We want people to have what Joseph Campbell calls "Aha!" moments. Where there are real moments of enlightenment, real moments of revelation. That's what we want with an audience. But those things can only happen if something is actually happening on stage. Like if something live is happening.

It is important to note that the image work never remains static, but rather through the points of focus the images are always experienced anew in the present moment of rehearsal or performance, evolving and growing with the process.

Most of the time what we do is we take words and we define them. We put them in cement. With image work what starts to happen is we actually go beyond the clichés and because [of this] we start to realize that the meaning in these words is profound. And we begin to enter the particular: our living experience of these words and images. That is what I want from the theatre.

Given the *experiential* nature of Latham's image work, and its use of the word "image," and given that Latham's work is one theatre practice among many, one may rush to link Latham's work to other practices in the landscape of theatre making. This inclination may be especially true of existing practices that are *experiential* or practices that also use the word "image" as their foundation, such as Stanislavski's affective memory,[1] Brecht's gestus,[2] Boal's image theatre,[3] or Lehmann's concept of *image* in the postdramatic theatre.[4] I wish to highlight some of the conceptual differences of Latham's image work from these existing practices and concepts.

In light of its focus on the present experience of language and its communication, Latham's work is easily differentiated from Stanislavski's affective memory work, which requires an actor to call on details of memory from a similar situation to that of their character and has the goal of arming the actor with emotion and personality for playing their role.[5] Also dissimilar is Brecht's gestus. Gestus is the characterization of an identified character attitude, expressed through word or action. Gestus implies a conscious search for expression of an idea (attitude) and the search for a means of expression.[6] Latham's work looks to circumvent intellectualization for the communication of much more immediate experience. Boal's image theatre is the representation of concepts and ideas through non-verbal shaping of bodies into image for the purposes of exploring issues of oppression.[7] Lehmann's widely read book *Postdramatic Theatre* outlines tendencies and traits in avant-garde theatre of the late twentieth century.[8] When Lehmann is referring to image, he is referring to the cultural shift from a text-based culture to a media-based culture of visual image and sound. Clearly this is entirely different from Latham's concept of image.

However, I would argue there are some potential connections between Latham's work and Lehmann's postdramatic paradigm. Lehmann surveys a range of approaches to text, from the "no plot, no character" text to the performance of dramas. Depending on the director and their intended relationship with the audience, Latham's image work could serve Lehmann's postdramatic paradigm very well. Latham's image work focuses on the moment-to-moment language experience of the actor and the sharing of that experience using the text – whether the text is dramatic or not, whether there are characters or not – as it is the actor's image relationship with the text that is privileged. In addition, Latham's image work tends to be inclusive of the audience in meaning-making as part of the theatrical experience – another hallmark of the postdramatic paradigm. There is clearly room for more rigorous investigation of the relationship of Latham's image work with the postdramatic paradigm, but such work is beyond the scope of this chapter.

Latham's image work is a radically powerful approach to bringing an ensemble and the audience directly to the language experience of the theatre. Through language, meaning is made experientially, moment to moment, within the structural container of the theatrical experience. The process demands that actors work with the raw material of their own relationship to the language, in the present moment. Why is Latham's image theatre a way forward for creating an essential theatre of rich, poetic language for our time?

First, from a practice standpoint one might well ask: What are the current obstacles to creating meaningful theatre of rich, poetic language? I would suggest that in most Western English-language traditions, our era is anaemic in terms of poetic language in the theatre. Our theatres are faced with chronic funding shortages, which translate into shorter and shorter time frames for creation. With the dominant process for preparing productions being Stanislavski-derived action/objective work, poetic plays often do not stand a chance of coming to life.

> *Whatever you use of Stanislavski, his theories and his work have a profound effect on our acting. But I do feel that so much of the work that is done even in language-based theatre is not actually language-based at all. It's usually to do with character and character objectives rather than the language itself.*

Action/objective work is often conflated with naturalism, and this results in some poetic pieces getting naturalistic treatment whether it serves the theatrical experience or not.

> *We have to respect the text in terms of – if you are doing a Greek play or Shakespeare, it's not naturalism. It's not to find a way to reduce the text so it becomes naturalistic. It's to do with finding a way the text can live in the world in which it lives. The container for our work is the world of the text, not interpretation of action.*

Few theatre-training programs prepare students to engage directly with poetic language, rather than indirectly through the interpretation of action. The impediments to a theatre of rich, poetic language, and work like Latham's image work, are deeply embedded in the infrastructure of Canadian culture and theatre. It is crucial to acknowledge that some theatre companies and individual productions succeed at creating theatre of rich, poetic language, but it is, in my humble view, surprisingly rare given the amount of theatre being produced.

When I look at the surface story there is always an action in the text that is specific. I want the actor to actually extract the action that is contained in the text, not an interpretation of the text. But the image work is the foundation of the process, not interpretive action/objective work. If we have discovered the image life of the word, and we've opened up that image life, we have all kinds of possibilities to work with. We can still work with objectives. As long as you can allow yourself to continue moment to moment to experience the image work, rather than sticking with: "I want it to sound like this. Because when it sounds like this I know that you/I are playing your objective." That is cementing the life of the word. Once you have discovered the image life of words, the poetic foundation exist[s]. It's just there. If we have that foundation, we can then do all kinds of things.

Latham's image work shifts the foundation of theatre creation from an action/objective paradigm to the poetic possibilities of the specific image world of the text.

Why are the poetic possibilities of Latham's image work so fitting for an essential, poetic theatre of our time? This work engages with the very poetics of theatre: the life of language, metaphor, the live experience, and impermanence. The poetics of theatre are particularly essential for the present moment.

A teapot is a teapot, something to make a brew in. Put it on stage it takes on a life of its own ... Everything put on stage will be read as a message – an actor who can't find their shoe will still go onstage on cue, and we will all try to work out the significance of the missing footwear ... At its best, theatrical metaphor can become a thing of real, sometimes unbearable beauty.
– Julian Bryant[9]

Theatre is a space where we make meaning. Words, actions, images, lighting, sound, – everything that is presented in a theatrical experience is assumed to have meaning. When choices are made to create meaning, the shared experience of the performer and the audience can be powerful and affecting. Such meaningful theatrical experiences can last far beyond the final moments of the performance. For some, the insights and memories of a theatrical experience can last for years. Whatever the particular genre, we look for meaning in everything we see and hear in the theatre.

Metaphorical thinking – our instinct not just for describing but for *comprehending* one thing in terms of another – for equating I with an other – shapes our view of the world, and is essential to how we communicate, learn, discover, and invent. – James Geary[10]

Rich, poetic language has a unique role to play in the meaning-making experience of theatre. There are many genres of poetic language for the theatre, such as contemporary dramatic and non-dramatic works, poetically rendered verbatim text, classical plays, and poetry. Poetic language rich in metaphor is a powerful tool for understanding and communicating meaning, in particular meaning that is difficult to understand and communicate. For example, rich text is very useful for communicating experiences, or complex feelings, or ambiguities. Rich text can communicate much more than information.

The art of the playwright is only one part of the rich, poetic language experience of the theatre. The art of the director and of the actor are also a part of this experience. Latham's image work pays particular attention to the director's invitation to the actor to partake in the art of creating meaning in the theatre. The actor's experience of the written word, and the communication of that experience, is the heart of David Latham's image work. Theatre happens in real time. It is transient and impermanent. It requires an experience between living human beings sharing a space and time together. I like to use the word "encounter" when talking about the sharing of time and space together in a theatre. The *Oxford English Dictionary* defines "encounter" as "a meeting face to face." There are multiple human encounters in the theatre: actor and actor; actor and the audience; audience member and audience member. They all meet "face to face." Complex and often contrasting ideas, arguments, images, feelings, and experiences are communicated in a theatrical encounter.

The theatrical experience has a beginning, a middle, and an end. The actor and the audience experience the overall structure, but they also experience each moment between the beginning and the end. David Latham's image work is about the experience of each shared moment and the nature of the communication that transpires in each moment. Latham would say, "There is the overall story, but then there are many, many stories taking place in each moment that make up the experience of the larger story. Each moment is its own story. Each word and the experience of each word is its own story."

"The Limits of My Stories Are the Limits of My World" – David R. Loy[11]

When the actor communicates his/her own experience or *image* of each word, using each word in the play, to an audience, layers of meaning are created that the writer might never have known or expected. I understand this experience as the invitation to the actor by the director. By bringing his/her own *images* to the theatrical encounter, the actor becomes a co-creator of meaning, along with the writer and director. The result for the actor and the audience is a depth of encounter with human complexity and vulnerability that is rare, in our society and in our theatre. It also potentially results in a rich and complex language experience for all present. In the best cases, it results in the creation of new meaning in the here and now between the human beings sharing in the experience together.

What are the broader implications of the poetic possibilities of Latham's image work beyond the theatre at this particular moment?

> In virtual worlds and computer games, people are flattened into personae. On social networks, people are reduced to their profiles. On our mobile devices we often talk to each other on the move and with little disposable time – so little, in fact, that we communicate in a new language of abbreviation in which letters stand for words and emoticons for feelings. We don't ask the open ended "How are you?" Instead, we ask the more limited "Where are you?" and "What's up?" These are good questions for getting someone's location and making a simple plan. They are not so good for opening a dialogue about complexity of feeling. We are increasingly connected to each other but oddly more alone. – Sherry Turkle[12]

Simply speaking, Latham's image work is a balancing force in an increasingly technological age. I would go so far as to say that this kind of work humanizes us. It makes us engage with our vulnerabilities, complexities, and contradictions and with those of others. It brings us into an intimate living encounter with the other. It reminds us of the life of the shared present moment and the life and complexity of words and language. This particular experience of live theatre is crucial in our time.

> The problem is that we have to understand ourselves and the meaning of our existence in a technological culture, but technological knowledge cannot supply us with this kind of understanding. – Wim Bollen[13]

Latham's image work brings us face-to-face with our stories, word-to-word, moment-to-moment, in the theatre. By doing so, we locate ourselves and make meaning within the arguments and conflicts of larger stories, stories that speak to timeless conflicts and arguments and to conflicts and arguments of our time: *Antigone, Hamlet, Scorched, If We Were Birds, Enron, The Middle Place, Crash, Seeds*. Theatre is the moment-to-moment practice of asking ourselves, What does it mean to be human *now*? We need to ask this question in an age when, for many, traditional canopies of meaning such as religion have lost their place as organizers of our beliefs, understandings, and experiences.[14]

Technology has other bedfellows. It is not the only contemporary force in our society that entreats us to discover the balancing influence of a meaning-making theatre of rich, poetic language.

> It is enough to say that the combined forces of technology, advertising, big business, and journalism have encouraged, if not produced, the linguistic crisis, which is upon us ... [In] our society it is more common for language to deceive and create obstacles to communication than for it to clarify or assist communication. I suggest that it is the responsibility of all the arts, and of theatre in particular, to address themselves to this situation. – Robert Skloot[15]

In his essay "The Theatre and the Crisis of Language," Skloot called for a reinstatement of the "morality" of language. For Skloot, the morality of language was meaning. His essay is both a lament on the breakdown of meaning in language and a call to arms for a theatre to address the language crisis. Journalist and cultural critic Chris Hedges argues the "crisis" of meaning in language still exists today:

> Those who seek to dominate our behavior first seek to dominate our speech. They seek to obscure meaning. They make war on language ... The reduction of popular discourse to banalities, exacerbated by the elite's retreat into obscure, specialized jargon, create internal walls that thwart real communication. This breakdown in language makes reflection and debate impossible ... This emptiness of language is a gift to demagogues and the corporations that saturate the landscape with manipulated images and the idiom of mass culture.[16]

The meaning-making and moment-to-moment experiential language power of Latham's image work is an antidote to what I am seeing as an obscuring of meaning, a manipulation of image, a diminishing of discourse, and the creation of obstacles to communication in our current moment.

David Latham's image theatre is a theatre of rich, poetic language. It makes meaning, communicates human experience – that which is especially difficult to communicate – and does this moment to moment in the theatrical experience with the audience. It also fosters the practice of complex and poetically ambiguous language and communication. Image work has a humanizing influence, and I would argue, through its power, commitment, and connection to language, it may also foster important democratic discourse as we struggle to negotiate multiple truths in a postmodern time.

To Conclude

In a 2005 interview, David R. Loy proposes that our relationship to time is also in crisis.

> The promise of consumerism is that something you buy or consume is going to fill up your sense of lack ... Consumerism never makes you happy. Yet, it's always promising to make you happy. It's always the next thing that's going to make you happy ... In the Western context, lack encourages us to live in the future ... We are preoccupied with the future because we think that's when our lack is going to be resolved. We think our projects in the present are so important because it is only by acting on them now that they can be fulfilled, and it is only by fulfilling them that we can resolve our sense of lack. But the future doesn't make the present real.[17]

Loy argues that part of the language crisis comes from the *story* that technology and consumerism will make us happy. He suggests that the future-oriented utopias of fulfilment through technology and consumption foster disregard for the rich experience and meaning created in the present moment. I have argued in this chapter that Latham's image work offers a balancing influence to utopias of the future by heightening and strengthening our experience of the present through the rigour of its moment-to-moment language use and meaning-making structures.

In a later publication, Loy further reflects on the place of stories in our lives, concluding "our stories make us meaning-creating beings ... We play at the meaning of life by telling different stories."[18] If these things are true, Latham's image work offers an important alternative to the dominant practice of naturalism in Canadian theatre, a practice that has not resided enough in a present to find its own poetry and metaphoric heft. David Latham's moment-to-moment, meaning-making image work offers us a precious place for considering the affective and imaginative power of language in a culture and a theatre practice which all too often leaches the life out of language and our experience of the present moment. Why theatre now? Because we simply cannot afford to defer it to a later time.

NOTES

1 Constantin Stanislavski, *An Actor Prepares*, trans. Elizabeth Reynolds Hapgood (New York: Routledge, 1989); the original work was published in 1936.
2 Bertoldt Brecht, "A Short Organum for the Theatre," in *Brecht on Theatre: The Development of an Aesthetic*, ed. and trans. John Willett (London: Methuen, 1964), 179–207.
3 Augusto Boal, *The Rainbow of Desire: The Boal Method of Theatre and Therapy*, trans. Adrian Jackson (New York: Routledge, 1995).
4 Hans-Thies Lehmann, *Postdramatic Theatre*, trans. Karen Jürs-Munby (Abingdon, UK: Routledge, 2006); original work published in 1999.
5 Stanislavski, *An Actor Prepares*.
6 Brecht, "A Short Organum for the Theatre."
7 Boal, *The Rainbow of Desire*.
8 Lehmann, *Postdramatic Theatre*.
9 Julian Bryant, "The Power of Metaphor," *Creating Theatre*, 27 October 2008, http://creatingtheatre.com/?p=36.
10 James Geary, *I Is an Other* (New York: HarperCollins, 2011), 3.
11 David R. Loy, *The World Is Made of Stories* (Somerville, MA: Wisdom Publications, 2010), 3.
12 Sherry Turkle, *Alone Together: Why We Expect More from Technology* (New York: Basic Books, 2011), 18–19.
13 Wim Bollen, "Technology and the Problem of Alienation" (paper presented at the 4S & EASST Conference, Paris, France, 25–28 August 2004), http://www.csi.ensmp.fr/WebCSI/4S/search/search_P/search_P.php, 9.
14 David R. Loy, *The Great Awakening* (Somerville, MA: Wisdom Publications, 2003), 3.

15 Robert Skloot, "The Theatre and the Crisis of Language," *Journal of Aesthetic Education* 6, no. 4 (1972): 65.
16 Chris Hedges, "The War on Language," *Truthdig*, 28 September 2009, http://www.truthdig.com/report/item/20090928_the_war_on_language.
17 David R. Loy, "Lack and Liberation in Self and Society: An Interview with David Loy," *Holos Forum*, 2005, www.holosforum.org/davidloy.html.
18 Loy, *The World Is Made of Stories*, 16–17.

7 The Box That Cannot Be Contained

CATHERINE BANKS

Theatre, it is said, is like a church. You enter it and the world is shut out for a time. The play begins and you are drawn into a story that the writer has held in his/her imagination for a long time. If it is a good play, it is deeply thought out, explores complex ideas that are expressed through richly authentic characters. You sit quietly having thoughts about what you believe against what is being played out before you. The playwright's full orchestra of ideas and feelings flows through and out from the actors, who have in rehearsal layered in their experiences and feelings, and all of it floods everyone in the audience. You hear the people around you laugh/shift about/cry and you think, am I with these people around me or am I different? This collective experience with the other members of the audience in the house – *house* because we are for the duration of the play living together – expands what the playwright wrote into something even larger for you to process and find connection to. It seems more than ever in this increasingly solitary world in front of a screen of blogging, tweeting, and texting, we need a place to gather to feel connection.

People now are constantly being given – we can say "posted" – information. Almost before you finish trying to absorb one bit of information you have postings on other, completely different and equally interesting topics. It seems like there is never enough time to integrate/synthesize this information so that we can understand how we ourselves think about what is happening around us. Theatre is a place we can take the measure of our humanity through the world of the play as we (safely) watch how the characters speak to and treat each other. These days there is a lot of talk about theatre dying out as an art form. I don't believe it for a moment. I do, however, believe that until theatre stops trying to razzle-dazzle audiences it will struggle. The virtue of writing for stage now is that it is like the slow food movement in a "fast-food" (information highway) world.

Everyone in the world, everyone, is worthy of close attention. I spend a lot of time listening to the voices of those around me hooking into feelings that I have experienced and feel the need to explore in the long process of creating a play. If I do my job well, there becomes a fragile, glowing beam of light from the person I overheard, passing through me (the playwright) and the director and actors and ultimately connecting to the person sitting in the theatre watching the play. I call this glowing beam of light authenticity. Theatre is a place where we can gather and experience what it is like to be inside the skin of another and come out into the night air, changed because we are connected more deeply to what it is to be human.

All my plays were initially inspired by moments of attentive listening, with a snippet of overheard conversation becoming the seed for the whole drama.

"Happy Mother's Day!" [laugh]

That greeting and more importantly the laugh that followed was the beginning of my play *Bitter Rose*. I had met a friend, a mother of five, at the grocery store on the eve of Mother's Day and the tension between her *knowing* "Happy Mother's Day!" and her laugh that followed – well, in that tension the character Bitter Rose stepped forward. For months after, Rose "followed me" and every experience I had, as a middle-class mother in a small town, became fuel for her monologues. It took three years of writing (and cutting) to create a 75-minute play that captured, for me at least, the nuance of the tension of those three words with that laugh. And, of course, to find the grace in Rose's story to be able to write, "I will not be bitter. I will not be a bitter Rose."

"… if you aren't having your period or PMS then you're ovulating, or you've got break through bleeding."

Krista and Chicky, two characters in *Bone Cage*, were seeded the day a friend repeated this line she had overheard at the river in the picturesque village where I was living at the time. The river was a community gathering place on hot summer afternoons, and I too had overheard lots of conversations among the 20-something crowd that came to swim, drink, and jump off the "high" – the top beam of the steel-framed bridge. I had lived and observed the people of the area for seven years, but the play jump-started, several years after I had moved away, when a feud between two men in a neighbouring community led to the beating death of one of the men. I happened to hear a newscast that ended with the reporter asking the question, "How could something so brutal happen in such an idyllic setting?" I felt that I could answer that question in a way that would not excuse the murder but leave an audience with an understanding of the despair under the surface of the idyllic setting.

"He hadn't bargained on marrying a failure."

This is something a friend said to me that stayed with me for 20 years. There is, of course, a world in that line ... a painful world. I started *It Is Solved by Walking* by writing a monologue for each of the stanzas in Wallace Stevens's *Thirteen Ways of Looking at a Blackbird*, but it wasn't until I began to create scenes around the monologues that I fully understood the territory I had entered. When I wrote the words "He hadn't bargained on marrying a failure" at the beginning of stanza vi, I knew that this line, perhaps more than any other, was the heart of the play. It embodies Margaret's overwhelming sense of failure and how that perceived failure resounds in her marriage.

The play that follows, *The Box That Cannot Be Contained*, initially sparked to life when I overheard a woman express dismay that the school had sent home fliers about a Beaver group at the local church. She didn't want her child contaminated by "Christian values" but then, in practically the same breath, she mentioned that her seven-year-old played online war games with his father and that was their father/son time. Her passive uneasiness about online gamers coupled with her strident rejection of Beavers in the United Church basement fired my imagination.

But all the ingredients I needed to write this play were seeded in the years parenting a son. When my son was under five in the early 1990s it was very unpopular to give boys toy guns. However, by the time he was seven, gaming systems were all the rage and a lot of the parents who didn't want their boys playing with toy guns seemed OK with them playing graphic war games in which the boys (on a screen of course) hunted down and "killed" each other. Gaming was huge for the boys at my son's school, and even though we didn't have a gaming system in the house, it had been impossible to prevent his exposure to that world. When he was in high school and old enough to buy a gaming system with his own money, online gaming had started. It felt so weird to hear him talking to and playing these killing games with other gamers, boys, men even, we knew nothing about. Meanwhile, every night on the news I watched video snippets of conflicts around the world: images of targets on a night-vision screen, video of rockets fired so deeply into border cities that the soldiers pressing the buttons did not see the carnage they were responsible for across whatever border was being assaulted. I felt that the video war games being played in family recreation rooms were desensitizing our sons, making them ready to fight the wars of the future. Of course there were some articles about the violence of these games, but mostly I saw good parents who were too busy to think about what the games might be really doing to our sons. After all, we all played with toy guns as children and most of us didn't grow up to kill anyone with a real gun, right? When I heard the mother make her comment about Beavers in the same breath as her admission about her husband and son's online gaming it brought back my thoughts about video games and war some 20 years ago when my son was young and also my own parenting during stressful times when the kind of parent I wanted to be got squashed by my need to get through the day.

This 10-minute piece took 20 years of thinking about children and video games and our role as parents before it got to a place ripe for the writing. I love that I can write in heightened language and impact the audience dramatically by creating the "impossible," in the case of this play, the bruised and bleeding body of a six-year-old "soldier," at once metaphorically present and also, poetically, in the future. Theatre is unique in this way. I write to try to communicate to the audience what it is like to be in the skin of the character I am writing. I wholeheartedly reject the notion that a character must be likeable, but I have not done my job if the audience does not understand a character's actions. The mother and father in this play are like a lot of parents, divorced or not, struggling to get through their day still sane.

In this short play, the mother's passivity and the father's aggressiveness grow out of many blurred lines, lines that, yes, are often easier not to think about as we struggle to get to the end of the day.

The Box That Cannot Be Contained

Mother, 35, and Father, 35, stand a distance apart on the stage. They do not look at each other but speak directly to the audience.

MOTHER: I got this notice from Andrew's primary class. A Beaver group is starting at the United Church. I am not comfortable with the whole militaristic thing, children 6 years old in uniforms, earning badges –

FATHER: I let her decide those things. I told him forget it, Tigger 1, they let girls in Beavers now.

MOTHER: Beavers leads to Scout *TROOPS*. I told him no.

FATHER: Six-year-old girls can kick little boy butt on things like earning badges. I figure his peter-meter doesn't need that.

MOTHER: And the motto is share share share – share what, Christian brain washing?

FATHER: My motto is let his mother capture the worthless flags and I'll get the ones worth having.

MOTHER: Besides Wednesday night is his night – Wednesday night supper and evening and one weekend a month.

Father puts on a gaming head set.

FATHER: I tell her it's not my job to take him places – if it's Wednesday night it's not happening. I am not driving to her place, and dealing with her attitude for starters. That's why I do Wednesday nights online. *Hey there Tigger 1 – how was school? Pizza there yet? Meatlovers special same as you little buddy.*

MOTHER: I – well it is easier not to have to deal with his pissedoffness. And Andrew says it feels like it is a real visit with his Father. I checked with him about it.

FATHER: Besides everything he needs to know about life he's learning playing Capture the Flag.

MOTHER: I don't actually like the Never-go-out-and-play-Box.

FATHER: I don't order a pizza for me. He'll find that funny when he's older. All those times we compared our rations but I made it all up. *Oh Tigger 1 they forgot the onions on my pizza. Maybe I should go to Pizza Heaven and set fire to their asses with this A-K machine gun, eh?*

MOTHER: I made rules and conditions.

FATHER: First rule – no rules, no conditions.

MOTHER: Andrew can only play online with his father. Otherwise it is like there are all these people that I don't know in his bedroom with him.

FATHER: I only let him play with my buds – people in my clan. We have this actual US army guy – he is serving in Iraq – he likes to play after he has been out on 36-hour patrol. He's hopped up and fearless. Tigger 1 loves that guy.

Father puts his hand over the headset mouth piece. He's excited.
    (whispers) He just came on. He's talking to Tigger 1.
    (mimics BadassUno) You ready to kill some hostile villagers Tigger1?
    (mimics Andrew) Yes sir BadassUno.
    (reentering the game) Yes sir BadassUno. Tigger 1 your lead.

MOTHER: I've actually seen some of the game that they play and it breaks all my rules. But I know he needs contact with his father.

FATHER: BadassUno tells Tigger 1 that he wishes he could hook him up directly to the war in Iraq. Says they would win in a month if his brain was running the show – cause he is so fucking crazy ass unpredictable and never dies. BadassUno has this theory if all the gaming 6-year-olds was harnessed directly into the war it would be good guys win, win, win – bad guys tits up.

MOTHER: I told him – I don't know if he heard me, I don't know how to use those headset things – I told him when Andrew is 10, when he *understands* what war means he can't play those games anymore. I mean that 15-year-old who died …

FATHER: She got all hysterical when that kid disappeared after his parents took away his gaming unit.

An undercover man with a security tag comes out and stands silently. There should be something about the man that seems cold/chilling.

MOTHER: I mean did you wonder if that whole thing was some sort of cover-up or conspiracy? Because I did. The kid disappeared and then the gaming company contributed $25,000 to a reward for information. Doesn't that seem like don't-look-too-closely-at-us money?

UNDERCOVER MAN: (reading a clipboard) The cause of death was determined through medical examination to be the result of injuries to the chest area that are consistent with a fall from a tree. Game over.

Undercover Man walks off.

FATHER: I said what do you think? – he was taken out by the CIA? Hey Tigger 1?

MOTHER: I mean we call it a game but to that boy, it wasn't a game.

FATHER: Where are you buddy?

MOTHER: Sometimes I just wish I could see inside Andrew and see what the effect these games are having on him.

FATHER: Tigger 1? Tigger 1?

MOTHER: (Calling) Andrew, tell your father it was your bedtime one hour ago.

Mother goes into Andrew's room. There is a long anguished scream.
Mother comes out carrying the broken, bleeding body of her son. She holds it out for all to witness.
Father sees his son and rushes forward.

FATHER: Tigger 1? Medic. MEDIC!

Undercover man comes out of Andrew's room, watches the scene briefly, then leaves unnoticed.

Lights down.

PART III

(En)Gendering Change

8 Recontextualizing

JACKIE MAXWELL IN CONVERSATION WITH
KATHLEEN GALLAGHER

*The following interview took place in Jackie Maxwell's office at the Shaw Festival,
Niagara-on-the-Lake, Autumn 2013.*

Kathleen: Let's start with your role as artistic director of the Shaw Festival.
Jackie: This is my eleventh season – and when I came here, my predecessor, Christopher Newton, had it in very good shape. He'd been here for 23 seasons and had really, I think, just lifted the whole playing field in terms of the kind of work produced here and it was a case of, "Oh, if it ain't broke, don't fix it." It was very respected. But I think the time was coming for a shift. And part of that was because of Shaw. So if we are the Shaw Festival, we were founded because of the passion that two men had for Shaw 50-odd years ago ... grown exponentially, of course, since then. But the notion of Shaw and who Shaw is – he's a very different figure than he was 50 years ago when this theatre was founded. He's not taught in high school anymore. He's not really known as a personality in the way that he was, of course, when he was alive or shortly thereafter. So a lot of people, a couple of generations at the very least, don't know who the hell our named playwright is. And probably don't know very many, if any, of his plays. So what does that mean?

Well, pragmatically it means that not as many people automatically come to see Shaw plays. So for me I have to deal with that programming-wise. I certainly feel very secure in his work because of the provocative nature of who he was, because of the fact that he was a man who was the mosquito in the flesh of the establishment. He was a man who challenged establishment, challenged assumptions. Because of this, many of his plays really live very well. *Major Barbara* is still, frankly, a very scary play to do, in the best way. *Mrs. Warren's Profession, Saint*

Joan ... these were plays that live. So it's not that he, as a writer, is irrelevant. It's just that he's not in the current zeitgeist, really.

For me, when I came here, when I was asked to apply for the job – and I had run a theatre before, Factory Theatre, which is a very different kettle of fish: very urban, totally dedicated to Canadian work and the development and production of that – I was very taken. I loved Shaw. I knew Shaw's work. I'd read it at university. I did a very academic drama degree. I knew that whole period. But what interested me was that Christopher said that the original mandate of the festival is the plays of George Bernard Shaw and his contemporaries. The guy lived 94 years so he had a hell of a lot of contemporaries. One isn't lacking for product, so to speak. The period he lived, 1856–1950, is the beginning of the modern world. So you've got a turn of the century from Victorian to Edwardian. You've got World War I. Everything. But what Christopher I think quite smartly did before he left is open the mandate to include contemporary plays *about* the era, as well as the era itself. And to be honest that's what really interested me in running the place. Not because I didn't love those of the period. I mean who doesn't want to do Chekhov and Ibsen and Coward and all those wonderful writers? But I want to see the creative friction that happens when you take a contemporary play about an era and put it alongside a play of its time. Have we gained anything in hindsight? How do we look at it differently? Even form-wise, we write plays so differently now than we did then. What does that do? So that really interested me. I thought that there were empty spaces, it seemed to me, in the programming and voices that weren't being heard. So the first set of voices, it seemed to me, were Canadian voices. I wanted to put Canadian plays into the programming. I wanted to bring playwrights into the company. I wanted to develop new work. I didn't want to take it over, I wanted it to be a strand of the programming. I feel any contemporary theatre needs contemporary writers attached to it. So that was one point of view. The other voice that I felt was very lacking was a female voice. And I thought to myself, I have to believe that there must have been female playwrights in Edwardian and Victorian times and thereafter. They happened. And sure enough, you go back into time and it didn't take very long to start finding *fantastic* plays that had happened and in some cases been very celebrated and then simply just left. So that was something I felt very strongly about.

Kathleen: Who did that research? Did you do it yourself?

Jackie: Yeah, pretty much. It was so interesting to do! And it's not that there aren't other people who are doing it. I mean there's a kind of wonderful, nerdy network of people who are going down these roads. And then I eventually brought on a wonderful associate, Edith Holmes, and then a literary manager, Joanna Falk. We all do this together. The other thing I wanted to do was to bring in more female directors. People always ask, "Are you a role model?" There hadn't been a woman running one of these big institutions before and I felt it was up to me then to try to –

Kathleen: Make the spaces.

Jackie: – because there was, or maybe still is, a huge imbalance. So in terms of artistic direction, my job was to start trying to fold in these kind of programming ideas. The Royal George Theatre had a formula which was that they did murder mysteries and sort of light operas. I was not interested in that. I think they'd really come to the end of their time. I didn't want to read or program them, frankly. And I felt that we could turn the Royal George into – albeit still a very populist space – but I thought that there was more that could be done in that space. And so I slowly started to turn it around. I started putting Shaws there. And then one other thing I thought of was in terms of musical theatre, that of course we could always do a big, populist musical, but also that it's such an interesting and wide-ranging genre that we could also start to look at more contemporary ones or develop our own. I soon discovered that you have to move slowly. You have to be tenacious, but you can't just slam stuff up. The audiences will just freak out. So being artistic director, as I say, there are the pragmatic things that I do. But I have to keep, also, looking ahead because I think we have to be a leader in the theatrical conversation in this country and the whole continent. And to do that, you have to keep going: Okay, how do we stay there? How do we maintain our relevance? How do we open up to more people?

Kathleen: Yeah. Even the question of gender is interesting because – as you say – when you inherit something or come into something that is so successful, so beloved, it's hard to hear the missing voices.

Jackie: Well, you have to prepare for the fact that you're always going to upset someone. But I wanted to be careful. I didn't want to blow the place up. I also wanted to maintain the intellectual rigour of the place that is matched with an emotional connection, the production values, the notion that design is important, the notion of an ensemble of actors that are tuned like an orchestra.

Kathleen: Well let's pursue that gender question, because obviously it figures largely in your selection of plays. To work with the plays of that era for a contemporary audience, what kinds of issues surface for you?

Jackie: All sorts of issues! One of the fascinating things, for example, in finding female writers *from* the time is – Well, for example, I discovered a wonderful British writer, a woman called Githa Sowerby. And she wrote a play called *Rutherford and Son* in 1908–9. It's about a kind of a man who – Rutherford is a dinosaur. He runs a glass empire. Industrialization is taking over. Though it's clear that he's a man shortly to be completely out of his time, he's not going down gracefully. He's a tyrant to his children, and his rather weak son has married this young woman who essentially in the end kind of takes him down. It's a fascinating and beautiful play. Emma Goldman saw the play when it was done in London and said it was one of the most extraordinary pieces of art that she had ever seen. So it was very celebrated and then it just fucking disappeared, right? The National Theatre had actually found it and I read it and went, *oh my god …*

But what was fascinating about it (and subsequent plays of hers that *we* then found) was that these *stories* were not necessarily new, per se. It's the kind of work that Galsworthy was doing, or Barker, or Shaw himself. But suddenly the whole point of view is flipped and it's really fascinating. Once we did that, it was very successful and people were really quite kind of bowled over by it. And so I kept thinking well where the hell are Sowerby's other plays because she apparently wrote five others. We eventually dug our way down and met someone who'd found some of her manuscripts languishing in the basement of Samuel French. It was a great kind of detective story. So the next play we did was a play that she wrote called *The Stepmother*. This was written later, it was in the early 20s. And it was done once. It was read once in 1923 and then it was never touched again, never published. This play is *fantastic*. So in it, we meet a young woman who's a dress maker and designer. She's independent. She's doing relatively well, financially. And she essentially gets to come live with this man who's a widow. He's a bad guy, a wastrel, a gambler. But he has two daughters, two young-ish teenage daughters. They get married. So the whole notion of "stepmother" you go: "uh oh." No, the daughters *adore* her. And in the end, he basically bilks her of all her money because of the way that finances work. The money became his. And there are these shocking scenes where she finds out that he has taken her money. I mean, the audiences here, people were like, "Oh! No! Oooh. Ah!" I mean, literally. And of course, the ending, which was so interesting. Normally, the ending would be (well, because she had fallen in love with another man) you would think well, either she has to die or she has to be pushed out or she has … BUT NO! The husband – the ne'er-do-well – is pushed off to America. She gives him some money and she ends up in a new life with these daughters. And the last line is so … literally, the oldest daughter she brings out some tea and she goes, "Tea?" And the mother goes, "Tea." So that's been just delicious. To be able to show historically, here's a point of view about a time in the world and we are not used to having that history from a female point of view.

And when you do a Shaw play they're gifts because his ideas about women were –

Kathleen: – were feminist!

Jackie: Absolutely! And often the women are so smart, usually far smarter than the guys. And yet interestingly, as a contemporary woman going in to do Shaw plays, which I adore, there is still a certain amount of shape-shifting that you have to do, or a point of view that you have to bring in. The sexual politics of a lot of the drama of this time is fascinating. But interestingly, I find it very heartening that you go to a writer like Noel Coward and find in a play such as *Design for Living* that he's actually espousing that three people can live together. I took my then-16-year-old daughter to the opening of that and she kept saying to me, "When was this play written?" Somerset Maugham, you know, is a very politically – Many of these writers were breaking ground. Even the so-called "comic" writers. So I think that as long as we try to approach them from a contemporary point of view, I don't mean "updating" them, I mean just going in and really looking at their politics.

Kathleen: So what about the kick-up with the Somerset Maugham this season? When I read the exchange in the paper between critic J. Kelly Nestruck and director Morris Panych, I was sitting with the question of the distance, that gulf between then and now. And also realizing that when I see a play, even if the play doesn't resolve hiccups for me, observing the space between where I'm sitting and what I'm seeing is an incredibly important, and engaging, and provocative experience. And I don't actually *need* the play to bridge anything for me, because it's sometimes the discomfort of the space that I'm looking for. That's what I want.

Jackie: Yes! That's exactly it. I don't think we need to spoon-feed people and go, "Oh, look, it isn't like this anymore." You're here. You're sitting here. You're watching it. I think it's up to us to really clearly contextualize the play. And I mean Somerset Maugham was pretty anti-American, pretty anti-British, he's pretty anti – I mean, he was a viperish satirist, you know? Nobody gets away scot-free as far as I can see. He says things in his plays that are still really shocking. That's what I need: writers who aren't afraid of ideas because that's what this place thrives on. And how active ideas are. And how compelling. So you have a contemporary writer like Ann-Marie MacDonald. I wanted Ann-Marie, who can take an idea, a hundred ideas and spin them in the air and so that's how we ended up with *Belle Moral*. And *Belle Moral* is exactly that. There's this wonderful woman in the middle of it who is essentially dealing with all of the ideas that were taking us from the nineteenth into the twentieth century.

Kathleen: What do you think will be the political legacy of what you're doing?

Jackie: If the festival's called the Shaw Festival, the very nature of almost all of the work has a political edge to it. Larger, bigger "P" to it. The work that we do, it requires engagement from the audience, you know? If you're going to sit and watch Tom Stoppard's *Arcadia,* you have to fucking *engage*, you know? And you may not understand absolutely everything about chaos theory or algorithms but you will understand the notion of what a story from the past can do when it's retranslated into the present. I hope that certainly we will have allowed the piece to be accessed in a way that, at the very least, will put those issues out there. And to my mind, I would like to think that I have been able to extend the notion of what that engagement is about. I want to send a billion signals. I believe in the spirit of this place. And in the spirit of the use of theatre. What is theatre for? It is here to make you rethink. It can completely turn your head around. It can give succour.

Kathleen: I had that experience in *Lady Windermere's Fan* last night. You could run away with so many of those timeless quotations. But when she said, "There isn't good and bad. We're in the same world," and I was suddenly thrown into the last 10 years of "us against them" and the "evil forces" and terrorism. And I thought, that's the idea! That's at the centre of it. It's been so dressed up and it's been so confused by so many other things, not the least of which is fear. Then in that sort of escape of three hours and the poignancy of that line, all of the messiness, the complexity suddenly became clear for a fleeting moment for me. And then I thought, well I mean *that's* socially engaged theatre. Because I had to reconsider everything that I'd been swimming in and couldn't see because we'd been swimming for so long. And it just took one turn of phrase in a context that *just* distanced me enough that I could see something I was swimming in. It's totally a fabulous and a very active, activated position to be in.

Jackie: Yeah! I mean who wants to go to the theatre and just kind of slump in your seat? I mean, even with the musicals. We did *Ragtime*. I mean *Ragtime* was a very moving and hard piece to work on, in a great kind of way. And if you're truly Shavian about it, you can get to engagement without hitting people over the head.

Kathleen: Right. I want to talk about education, but writ large. Not strategies, not initiatives for doing this, that, or the other thing, but what is theatre's teaching or pedagogical function that you think you've given some attention to while here?

Jackie: I think that the biggest thing we can do is either change someone's point of view or if not change it, actually stop them for a moment and make them rethink or re-examine why they're sitting in a certain place. I think that is what theatre can do brilliantly. There's a point where that person goes, "Oh, I recognize that. I recognize what's being questioned, or what's being assumed or that behaviour." Then that's where the door opens, that's where the questioning happens. I don't mean to *change* people. You might say, "Well, does theatre change people?" Well, theatre opens the potential for people to re-examine something that might make them actually ultimately change themselves.

Kathleen: Right. Right. So here's something I'm interested in. There's often a dichotomy in theatre between this sort of intellectual, idea-based, distanced, cool kind of theatre that you talked about – which is a little bit Shavian – and a kind of affective theatre, where emotion and affect are significant drivers in its creation. And normally these things are dichotomized, a little bit of a gulf between them. Over the last five years, I would say that gulf is narrowing considerably and I don't know how much of that is theatre and how much of that is me, but I feel like some of the most politically engaged theatre I've seen is also very affectively attuned and I don't think that's always been the case.

Jackie: I think that's an astute observation. You could go back to Brecht's alienation effect and then you go and see *The Caucasian Chalk Circle* and watch two women pull a child apart and of course you're completely wrecked –

Kathleen: – Not feeling so distant!

Jackie: – not feeling very alienated right now. I think these two ideas have always, they're always regarding each other in one way or another. I certainly notice the actors here now – the notion of viscerally connecting to what you're intellectually saying is vital. Even though Shaw is cool, there is a huge passion –

Kathleen: Heat.

Jackie: And frankly, sex is under *everything* in Shaw. I'm completely and utterly convinced that's ultimately what drives a huge amount of it. It's kind of the potency of emotion versus argument. And so it's somehow trying to always not let one overcome the other, it seems to me. Because I think they can and should coexist but sometimes you think, are you manipulating people? I don't know. Sometimes I wonder. I'll put in a sound cue and then I'll go, Oh fuck, I'm really turning the screw there. Maybe I should pull that back a little bit.

Look, it's interesting, I went to see *Angels in America* at Soulpepper, which I hadn't seen for years. And it was interesting now (not that the issues aren't around but it isn't the heat of the time in which it was written in terms of AIDS and so on). So I'm sitting there and I'm going okay, so what am I – I'm enjoying this, and as always with Tony Kushner who's so brilliant I mean there's still just stuff that gets said where you just go, "Okay, well that's fantastic." But then I'm going, "Okay, what am I finding old-fashioned?" I'm finding the structure, the episodic nature of it a bit of a thing of the past. Somebody asked me, "Do you really like these AIDS plays?" I really don't think we can be quite *that* blasé about it. I was very happy to be there watching it, but I was not actually completely and personally engaged in it. But I didn't mind that. I don't feel that every time I go to the theatre I have to leave weeping. On the other hand, I went to Soulpepper to see *Death of a Salesman* that I've seen many, many, many times and by the time I got to the scene where Joe Zeigler, who played Willy, is being told he didn't have a job, I was so – I couldn't even look. I saw Joe afterwards and of course all I did was just burst into tears. I've seen it a *million* times and I kind of suddenly – Whatever they found in that, whatever core, completely demolished me. So it's very personal. But when I'm working on a play, I really do work at times to deliberately make myself mistrust the moment of "oh-that-will-get-people." To me, it has to be so fucking earned.

Kathleen: That's what Richard Sennett says in his last book about the idea of rehearsal – that those moments are earned. In the Renaissance workshop they were earned. And they have to be earned now.

Jackie: It all has to be earned. And that sounds very moralistic. It's not. I don't make art. I guess I translate art, but I hope in the end the creation ultimately is art, or artful. You have to go on a journey. You have to turn over every fucking stone. You have to find a way of reconstituting and rediscovering a narrative.

Kathleen: As you know, the overriding question of our book is "Why Theatre Now?" And for us – my co-editor and I – both the why and the now were central to that question. So if I pose that question to you, what would you say?

Jackie: I think we have to continue to keep proving it, but for me, theatre *now* is vital. Why? Because it is a place where a community of people can be brought together in a live experience, to experience a story in whatever form it is that potentially will radicalize, question, clarify, anger. I think that if we don't have that, there's the potential now, because of the global world that we live in, first of all for homogenization. But there's also the problem that knowledge is given and received so quickly. We need to be able to sit in a room (importantly, with other people) and to see that knowledge can be reconstituted into a narrative that requires time and thought. It's vital that we find another way to look at our experiences and the information that is around us.

Kathleen: Where does your confidence in theatre to make us see anew come from?

Jackie: So I was born and brought up in Belfast and all my teenage years were right in the middle of the troubles, when they were at their height. I was very aware of it and it was the mid-sixties to late sixties and into the early seventies. I remember being in school and like a teacher coming in and often they would say girls (I went to this all-girls grammar school that I got a scholarship to go to) and they'd say, "Girls, there's been a bomb scare, can we check your bags and desks." And I'm thinking, well like what would you do if you *found* a bomb? So there was a necessary casualness about it, in a funny way. You got used to the fact that if you went into town you had to go through security and if you went into a store you had to go through security. But then I thought about it, you know, later for my mother and what it's like bringing up teenagers, period. Well of course my mother's at home, knowing there's been a bomb in downtown Belfast and that's where I … and she doesn't know until I walked in the door. There were no cell phones. And I think about that and I thought, fuck that must've been just terrible. I mean I was just like 15. But the other thing is that's where my love of theatre and words started. In Belfast. Because my mother taught theatre and English and art. She was very big in community theatre so there were always people in the house making props and all that kind of stuff. So I joined a youth theatre, the Lyric Theatre, which is the main regional theatre in Belfast, and there was a Lyric youth theatre and it was run by this woman called Mary O'Malley, who was the founder of the Lyric and she was this sort of scary woman for me – I was only nine. She was a *staunch* Irish nationalist. And the only thing that we did was Yeats. She believed [putting on a thick Irish accent] "the only person for any child to learn about in theatre was Yeats." Fucking Yeats. So every year, we would do these Yeats one-act plays. So I would come home and my mom would say, "So now Jacqueline, what play are you going to do this year?" And I'm going, "We're going to do *At the Hawk's Well*." And she'd go, "Oh for God's sake! What the hell?!" And there we'd be "Who can have trod in the grass?" Doing these crazy fucking Yeats plays.

Kathleen: And that's why you're in theatre now, there's no question about it.

Jackie: Of course! I mean, absolutely. And in the end I think somewhere right in there, that seed, of all of those words, those torrents and torrents and torrents of words, half of which I really didn't understand. But nevertheless. And then because I became the local kid actor. I got my equity card, so any play that was happening that needed a kid in it, I would be the kid. So I was in some good and some *terrible* plays. I remember a play called *The Famine*. I remember mom saying, "Jacqueline, that has to be one of the most turgid plays I've ever seen." You know? Where it was all about the potato and I played a corpse, and a keener, and – prophetically – someone immigrating to Canada. So the notion of the theatre and words and words and words and words was something I grew up with. I went to Manchester University in England, quite convinced that it was just a stop on the way to becoming Juliet at the RSC. Manchester University was fantastic because we had this little studio theatre and this was now in the early seventies. And it was on the circuit of all the political theatre companies that were just starting up. So like, Caryl Churchill's *Monstrous Regiment, Joint Stock, 7:84* from Scotland, they all came and we tore the tickets. We had to run the studio. So suddenly I started seeing this stuff and going, "Ohhh … Okay."

Kathleen: Where's Yeats?!

Jackie: Yeah! And it took me a long time to put the two things back together again, you know? But that was it. I went, "Oh, okay. That's what theatre is! That's what theatre is."

9 Performance as Reappearance: Female Blackness in History and Theatre

NAILA KELETA-MAE

and ...
and ...
It will be good this time.[1]

Theatre has an uncanny ability to examine perceptions of what was then and what is now, to face the past as the present and the present as the past. It is through the sustained engagement with then and now that theatre reveals, especially in Canada, its remarkable capacity to expose historic omissions in dominant epistemes and stage productive contestations against established narratives. In this chapter, I will examine the play *Angélique* by Lorena Gale as it accomplishes, I will argue, what all theatre has the potential to accomplish – turn a little-known historic moment into a compelling contemporary narrative that is relevant and necessary. *Angélique* demonstrates that for people in bodies read as female and black in Canada, theatre can provide a departure point from which to examine how the parameters of social performance have influenced female blackness – from slavery, to the early days of the civil rights era, to contemporary Canadian life.

Gale's acclaimed play *Angélique* is based on the historical account of Marie-Joseph Angélique, born into slavery in Madeira, Portugal, circa 1710, sold into slavery in New France in 1725, and accused of burning down the city of Old Montréal in 1734. Once convicted, Angélique was tortured, hanged, and burned.[2] As much as Gale's play is a historical representation, it is also invested in producing the present; this is made explicit in the *dramatis personae* that describes the play's time period as "The present and 1730s. Then is now. Now is then."[3]

Gale's constant blurring of the lines between past and present (through costumes, music, and references to current affairs) transforms the play from a dramatization of Angélique's life in New France in the early eighteenth century to an exploration of the lives of people in bodies read as female and black in Canada today.[4]

Angélique is a mix of fact and fiction that centres primarily on Angélique's life in the 1730s as an enslaved black person in Old Montreal, where the ownership of people was mostly a symbol of wealth and social standing. When the merchant François Poulin de Francheville sees Angélique for the first time he is immediately attracted to her female blackness in the form of her "elegant shapes" and "chestnut skin."[5] De Francheville purchases Angélique for 800 pounds to make his wife, Thérèse de Couagne, the "envy of female society."[6] In the *dramatis personae* Gale indicates that, unless a stage direction states otherwise, Angélique is seen working whenever she is visible on stage[7] – conspicuous labour is central to her social performance. As such, de Couagne is conferred an elevated social status because de Couagne can be a spectator while Angélique performs unceasing labour. In addition, Gale makes clear that de Francheville's acquisition of Angélique is not only about fostering the jealousy of his wife's contemporaries, it is also about his ability to ascribe authority to himself. In a monologue describing his first encounter with Angélique he asks, "Do you know what it's like to be flush? To say, 'I want that!' And without giving it any more thought, to just reach out and take it. To be able to buy anything or anyone … there is no more powerful feeling in the world!"[8] The couple's genders, class, and whiteness are affirmed, and to some extent conferred upon them, by the ability of Angélique's body to be read as female and black in New France. In this instance, *Angélique* demonstrates the complex impact of spectatorship and geography on the social performance of female blackness. It is precisely the presence of others attuned to the culture of a specific place that makes Angélique's female blackness at once possible and necessary.

The confluence of spectator, geography, sex, and race on the performance of female blackness generates what I call *perpetual performance*.[9] Writing in the early civil rights era, Zora Neale Hurston made an observation in a short essay entitled "How It Feels to Be Colored Me" that describes the experience of *perpetual performance*: "It is thrilling to think – to know that for any act of mine, I shall get twice as much praise or twice as much blame. It is quite exciting to hold the center of the national stage, with the spectators not knowing whether to laugh or to weep."[10] Hurston insists that "any act" performed by her body (which was at the time read as coloured and female in the United States of America) occupies prominent "stage" space and engenders audience response.[11] What Hurston powerfully implies, then, is that her "acts" do not require professionalized performance training and formal performance contexts to be read as acts, nor does her "stage" have to be an official, public space replete with costumes, lighting, paying audience, and the like. Quite the opposite, Hurston asserts that in the mundane activities of everyday life, her gendered, racialized body moving through society is a social performance that creates an audience that thrusts her onto the stage to simultaneously affirm and to some extent confer upon them their individual and collective identities.[12] Gale makes a similar assertion to Hurston's; *Angélique* is rife with moments that depict her in everyday life, and in all but one brief scene her actions are witnessed by others either who she knows are present or who, according to stage directions, lurk in the shadows. The social performance of Angélique's gendered, racialized body moving through everyday life in New France in the eighteenth century results in her almost always being watched and thus thrusts her, involuntarily, onto the public stage. The sensation of being watched, and the social performance that accompanies it, extends through to my experience of being in a similarly gendered and racialized body as Angélique and Hurston, but moving through contemporary Canadian society. The mundane acts that constitute everyday life in a body read as female and black in Canada elicit, from others, the heightened scrutiny that being an audience member permits. The performer's margin for error is slim and the potential to receive unsolicited commentary is high – especially whenever social performances of female blackness deviate from expected or stereotypical scripts in ways that challenge audience members' abilities to affirm their own identities. For people in bodies read as female and black in Canada who read, watch, or perform *Angélique*, there is nominal personal or professional risk at stake as they examine the impact of social performances that the play makes visible. *Angélique* provides a safe space for deepened contemplation of these impacts through Gale's efforts to connect past with present experiences of female blackness. *Angélique* is important today because it does what all theatre has the potential to do – provide formal stage space for readers, spectators, and practitioners to examine the complexities of their roles as social actors.

Angélique demonstrates that for people in bodies read as female and black in Canada, theatre can also address systemic omissions in dominant epistemes – namely in history, scholarship, and education. Attempts to control female blackness have occurred in the Americas since, at least, the advent of the transatlantic slave trade in the sixteenth century. Identifying the impact of the transatlantic slave trade on contemporary life is particularly difficult in Canada, where the dominant narratives of the nation's implication in this historical episode is that of Canada as the place to which runaway slaves from the United States of America escaped to be free. This narrative holds within it telling omissions. *Angélique* challenges this historiography because, as Katherine McKittrick asserts in her analysis of the play,

> [Angélique's] story documents Canadian slavery as well as the lengths to which local communities will go to secure racial, economic, and gender hierarchies. Angélique [the historical figure] also calls into question the workings of the Canadian nation by shattering the safe-haven myth – one of the key ways in which the nation secures both its disconnection from blackness and its seeming exoneration from difficult histories. By exposing how transatlantic slavery played a key role in the making of the nation (through enforced labor and the entrenchment of racial hierarchies), Canada is exposed as both materially complicit to, and discursively innocent of, racial domination. More clearly, Angelique's narrative suggests that slavery is possible, but that this possibility holds in it a series of comfortable erasures, in which the nation is always positioned as opposed to both blackness and racial domination.[13]

Given the persistent presence of this "safe-haven myth" in the national narrative, one of the most prevalent stories of female blackness that emerges is that of Harriet Tubman, famed for her leadership of a secret network called the Underground Railroad. Born into slavery in the United States circa 1820, Tubman escaped and went on to lead other runaway slaves to freedom in northern parts of the United States (where people in bodies read as black were legally allowed to be free). Slavery was abolished in Canada in 1834 but Canada only became one of Tubman's destinations on the Underground Railroad after 1850, when the Fugitive Slave Act was passed in the United States requiring that runaway slaves be returned to their owners. Even though Angélique is bought, further exploited, and hanged in Old Montréal 125 years before Tubman crosses Canadian borders to lead slaves to freedom, it is Tubman and her exceptional courage that occupy centre stage in established recitations of Canadian history – it is Tubman who emerges as the protagonist in the "safe-haven myth." The emphasis on Tubman as representative of histories of female blackness in Canada is specious in at least two ways: it erases the presence of black slaves and labourers who were in Canada long before the advent of the Underground Railroad; and it incorrectly locates the origins of female blackness in Canada solely in the United States. *Angélique* challenges these misleading occlusions head on; and the play's national and international production successes indirectly address a second area of systemic omission of the presence of female blackness in Canada – scholarship on black cultural production.

As noted by artists and scholars in Canada, very little theatre, performance, feminist, or critical race scholarship thoughtfully considers black cultural production in Canada.[14] Djanet Sears describes the constant lack of documentation as "serious patterns of omission."[15] Despite substantive material differences, black cultural production in Canada, as a site of critical inquiry, is usually collapsed into examinations of African American, black British, and black Caribbean cultures. To some extent, this recurrent under-examination is a conundrum; on the one hand, the aforementioned diverse geographical regions of blackness provide very useful theoretical and methodological modes for the study of blackness in Canada. On the other hand, the reliance on and referencing of blackness elsewhere can also contribute to the lack of critical work on blackness in Canada. At stake in these complex and "serious patterns of omission" is the opportunity to carefully contemplate a geopolitical context where various ethnic, linguistic, national, and religious modes of female blackness have collided with dominant epistemes for centuries. These collisions contain insightful perspectives that are not only pertinent to the integrity of academic scholarship but are also integral to the credibility of a national identity. The particularities of Canada's politics of sex and race are generally referred to as exemplary by disseminators of dominant discourse and as exclusionary by those with little to no influence on the shaping of prevalent narratives. At the heart of this chasm of perceptions (as it pertains to female blackness in Canada) is the systemic occlusion of female blackness from the national imaginary. But when theatre exercises its potential to expose historic omissions the results can be arresting – Gale places Angélique on centre stage and, as Alan Filewod observes, the playwright "uses the moment of performance to destabilize the narratives that have historically secured Canadian nationhood."[16]

Theatre's ability to directly address modes of exclusion has been no more evident to me than when *Angélique* is brought into the classroom. I have taught *Angélique* to undergraduate theatre students since around 2010, either as a formal course syllabus entry or through informal conversation. I have yet to teach a student, educated in Canada, who has not heard of either the Underground Railroad or Harriet Tubman, but in almost every instance when I teach the historiography of Angélique, students are surprised to learn of her existence and shocked that the transatlantic slave trade took place in Canada. Inevitably, the students' surprise leads them to pose some iteration of the question "Why wasn't I taught this in school?" Like many of my students, I attended public elementary, middle, and high schools in Ontario, and these aspects of Canadian history were also absent from the curricula that I was taught. Like many of my students, I too was surprised when I first heard the story of Angélique; though I had learned, outside of the classroom, that the transatlantic slave trade had operated in Canada, reading *Angélique* concretized this knowing in visceral ways. According to McKittrick, the experience of surprise that my students and I share is particularly telling of how blackness is often constructed within narratives about Canada:

> Blackness is surprising because it should not be here, was not here before, was always here, is only momentarily here, was always over there (beyond Canada, for example). This means, then, that black people in Canada are also presumed surprises because they are "not here" and "here" simultaneously: they are, like blackness, unexpected, shocking, concealed in a landscape of systemic blacklessness ... In Canada, blackness and black people are altogether deniable *and* evidence of prior codes of representation that have identified blackness/difference as irrelevant. But black existence is an actuality, which takes on several different forms that do not (much to the surprise of some) always conform to the idea of Canada.[17]

Angélique consistently appears on my course syllabi because it dramatizes Canada in ways that challenge students to productively contemplate relationships between history, gender, race, and nation. I teach *Angélique* because its analysis consistently challenges students to reflect critically on how their understanding of themselves and the nation is affected by what is and is not omitted in prevalent discursive formations – from historical records, to academic scholarship, to public school curricula. *Angélique* is relevant today because it does what all theatre has the potential to do – challenge various forms of systemic exclusion.

Angélique demonstrates that for people in bodies read as female and black in Canada, theatre can also be a productive site of contestation that shifts the emphasis of official narratives, imagines personal agency, and explores the conditions that make hope possible. Gale uses a nuanced combination of imagery and language, in the short opening scene of

Angélique, to contest an authoritative account and shift its emphasis. The stage directions that signal the beginning of the play call for "[t]he featureless silhouette of a woman dancing with a book against a backdrop of red, oranges and yellow, suggestive of flames. VOICEOVER – building in a rapid repetitive delivery."[18] Gale makes the woman on stage, presumably Angélique, indistinguishable apart from her sex and instead emphasizes the presence of an authoritative document – a book. The presence of the woman on stage is further usurped with the play's opening words, which come not from her mouth but from a voiceover that states, presumably reading from the book, "And in seventeen thirty-four a Negro slave set fire to the city of Montreal and was hanged."[19] With this utterance, Gale reproduces what was, at the time,[20] the official interpretation of the facts that led to Angélique's conviction and sentence. However, Gale's reproduction of this dominant narrative contains a subtle disruption that throws into question the context within which the statement of facts takes place. Gale starts the sentence with a conjunction ("and") but does not include the requisite preceding phrase or clause with which the conjunction would connect – this signals to readers and spectators that information is missing; the larger idea is incomplete. Gale then proceeds to further contest the authoritative account with a methodical exercise in revision and repetition:

VOICEOVER. And in seventeen thirty-four a Negro slave set fire to the City of Montreal and was hanged.
In seventeen thirty-four a Negro slave set fire to the City of Montreal and was hanged.
Seventeen thirty-four a Negro slave set fire to the City of Montreal and was hanged.
a Negro slave set fire to the City of Montreal and was hanged
slave set fire to the City of Montreal and was hanged
set fire to the City of Montreal and was hanged
fire to the City of Montreal and was hanged
to the City of Montreal and was hanged
City of Montreal and was hanged
Montreal and was hanged
and was hanged
was hanged
hanged.[21]

Gale contests the dominant narrative by shifting its point of emphasis. Her painstaking exercise of removing the first word or two of the opening sentence and restating the remainder only concludes when the voiceover delivers the single word "hanged." Gale draws readers' and spectators' attention away from the historical era, the slavery, the location, and the fire and places it firmly on the state-sanctioned killing of Angélique. When theatre establishes the interchangeability of then and now, a seemingly simple shift in focus can catapult a play from the contemplation of a specific historic moment into a provocative conversation about the activities of the state in contemporary times. The scene ends with a stage direction, "The crackling sound of fire."[22] And while this certainly alludes to the burning of Old Montreal, it can also be read to suggest, through images and performance, what all theatre has the ability to do: burn away an authoritative account, raze over of an official historical narrative to shift the focus of the story that will be told.

Angélique also demonstrates contemporary theatre's capacity to be a productive site of contestation in the moments when Angélique imagines the scope of her own agency. Gale does not stage these moments as forceful declarations that might temper readers' and spectators' engagement with the difficult conditions that shape Angélique's life. Instead, Angélique's imaginings occur in tentative, hushed tones. One of these key moments takes place in a conversation between Angélique and César, an enslaved black man in New France – a man with whom she is forced to have sex in order to procreate and thus produce new property for their owners.

ANGÉLIQUE. I remember. Before this Montreal. This New France. Before this Canada. I remember Madiere. Picking coffee with my mother and my father. The coffee beans. Their tender green. Their firmness between my little fingers. We toiled for them. Yes! But it was work. Just work. Hard work is a part of life. And at least we were together.

On the days of rest and celebration we would all descend on the beach. We would build a fire in conjunction to the line of the horizon. As the sun set, the orange and red and yellow of day's transition into night, would blend with the colours of the fire. Everyone would gather round. And to the beating of a drum, they would tell the stories of our ancestors. Our warriors dancing the great battles. Our hunters re-enacting their kills.

The little me would stand on the sandy shore and look out across the inky water. And imagine I could see the land of my ancestors. It was that close. It was that far away. [pause] I cannot understand this cruelty. I may have always been a slave. But I did not feel like one until I came to this land ... [carefully] We could run.[23]

Gale concludes Angélique's comparison of slavery in Portugal and New France with an indicting attestation of the brutality of the treatment in the latter. Yet Angélique does not propose that she and César match the violence of their owners with their own – instead, Gale's protagonist imagines the possibility of freedom. "We could run," Angélique cautiously suggests – a clear disruption of the narrative that Canada was a place that slaves only ran to. "We could run," Angélique says, cognizant of the vicious physical punishments they would suffer if captured. "We could run," Angélique says anyway – a lucid example of the glimpses of agency that can exist even within a context as violent as slavery, where the litmus test for whether or not one is treated as a human being consists of the visibility of the melanin in one's skin. "We could run," Gale writes – a poignant reminder to readers and spectators, especially those in bodies read as female and black, that alternate realities can be imagined even in circumstances laden with gender and racial oppression.

Angélique also demonstrates contemporary theatre's capacity to be a productive site of contestation through Gale's unflinching staging of the conditions within which hope can arise. For readers and spectators of Angélique the reward, and relief, that a moment of hope can offer does not come easily; Angélique insists that the story's unfoldings be witnessed in, at times, deeply disturbing ways in order for the complexities of hope to be made visible. Filewod contextualizes the witnessing that Gale's play demands:

> Angélique works a ruthlessly effective critique of the naturalised fictions that historical narrative so often conceals. The conventional mode of historical narrative in the theatre – at least on Canadian stages – is one in which revelations of past crimes speak to present injustice. The mapping of past and present tends to result in a "living history" form of dramatic realism that dehistoricises the past. Lorena Gale deliberately dismantles this convention with a strategic play of spectatorial politics in which every moment of the drama is constructed through frames of testimony and witnessing.[24]

Angélique requires audiences and spectators to witness a wide range of violence – from the sale of a human being, to rape, to infanticide, to torture, to hanging. But what I found most unsettling was Gale's insistence that readers and spectators witness Angélique's articulation of her hopes for a life in slavery that includes some modicum of human dignity. Angélique's articulation of her hopes for a different future occurs in her first of five monologues, delivered soon after she is purchased by de Francheville, introduced to his wife, and given an exhaustive and exhausting list of the domestic labour that she will be forced to perform. Regardless of whether or not readers and spectators are familiar with the historiography of Angélique, by the time she delivers this monologue Gale has already foreshadowed that, at the very least, Angélique will be enslaved, she will be raped, and she will be killed. Against this backdrop, readers and spectators are forced to witness Angélique say,

This time will be different.

This time everything will work out for me.
This time, I will not just
"live in."
This time, I will
"live with."
I'll make this strange new land – my land!
This house – my home!
These new people,
My people!
This time I will live in reasonable peace.

These people will be different.
These folk will be decent and good.
This mistress will be firm but gentle.
This master will be honest and fair.
There will be no
Harsh looks or cruel words,
This time.
This time,
I will be treated with loving kindness and understanding.

I will work hard.
From sun to sun.
Do exactly as I'm told.
I will perform each duty with pride and obedience.
I will maintain their order.
Everything will go smoothly.
I'll know my place.

I will give freely of myself.
Repaying their humanity with loyalty.
Earning their protection and their care.
They'll wonder how they ever lived without me!

Life will be different this time.

There will be holidays ...
and happy days ...
and good times ...
occasional laughter ...
and private moments ...
and ...
and ...

It will be good this time.

This time will be different.
This time will be different.
This time will be different.[25]

Angélique's monologue is rooted in a measured and strategic hopefulness – one that is shaped by her assessment of the possibilities afforded to her given her sex, skin colour, and the geographic location that informs her audience's perceptions of her corporeality. Her hopefulness is grounded in an astute assessment of the limitations and possibilities before her. The monologue opens and closes with the sentence "This time will be different," a clear indication that Angélique is not interested in reliving whatever happened the last time. Clearly she survived that experience, but now she aspires to something different – something simple that readers and spectators know is unequivocally impossible – a life that is "good." Angélique's hopefulness is pragmatic, and in order to actualize it she commits to being obedient, maintaining her master's and mistress's order and knowing her place. And despite having been born into slavery in Portugal, Angélique is hopeful that a different kind of slavery might be possible in New France – one in which she could experience a sense of belonging to the land and its people and one where her owners would recognize her hard labour with fairness, protection, and care. Angélique's hopefulness is specific; she describes the mundane, everyday activities that in her purview would make her life "good" – holidays, laughter, and private moments. And when she attempts to articulate the kinds of experiences that would constitute a good life beyond the possibilities that life in her body has thus far permitted, she runs out of concrete examples and says instead,

> and ...
> and ...[26]

But Gale insists on hopefulness in these moments too – she uses ellipses and full returns as placeholders for the possibilities Angélique's future might hold. In a play in which "Then is now. Now is then,"[27] these ellipses and full returns can also resonate profoundly in the contemporary lives of readers and spectators. Gale's placeholders can act as a reminder that there is a shared present and future that has yet to be realized but for which there is ample room to be hopeful in measured and strategic ways. *Angélique* is necessary today because it does what all theatre has the potential to do – productively stage contestations of dominant narratives.

Angélique demonstrates that for people in bodies read as female and black in Canada, theatre can provide a departure point for the examination of the influences of social performance, address systemic omissions in dominant epistemes and be a productive site of contestation. Theatre holds the potential to expose historic omissions in dominant epistemes and stage productive contestations of established narratives because theatre has the remarkable ability to summon an audience to face the past as the present and the present as the past. When there is no clear delineation between then and now, theatre has the potential to intervene in the lives of its spectators, readers, and practitioners and unmoor them from the constraints of the past. It is precisely in these moments that theatre can inspire us to work and hope, in measured and pragmatic ways, for a more just future.

NOTES

1 Lorena Gale, *Angélique*, in *Testifyin': Contemporary African Canadian Drama*, vol. 1, ed. Djanet Sears (Toronto: Playwrights Canada Press, 2003), 14 (original work published in 1999).

2 Gale, *Angélique*; Afua Cooper, *The Hanging of Angélique: The Untold Story of Canadian Slavery and the Burning of Old Montreal* (Toronto: HarperCollins, 2006); Katherine McKittrick, *Demonic Grounds: Black Women and the Cartographies of Struggle* (Minneapolis: University of Minnesota Press, 2006).

3 Gale, *Angélique*, 7.

4 I use the term "people in bodies read as female and black in Canada" in an effort to make visible the roles of spectator and geographic location in the performance of female blackness. I also place the word "female" before the word "black" in order to foreground gender as a primary site of inquiry.

5 Gale, *Angélique*, 10.

6 Ibid., 10.

7 Ibid., 7.

8 Ibid., 10.

9 Andrea Davis, "Sex and the Nation: Performing Black Female Sexuality in Canadian Theatre," in *Critical Perspectives on Canadian Theatre in English*, vol. 2, *African-Canadian Theatre*, ed. Maureen Moynagh (Toronto: Playwrights Canada Press, 2005), 107. I include the word "performance" in the term *perpetual performance* to signal the radical possibilities of performance and to assert that performance is an integral way of knowing, particularly for people in bodies that are simultaneously gendered and racialized. My intention is not to superimpose agency on gendered and racialized bodies that are often strategically used as symbols of oppression. Instead, I am interested in exploring how *Angélique* uses formal stage space to proffer that agency has long been and continues to be present for people in bodies read as female and black in Canada.

10 Zora Neale Hurston, "How It Feels to Be Colored Me," in *I Love Myself When I Am Laughing ... And Then Again When I Am Looking Mean and Impressive: A Zora Neale Hurston Reader*, ed. Alice Walker (Old Westbury, NY: The Feminist Press, 1979), 153 (original work published in 1942).

11 Ibid.

12 Sherene H. Razack, *Looking White People in the Eye: Gender, Race, and Culture in Courtrooms and Classrooms* (Toronto: University of Toronto Press, 1998). See *Looking White People in the Eye* for a detailed discussion of the ways in which the gaze generated by the colonizer simultaneously creates both the colonizer and the colonized – establishing the superiority of the former through the subjugation of the latter.

13 McKittrick, *Demonic Grounds*, 119.

14 Kaie Kellough, conversation on 12 February 2010; Maureen Moynagh "African-Canadian Theatre: An Introduction," in Moynagh, *African-Canadian Theatre*, vii–xxii; Leslie Sanders and Rinaldo Walcott, "At the Full and Change

of CanLit: An Interview with Dionne Brand," *Canadian Woman Studies* 20, no. 2 (2000): 22–6.

15 Djanet Sears, "Introduction," in *Testifyin': Contemporary African Canadian Drama*, vol. 1, ed. Djanet Sears (Toronto: Playwrights Canada Press, 2000), i.

16 Alan Filewod, "'From Twisted History': Reading Angélique," in Moynagh, *African-Canadian Theatre*, 31.

17 McKittrick, *Demonic Grounds*, 93.

18 Gale, *Angélique*, 9.

19 Ibid.

20 In the years following the initial stage productions and publication of *Angélique*, historians' analyses of relevant historical documents brought into question whether or not Angélique set the fire and whether or not the fire was an act of arson.

21 Gale, *Angélique*, 9.

22 Ibid.

23 Ibid., 31–2.

24 Filewod, "From Twisted History," 37.

25 Gale, *Angélique*, 13–14.

26 Ibid.

27 Ibid., 7.

10 Unspeakable Vulnerability: Theatre Mattering in Men's Lives

JULIE SALVERSON

"Everything is a threat when you are a man." My husband studies me across a corner table in our favourite bar. We've just seen *The Place Beyond the Pines*, a smart and challenging American crime drama about fathers and sons. "I've waited months for this movie," he says. "Finally something intelligent that doesn't make men out to be assholes." Now he's waiting for my reaction.

I've never paid attention to men's lives. I was a young feminist; we had ourselves to look out for, and even though I knew that what happened to men played a significant role in what happened to "*us*" that was as far as it went. Although, when I think about my years as a theatre artist in schools and community projects, it's the boys I remember.

There was Jesse, a slim grade seven terrorist with shiny black hair, brilliant wit, and a gentleness under all the agitation. He loved improvisation and would stumble over himself getting all his ideas out. He couldn't stand it when others had the spotlight and would mercilessly joke at their expense. I did something stupid with that kid, made one of those rules: "One more mean crack and you're out of here!" Sure enough, Jesse blew it and I had to play my role in the restrictive bargain I had created. I told him, in front of the whole class, "You're out of the play." I watched him march proudly out the door and I hated myself. The child was desperately lonely and wanted to be there. I learned my lesson about absolutes, but it didn't help Jesse.

There was the skinny freckled fellow in grade three who broke pencils drawing pages and pages of exploding buildings. I don't remember his name but he rarely spoke – except, his teacher told me, in the theatre workshop. And the frantic teenager pumped with Ritalin whose exhausted parents couldn't believe how drama calmed him down. All of us who have been lucky to create theatre with people not usually exposed to it carry around these stories. I don't know why the moments that stuck with me were about boys. Maybe it's because I had a bad feeling that, for those particular kids, things were going to get worse.

I have worked in theatre all my life. I have always hated being asked, on panel after panel, to explain why it matters. It has seemed to me painfully Canadian to be reduced to arguing that the arts create jobs, and I envy European colleagues their curious audiences, generous funding, and ample rehearsal schedules. Because of this exhaustion of explanation, I hesitated to contribute to this book. But then I realized that, like it or not, we live in a time where the ability to feel – ourselves, others, the world we live in – is disappearing. Without this essential faculty, so central to the language of theatre, we lose our ability to know who we are and what matters.

Catherine Malabou says that exhausted identity and impoverishment are the battlefields of contemporary society. In her book *The New Wounded*, the philosopher describes a cultural landscape of "emotional coolness"[1] inhabited by subjects who are both traumatized and disconnected from their affects. This is a world I sense in the increasingly outcome-driven bureaucracy of my university, in the increased impoverishment of the humanities, and in the removal of liberal arts leadership training from military budgets. Malabou calls it a "paralysis of touching"[2] where "the impossibility of feeling anything blurs the mirror that connects us to ourselves and others."[3] If there is one thing we know about theatre, it is that human beings do it together. Theatre confronts us with the face to face.

The invitation to write this essay comes at a time when I am surrounded by men. Every fall for almost 20 years the Royal Military College of Canada (RMCC) English department invites me to give a theatre and story-making workshop for first- through fourth-year students. I bring members of my Queen's University drama class and they exchange stereotypes and assumptions each has about the other. They laugh. They ask questions. The Queen's students say everyone thinks they're rich and only want to drink. The RMCC students say everyone thinks they're brainwashed and only want to fight. Then the stories get more layered, more complex, more true. One military student says, "When I go home for Christmas everyone thinks I'm the same as when I left. I'm not." Another talks about visiting a local restaurant with his girlfriend and being refused service because he is in uniform. We talk about making a performance to show people in Kingston about what it means to be in the Canadian military and who these young people really are.

Then, in the winter of 2011, our dream of a military play became a reality. I served as artist in residence at RMCC for one term and am a designated adjunct until 2015. I am glad to be doing this, because living in Kingston, Ontario, means living in a military town. Downtown is Queen's University, where I teach the brightest and the best, as the administration is fond of reminding us. On the other side of the causeway, where the St Lawrence River meets Lake Ontario, are the limestone buildings and parade squares of RMCC. Farther along the river is the army base, where families live. And where, until very recently, families waited while their loved ones served in Afghanistan. Now they wait for something more invisible to the public, less straightforward. To see what it means for their loved ones to come back home.

I am curious to discover what drama means to these students. I don't know anything about the military. Like so many Canadians, I've grown up on American movies about war. I could say a lot about what I have learned doing this work, but that isn't the purpose of this essay. Instead, I want to focus on what makes an officer in training, who has classes from 8:00 am to 6:00 pm and drills and duties until the wee hours, *make* the time to create and rehearse a play. Because, believe me, I thought that the Queen's students were busy, but it's nothing compared to the life of an RMCC student. And yet they did it. So how come?

RMCC is where officers are trained in Canada. There are lots of women here now, but they tell me they are supposed to behave like men anyway. So the question of how men are socialized, what is expected of them, and what narratives are acceptable for defining men's lives matters to the men *and* the women at this school. Gender studies is not my field, but a few words about theories of masculinity are important. Gender became an academic focus in the mid-1970s and was situated within a feminist framework. Andrew Tolson's *The Limits of Masculinity* was a combination of personal accounts, anecdotal evidence, qualitative data from conversations with young gang members, and analysis.[4] It was "the first attempt to define a 'problem of masculinity' involving an adjustment to disintegrating images of self, and was pivotal in encouraging the previously female-dominated and feminist gender studies to embrace the study of men and masculinity."[5]

Tolson drew on sociologist Erving Goffman's examination of how people institutionally perform social roles.[6] Goffman's groundbreaking study of asylums and mental institutions looked at the processes through which people maintain certain behaviours as inmates and guards. What's relevant here is how Tolson's work on masculinity provided an early contribution to performance studies, describing certain behaviours as performances or presentations: "The working class boy 'expresses himself, not so much in an inner competitive struggle for achievement, as through a collective toughness, a masculine "performance" recognized and approved by his "mates.""[7]

Male students of all backgrounds are subject at RMCC to the need to appear manly and confident and to make decisions swiftly. Ciara Murphy describes the female body's inability to fit into Western societies' social and cultural image of the warrior as women's greatest remaining hurdle in the military.[8] Murphy, herself a navy reservist in her thirties, cites Karen D. Davis and Brian McKee's characteristics of the male warrior: "superior physical and moral attributes, aggressive nature, proclivity to violence ..., embodiment of virtue," and a "will to kill."[9] In some communities – the world of the academy, intellectual society, high arts, and culture – we have come a long way towards expanding and complicating Tolson's 1977 discussion of masculinity. But how ingrained are these restricting expectations on men in the broader culture, the everyday?

Katrina Onstad writes in the *Globe and Mail* that nobody likes Angelina Jolie. She has been called "smug, aloof, arrogant and snotty."[10] This narrative became unstable in May 2013 when Jolie revealed her double mastectomy to the public. Onstad quotes Facebook CEO Sheryl Sandberg on the "likeability penalty," which penalizes women professionally for behaving in "masculine" ways:[11] exhibiting decisive and strong leadership, not being concerned with popularity. Jolie has "got better things to do than worry about you liking her," says Onstad. "Good girls who live in fear of being unlikeable, who scramble to say and do the nice thing rather than being true to themselves, lose out on power. Life gets smaller and less thrilling when being liked trumps being real."[12]

This is empowering for women, but what does it say about how – and what – men are still expected to be? When I tell my husband about Tolson's book and the impact it made – understanding masculinity as having many forms, restructuring and reconceptualizing gender relations, and acknowledging "an adjustment to disintegrating images of self"[13] – he looks at me in surprise. "That's news to me," he says. My husband doesn't think popular culture offers "multiple narratives" for men's lives. He sees no public discourse that allows for vulnerability or variety. "This may sound old and tired, but men are portrayed as either tough loners or goofy geeks, lovable idiots or deliberately oppressive and insensitive. There is no nuance."

Major Hans Christian Breede does me a favour. He agrees to speak to the first meeting of the RMCC drama club. In Afghanistan, this gracious and intelligent young man was faced with the loss of soldiers under his command and the challenge of helping his unit deal with their loss. His experience with drama while studying at RMCC helped him in this challenging situation. Breede makes an encouraging pitch to these students and tells them that drama is not just a hobby. It was one of the most useful things to him in the field.

> You need to persuade people to follow you and this ability bears a striking relationship to what an actor does on stage. The analogy can certainly be taken too far, as out-right "acting" in front of the soldiers you desire to lead will result in failure. However your ability as a leader to be at ease in front of a group of people who may have doubts about outcomes or events is vital. Drama – in both high school and university – most likely helped me in my role as an officer. When I have to brief my soldiers on difficult news or issue orders, it is to some extent, a performance. I have to convey the right/appropriate emotions and sometimes hold mine in check – all things that drama helps us do.[14]

Over a period of weeks I do workshops with the military students to explore material for their play. They have decided to use *Romeo and Juliet* and examine the challenges of having a relationship at the college, or in the military more broadly. The students are playful and emotional, and we use melodrama to allow for ranges of feeling: despair, anger, hopelessness, passion. In the context of an "over-the-top" game, the students act out their fears and frustrations, laugh, and then say how real it all is. Men and women acknowledge the value and the pleasure of listening to each other and anticipating a performance where they can be heard by a wider audience. They are very aware of what they mustn't say, and some of the improvisations are "for rehearsal only." But inside the workshop, at least, it looks to me as if they are being heard.

"Men's bodies may be appropriated as well as women's," writes Arthur Frank.[15] I think about this as Pierre, a tall first-year cadet, enters the circle to make an image showing why he entered the military. He stands awkwardly, looking at the 28 people around him, his new family. Two months ago he was bringing in hay on his farm in rural Quebec; now he has just completed the gruelling initiation week of around-the-clock endurance that is the RMCC entrance ritual. It is modelled on the orientation at the US Military Academy at West Point, New York.

Pierre snaps to attention, salutes, and offers his hand, as if he was helping someone across the street. "I want to help," he says. "I want the world to be better. I want girls to go to school." It strikes me, not for the first time, that many of these students have the same aims as the more socially conscious of my Queen's students. They all want to save the world, they just see different ways to do it.

Next Andrew comes into the circle, a man in his thirties built like a boxer with a rash of freckles across his broad cheeks. Andrew has been in Afghanistan and is back at school to upgrade his education and become an officer. I ask if he remembers his first trip home after his tour of duty. He grins and raises an invisible glass. "Cheers! So, did you kill anybody?" The class laughs, and Carl speaks up. He's a first-year. "My girlfriend just wrote me and asked the same thing. Are you learning to kill people?" They laugh some more.

This 50-minute English class has been moved from their usual class-room to a lovely old wooden gymnasium. Above us are rows of plaques commemorating the students lost in past wars. The teacher tells me later that in the early days the students came from the best Upper Canada fami-lies. "Now the demographic has changed entirely. Now they come from everywhere, but the elite don't send their sons the way they used to." The class finishes and the students collect their belongings, piled neatly on the tables by the wall. Several of them come to me, shake my hand, and thank me for the workshop. This is common behaviour here, and I like it. Something about these old-fashioned manners reminds me of my father.

I drive home across the causeway, passing a car with a yellow-ribboned bumper sticker that reads "I support our troops." *Do I?* I catch a glimpse of the driver's red curls and careful concentration, a toddler strapped to the back seat, a teenager furiously texting in the front. My preparation for working with the military suddenly seems ridiculously inadequate. What did I know about war when I was the age of these children?

My father, George Salverson, couldn't serve in World War II because he was deaf in one ear, but he wrote radio plays full of government-dictated propaganda. His script briefings were probably supervised if not authored by Ottawa Minister of Munitions C.D. Howe. When I was an adult he showed me a file containing blue sheets of paper in faded type with official Ottawa letterhead. One sheet contained a list of what must be included in each broadcast.

It was Dad who took my brother and me to all the World War II mov-ies. I was six when the Hollywood blockbuster *The Guns of Navarone* was released, so I must have seen a rerun. I remember holding tight to my father's big hand as Gregory Peck and Anthony Quinn hauled them-selves by rope up a steep cliff in the dark of night, risking certain death from a German gun or the raging ocean below. This was our favourite film. As we watched the dashing American and the exuberant Greek, my imagination was captured. Peck, Quinn, and Hollywood itself stood for everything heroic and glorious about the fight for justice.

Alistair MacLean's 1957 novel *The Guns of Navarone* was set on the Greek island of Leron. The plot was a fiction and Navarone didn't exist, but that hardly mattered. Dad never spoke of his real experience during that war – I doubt it would have occurred to him and I never asked. He was an old-school documentary writer; he believed that his opinion and his story were irrelevant. There were the facts, and then there was Hollywood. Both were necessary and both had their place. There was no reason to mix up good inspiring fun, which was hard to come by, with truth – impossible to escape.

> As children, my sister and I knew that there were certain things we couldn't do with Dad. We were not allowed to wake him up when he was sleeping, unless we called out from across the room, as he often woke startled and flailing, regaining composure moments later when he realized he was not in the desert but rather on his own living room couch. We could never ask questions about what Dad had done when he was overseas.[16]

Some of the RMCC students are here because their families are in the military. Many of them have parents who are consummate professionals in public. Only the family sees the other side. The Canadian military knows that mental health is a big problem. In 2010 a call for help went out across Canada and beyond, under the umbrella of the Canadian Institute for Military and Veteran Health Research Forum (MVHR). At the first of what has become a sold-out annual conference, I presented a paper about the potential for the creative arts in addressing military trauma.[17] A military nurse was in the audience. Susan Ray had collected and analysed testimonies from six soldiers, two chaplains, one medic, and one female nurse who had sought treatment for trauma resulting from deployments to Somalia, Rwanda, and the former Yugoslavia. She asked if I was interested in creating a play from these testimonies. I suggested doing something with my students. This resulted in my testimony and ethics drama class performing drama as research at the 2011 MVHR conference in Kingston.

The students arrived at the Ambassador Hotel by car. The halls and conference rooms were filled with uniforms. Dustin, the only young man in the group, came up to me immediately. "I'm really nervous," he said, clutching his Tim Hortons. "They might think we are being too critical." Dustin was worried that the testimonies in their performance were angry.

The soldiers interviewed had felt let down, let go. The class was being true to what had been recorded, but now it was real, and they were face-to-face with people who knew much more than them what this was about.

We were second on the program. First, two men from Vancouver spoke about a therapy drama program for men. The therapist, Marvin Westwood, described the UBC Veterans Transition Program. Westwood was inspired to start the program when a member of his own family and other veterans of World War II said how relieved they were when they could tell their stories. They wished they could have done it earlier. "So I just said, let's not wait," says Westwood. "Let's offer this when people come back."[18]

Tim Laidler, one of the participants in the program, explains what it meant for him to take the risk to come to a group, to work with drama. Laidler is quoted in an article in the *Ubyssey* saying that when he first came back from Afghanistan he kept to himself.[19] Then he came to the group. Laidler elaborates:

> When you get on the program, with these other vets, they tell their stories with their head, and then they express how they felt about it through their emotions. And that can mean through tears … And that's what screws me up, especially as a guy, seeing these guys who are hardcore, big dudes, and they can actually cry and be strong. It doesn't mean weak, that's what I found out. It actually means that they're stronger, that they can process that stuff and put it out there.[20]

Then Westwood screens a film that documented some of the process, *War in the Mind.* I glance at my students; some of them are in tears. When the film is over, there are questions and then it is their turn.

Script directions:[21]

> We begin as one being, representing a person. We don't necessarily need to look like a person but it needs to be seen through some sort of movement sequence that we function as one. We move strongly and confidently.

I can tell that they are nervous, but they are, yes, moving strongly and with confidence. Vulnerable, that's what I think: standing so young and speaking these difficult testimonies in a room full of uniforms.

CLICK for SLIDE CHANGE (SLIDE #1)

A slide comes up of a familiar drawing from *Alice in Wonderland.* It is the White Rabbit, crouching down and pointing at his stopwatch.

STUDENT 1: I shouldn't have been surprised when I got to the military. The message is shame. In the military context, it's the doctor that informs the military that the member is sick which starts your release process that spirals down, down that chute, down the rabbit hole.

The text appears on the slide:

In another moment, down went Alice after it, never once considering ... how in the world she was to get out again. Down ... down ... down ...

STUDENT 2: Like Alice in Wonderland, the military send them down the rabbit hole. You're sort of half way down when you realize, I'm all by myself. There is nobody here with me. And then you're flushed out and that's it.

The students continue, performing stories of soldiers returning home. They have worked on this for weeks, lots of late-night rehearsal, lots of nerves – "Will we get it right, do we have the right ... ?"

STUDENT 3: The very fact that you have a trauma isn't because you went to Wendy's on a Thursday night and you watched a car accident. It's all these things that were on my chest. People said, "Oh, he must be so lucky." I say, "You know what? No." There's a price you pay for this stuff. There's a cost. No, it's because you put on a uniform and were sent to some God forsaken country that you never knew even existed, and for what? For a nation that really doesn't give two God DAMNS anyway. That's okay, I suppose. I mean you didn't expect them to care really.

STUDENT 4: I have more anger around, well, the church and the Department of National Defense, because neither one would speak to me when I came back, at all.

Another slide, Alice looking very lost and confused in her black-and-white sketched party dress.

"I can't explain myself, I'm afraid, Sir," said Alice. "Because I'm not myself you see."

One of the young women in the group asked her grandfather if she could record him talking about his war experiences. She had never heard these stories from him before. She was profoundly moved and then asked if he minded if she played some of the recording at the end of the scene. He agreed. Their final rehearsal was late at night in our drama department's proscenium theatre. When I arrived, they were going through the ending, and they asked me to watch the whole thing. I saw how passionate they were; they wanted to get it right. They were much more nervous than the rest of the class, who are also performing testimonies but only for each other. They are brave, this group, and perhaps they didn't quite realize what they were getting themselves into. Now, at the Ambassador Hotel in Kingston, it is all too real.

The final slide: There were doors all around the hall. But they were all locked.

The scene ends with the students introducing themselves. They say why each of them has come, what they care about. There is a smattering of applause, and the moderator asks for questions. A tall, mature man in uniform stands. "These students mean well, but this is wrong! This happened after Bosnia. It doesn't happen anymore. It isn't fair to accuse the military of something that doesn't happen anymore." My students turn pale. Dustin glances at me as if to say, "See ... see! I knew we shouldn't do this!" A woman in an orange dress raises her hand. "Excuse me. I am a trauma counsellor. I disagree with this officer. I see these problems every day in my office in Ottawa. Nothing about this is old, and nothing about this is over."

For the next 15 minutes an animated discussion breaks out. As someone points out, unlike most conference sessions where the dialogue is back and forth between presenters and audience, this time it is all between session members. They seem to forget that we are here. Just before the session ends, a tall, distinguished man in full uniform, perhaps in his late sixties, stands up. The room grows quiet. "I was in charge of things in Afghanistan," says the general. "We have to take responsibility for what has happened to our men and women, we have to help. And we should thank these young people for showing this today. Reminding us. Thank you."

My students are shocked. They all send me emails about this general and what he said. When we meet several days later to debrief, they are still teary. "It is the first time I realized theatre could really change things, could matter," says one young woman. This is the gist of it: they made a difference.

As I write this essay, I send a note to Dustin, the only man in the group. I ask him to tell me a few words about what drama means to him and what the experience of doing this military project was like. He answers immediately, even though he is busy preparing to start his new job as an elementary school teacher.

Looking back over my entire undergrad – that one project had the most impact on me. I believe all art has meaning and a chance to trigger raw emotions that provoke discussion. This was scary to be a part of ... As I was not in the military, I had no idea what was occurring and how people were really feeling. . . Drama should be used to make a difference, get people talking, and this is exactly what the project accomplished.[22]

I think what was going on for my students in this encounter was the powerful experience of being seen. Yes, they had been able to express emotion, think laterally, engage their bodies – many things that we understand to be so valuable about the dramatic arts. But their nervousness as they prepared the pieces came because they were saying something. When they saw the uniforms in the room, the fact that not only does theatre speak but *they* were speaking hit them hard. They spoke, and the room changed. People got angry, excited, for a while they forgot the students and the theatre that had started the whole process. The students watched all this, amazed. This animated exchange had been set off by them and their drama! As Dustin wrote,

Standing in that room full of military personnel, management, scholars and public and to perform such a dramatic piece was truly inspirational – in the sense I became inspired by what people were saying ... As "hot button" as our performance was, the fact is it really got the discussion started ... Standing there listening to many different viewpoints was outstanding and I encourage current and future drama students to strive to make such art in their lives.

I wrote Dustin back and asked if he thought there was something particular to how drama was important to men or to him as a man. Here is his answer:

The only thing I honestly can think is that theatre/drama helps break down barriers and stereotypes. I know there is a stereotypical belief drama/theatre is often for females or gay males, maybe by having more men doing theatre/drama will help eradicate those beliefs? Drama was something I always enjoyed since I was a very young kid ... Over the years I began to develop a deeper understanding of drama and the potential to use the art form to make statements and call things into question. I think drama is an avenue to express yourself even when you might be at loss for words. I think some men (obviously not all, and I do not know any statistics) have difficulty with expressing their feelings, but yet they are able to "act" it out in theatre/drama, and therefore they can still express their thoughts and emotions through their work. I think artists look for connections between their life and their work – at least I try to – and that is how drama is helpful to men.[23]

It is worth taking a moment to notice what was happening to the audience in that hotel conference room in 2011. They were agitated and engaged and they cared. I said at the outset of this essay that I envied my European colleagues because of the vibrancy of their cultural community. As I am completing this contribution to *In Defence of Theatre*, a phone call makes me think more deeply about the audience's part in this question.

Vancouver theatre director Steven Hill is spending a few months in Berlin. He calls to tell me that he has recovered his love of theatre "because of the audiences. People are jammed in here, theatre isn't decoration or mere entertainment." Someone in Berlin told Steve that, in Germany, theatre was born out of politics. He asks me, "Could that ever be true for us in Canada? Could theatre be dangerous, have real political power?"

I sit at the back of my Queen's drama class watching the handful of young men presenting project ideas. They are a small percentage, but they are among the most committed. Does making theatre allow them to see the depth and possibility in their own lives, even if they wouldn't put it this way? Why else would young men in my classes flee other pursuits and exclaim their willingness to spend their twenties earning no income and little respect or understanding? How do the military students I work with find inspiration, confidence, and a sense of identity when they create a play? What kind of futures do these young men imagine, and how does their engagement with drama contribute to how they anticipate living their lives?

Actor/director Brenda Bazinet works with students at George Brown College, Equity Showcase, and the Citadel Young Company. She tells me it is often hard for young male actors to feel and show their emotions. She describes a very difficult modern tragedy she acted in recently. A major role was played by a man in his early thirties. "The actor was so emotional, he cried easily, all the time actually, in rehearsal he talked openly about his feelings. It was a shock, it made me realize that I had never seen a young man expose himself emotionally like that."[24] Usually she finds her students very protective of themselves, careful not to reveal their fears, their vulnerabilities. This young man was the exception. "He showed us his feelings openly. You never see that. Never."

I remember my failure to keep Jesse in my drama workshop so many years ago, and I wonder what options he really had in that classroom. What narratives were he and the other boys offered as options for their lives, as role models? In Rosemary Jolly's work on gendered masculinity and heroic narratives inside the anti-apartheid struggle in South Africa, Jolly discusses subjects who make demands that are not considered to be in the public interest.[25] She says we are not able to *hear* all stories, and I think this plays a part in the poverty of narratives offered to men, to boys like Jesse, and to the young men who find their ways into my drama classes. We need to "critique narratives as forms of listening that can *hear* or capture certain subjects" while ignoring or not recognizing others.[26] Jolly calls this a form of cultured violence, "deaf listening."[27]

At the end of the workshop at the military conference, Dustin was approached by a man who told him what the performance had meant. He remembers this two years later and writes me another email that he asks me to pass on to anyone who will listen:

> Lastly, what cemented the importance of this project to me was the man who approached us. He told us that his superiors were in the room and he felt that he could not come out and speak his mind. He wanted to thank us for our performance because we touched on things that he was personally feeling and how he can finally realize he is not alone and that he can now find some comfort in that! What he said meant the world to me, and I will never forget it. Theatre has the ability to elicit such gut reactions and as artists please strive to make such meaningful art, because it really can make a difference to someone in need.[28]

The answer to the question "Why theatre *now*?" may lie in the crippling emptiness of contemporary Western culture. Patricia Fraser, a Vancouver-based theatre and digital media artist and writer who has mentored community stories for many decades, writes about imaginative practices in which we can feel the revelatory presence of the world. Fraser evokes our reckless need for certainty, our drive to produce conceptual language to prove everything. In her PhD thesis, she draws on Hannah Arendt's warning that since Galileo's telescope we can no longer trust what we see: "[This] measuring gaze [leaves us] with a universe of whose qualities we know no more than the way they affect our measuring instruments."[29]

We are in danger in our universities, with their increased obsession with outcomes and grids of evaluation, of imposing narratives of comprehension on all experience and learning. We have to beware of domesticating our students' experience or asking them to tell stories as "evidence of progress."[30] Fraser speaks of "missing the dark"[31] and situates how she narrates her drama work with seniors in Vancouver within the context of the deaths of her parents because death cannot be domesticated.

My students' performance piece on military trauma was called "Fracture." It was difficult for the students and the audience; it stirred things up, was unfinished, probing, visceral, and angry. This kind of dramatic enactment illuminates disturbing corners of our lives but it does more than this – it helps us feel.

> We're all human beings struggling with the same emotional dilemmas: loneliness, isolation. I think isolation is an unspoken tragedy of what it means to be alive in modern society right now. Our yearning to connect, and the loss of that.[32]

In my acting class at Queen's we study clown and melodrama. The students are thrown into a bewildering chaos: they improvise not through building characters, but by revealing themselves. The students are pushed relentlessly to follow their impulses, to respond to the behaviour of fellow players, and, above all, to be vulnerable. This is particularly challenging to the men, many of whom are used to achieving success by playing clearly identifiable roles. One man writes about a release he has after a physical exercise that is "emotionally and psychologically demanding. I was truly pushing myself to my limit giving it everything I had, keeping such an intense focus on the tasks at hand and *not allowing myself to be weak*" (emphasis added). He was overcome by emotion, pushed back tears, and then had to leave the class to sit outside. "I ran through those doors and I wept. I wept, but I felt SO alive. I felt as if my emotions overpowered me, but in this moment of being so vulnerable, scared and uncomfortable, I also realized that this was a good thing, I was alive and breathing."

Theatre is vital in a profoundly damaged world in danger of disappearing itself. Perhaps the men – the soldiers willing to open themselves to a drama workshop, the students nervous but brave in their vulnerability – are our canaries in the coal mine. My husband waited for a film that would reveal men's emotional and psychological complexity. The military audience who watched my students' presentation saw theatre that stirred and challenged them viscerally, politically, and immediately. Participating in drama and theatre in any role – writer, designer, community animator, technician, producer, actor, audience member – allows fuller and richer narratives and can defy confining roles or the safety of domestication. "What a gift," says actor Ellen Page, "that my job is about getting to feel."[33]

NOTES

1 Catherine Malabou, *The New Wounded* (New York: Fordham University Press, 2012), 168.

2 Ibid., 161.

3 Francoise Davoine and Jean-Max Gaudilliere, *History Beyond Trauma: Whereof One Cannot Speak, Thereof One Cannot Stay Silent*, trans. Susan Fairfield (New York: Other Press, 2004), 65; quoted in Malabou, *New Wounded*, 161.

4 Andrew Tolson, *The Limits of Masculinity* (London: Tavistock, 1977).

5 Yvonne Jewkes, *Captive Audience: Media, Masculinity, and Power in Prisons* (Devon, UK: Willan Publishing, 2002), 48.

6 Erving Goffman, *Asylums: Essays on the Social Situation of Mental Patients and Other Inmates* (London: Penguin Books, 1961).

7 Tolson, quoted in Jewkes, *Captive Audience*, 52.

8 Ciara Murphy, "Playing Soldier? Combining Theatre and Theory to Explore the Experiences of Women in the Military" (master's thesis, Queen's University, 2011).

9 Karen D. Davis and Brian McKee, "Women in the Military: Facing the Warrior Framework," in *Challenge and Change in the Military: Gender and Diversity Issues*, ed. Franklin C. Pinch, Allister T. MacIntyre, Phyllis Browne, and Alan C. Ikros (Kingston, ON: Canadian Defence Academic Press, 2004), 52–75; quoted in Murphy, "Playing Soldier?," 32–3.

10 Katrina Onstad, "Love to Hate Angelina Jolie," *Globe and Mail*, 16 May 2013, http://www.theglobeandmail.com/life/celebrity-news/love-to-hate-angelina-jolie-maybe-not-after-her-mastectomy-disclosure/article11968519/.

11 Sheryl Sandberg, quoted in Onstad, "Love to Hate Angelina Jolie," L3.

12 Onstad, "Love to Hate Angelina Jolie," L3.

13 Jewkes, *Captive Audience*, 48.

14 Major Hans Christian Breede, email to author, 28 October 2013.

15 Arthur Frank, quoted in Tarja Väyrynen, "Keeping the Trauma of War Open in the Male Body: Resisting the Hegemonic Forms of Masculinity and National Identity in Visual Arts," *Journal of Gender Studies* 22, no. 2 (2013): 137–51.

16 Joan Dixon and Barb Howard, *Embedded on the Home Front: Where Military and Civilian Lives Converge* (Victoria, BC: Heritage House Publishing, 2012), 36.

17 Julie Salverson, "Social Suffering in the Military and Possible Uses for the Creative Arts" (paper presented at the Military Veterans Health Research Conference, Kingston, ON, 14–16 November 2011).

18 Westwood, quoted in Arshy Mann, "War in the Mind Puts Focus on the UBC Veterans Transition Program," *Ubyssey*, 16 November 2011, http://old .ubyssey.ca/culture/film-follows-veterans-in-ubc-transition-program6230/.

19 The *Ubyssey* is the official student newspaper for the University of British Columbia.

20 Laidler quoted in Mann, "War in the Mind Puts Focus on the UBC Veterans Transition Program."

21 Sue Del-Mei, Dustin Garrett, Kylie Gilmour, Smita Misra, and Lauren Weinberg, "Fracture" (unpublished manuscript, 2011).

22 Dustin Garrett, email message to author, 1 November 2013.

23 Ibid.

24 Brenda Bazinet, personal communication, 20 October 2013.

25 Rosemary Jolly, *Cultured Violence: Narrative, Social Suffering, and Engendering Human Rights In Contemporary South Africa* (Liverpool: Liverpool University Press, 2010).

26 Ibid., 5.

27 Ibid., 3.

28 Dustin Garrett, email message to author, 6 November 2013.

29 Hannah Arendt, *The Human Condition* (Chicago: University of Chicago Press, 1958), 261; quoted in Patricia A. Fraser, "Postcards to the Beloved: An Inquiry into Our Shared Worldliness through the Practice of a Story Mentor" (PhD thesis, University of British Columbia, 2012), 18.

30 Fraser, "Postcards to the Beloved," 8.

31 Ibid., 14.

32 Ellen Page, quoted in Johanna Schneller, "The Gift of Feeling," *Globe and Mail*, 5 October 2013, R3.

33 Ibid.

PART IV

Breaking Down Barriers

11 It's Time to Profess Performance: Thinking Beyond the Specialness and Discreteness of Theatre

LAURA LEVIN

[It] is depressing indeed that here in Canada there has been a singular failure to respond to one of the most vibrant and relevant intellectual pathways of our time.

Susan Bennett[1]

I'm starting to wonder if Rob Ford is secretly the greatest performance artist in the history of Toronto. I can dream, can't I?

East Yorker[2]

The question "Why theatre now?" immediately calls to mind anxieties that have been swirling around the future of theatre studies as an academic discipline. These anxieties stem, in part, from the glut of theatre PhDs currently floundering on a bleak job market, an oversupply that has prompted cynics like Jody Olson (pseudonym) to opine that universities should "act to close Ph.D. programs in theater."[3] They also flow from budget crises rippling through North America, which have led to the unfortunate closing of theatre and other arts departments. This threat was realized in Canada in 2013 when the theatre program at Mount Royal University was suspended as a cost-saving measure in the face of a 7.3 per cent reduction to the school's provincial funding.[4] Meanwhile, other Canadian theatre programs have become vulnerable as more and more universities decide that the tenure-track positions of their retirees will not be replaced. Theatre departments thus find themselves embroiled in the wider "crisis" within the theatre community at large that the editors of this book cite in their introduction, in the context of which questions of value have tended to come to the fore.

Olson believes we should accept that the academic study of theatre is now passé. If theatre departments are to survive, he says, it will be as mere factories for training actors, directors, and designers in professional theatre craft.[5] Instead of caving to this pessimistic view, I want to take up Richard Schechner's recent and provocative claim that, if theatre departments find themselves in crisis, if they seem too outdated to higher-ups at our universities, it is in part because they have not gone far enough in addressing the challenges posed to theatre by "an increasingly performative culture" – a culture in which theatre is found not just on the stage but also, now almost insistently, in the spaces of everyday life.[6]

As an inter- or post-discipline, performance studies has, since its inception in the 1980s, offered a powerful set of tools for parsing this more expansive understanding of theatre. It asks us to view theatre on a continuum with a broad range of cultural behaviours, from ritual to popular entertainment to public demonstrations to the enactment of identity in interpersonal encounters. "Professing performance," to borrow Shannon Jackson's useful phrase, requires that we acknowledge the complexity and site-specificity of "performance" as it traverses a number of disciplines. As she points out, performance means embodiment to a kinesiology professor, postmodern experiment to an art historian, and a speech act to a linguist.[7]

Schechner's reference to an "increasingly performative culture" implies that performance studies has become even more relevant in the twenty-first century, as individuals are routinely, almost inexorably, summoned by digital culture to participate in collective rites of public display.[8] Yet, especially in the Canadian context, the introduction of "performance" as a theoretical lens has not, I believe, significantly radicalized what we now think of as theatre. As Susan Bennett convincingly argued in her assessment of the field, performance studies in Canada exists, "insofar as it exists at all, as an add-on or stream within existing departmentalized disciplinary fields, most typically theatre or communications, or as a non-departmentalized collaborative program."[9] This add-on approach can simply use an ampersand to bolt a foggy notion of "performance" to an existing theatre program.

While three performance studies graduate programs have been formed at Canadian institutions since Bennett offered this insight – at University of Alberta, University of Toronto, and York University (where I teach) – it remains to be seen whether they will be able to overcome the ampersand problem that plagues the development of the field.[10] Schechner notes that many theatre departments in North America transform themselves into "Theatre & Performance Studies" programs, or some variation of this compound, in order to capitalize on the performance studies brand that seems to stand in for the "new," thus serving as a recruitment tool for students looking to align themselves with the latest academic trend.[11] While a change in a theatre department's identity might be signalled through the "and" or ampersand, and perhaps through an added course or two on a performance studies topic, it is not necessarily accompanied by a more fundamental shift in the way that theatre is taught or thought about in both graduate and undergraduate contexts. Accordingly, a similar problem arises when the addition of the term "performance studies" – even without an "and" – at the graduate level is not mirrored in either the title or curriculum of the associated undergraduate program.

In practice, this "halfhearted gesture of reform" covers up persistent beliefs in the sacrosanct nature of theatre as an endangered art form.[12] In this formulation, theatre is primarily defined as that which takes place on a stage, with a text, and before a static audience. The apparently self-evident conclusion is that this magical configuration needs to be protected at all costs. These beliefs are regularly announced in curriculum meetings, as educators wax poetic about the specialness and discreteness of theatre, invoking an elitism and exceptionalism that is incompatible with the *ubiquity* of the activities over which they claim to have dominion. Such pronouncements, often trotted out to argue against restructuring core theatre courses to incorporate performance studies developments, are out of touch with major changes taking place within the fine arts and the critical humanities more broadly.

What would it mean to take seriously the challenges posed by the term "performance" to the idea of "theatre"? How can we expand our conception of what might be taught as theatre in our courses, or what could be viewed as theatre within our cities and communities? How might this thinking put theatre more in touch with the many publics that it hopes to reflect and serve? Asking these questions will help us properly prepare students to face head-on the shifts that are being brought about by today's performative culture – shifts in consciousness, artistic practice, and modes of relation that are growing more complex each day.

Now, more than ever, it is time to profess performance. It is also time for performance studies scholars to get better at articulating *why* performance is important. In what follows, I outline some of the more compelling reasons for kicking the ampersand habit and giving performance studies the respect that it is due.

Today's Theatre Exposes the Ubiquity of Performance

The claim that theatre is an art unlike any other has much to do with its own self-image as a scrappy underdog struggling for recognition within the field of humanities. Janelle Reinelt and Joseph Roach explain: "the history of the discipline of theater studies is one of fighting for autonomy from English and Speech departments, insisting on a kind of separation from other areas of study. It was necessary, politically necessary, to claim this distinctiveness, even at the expense of becoming somewhat insular and hermetic – a result that unfortunately became true of many departments of theater."[13] This feeling of insularity, in some ways, echoes the architectural form that has come to be associated with many of our departments: the windowless black box theatre, the beloved site where theatre students sequester themselves for hours to prepare for a show. Jill Dolan observes that this sense of isolation is also fostered by the frequent segregation of theatre buildings from the rest of campus. From a planning perspective, it is expedient to place university theatres in remote locations to allow for "ample parking and room to build shops, fly lofts, and large auditoriums."[14]

In Canada, theatre studies' battle for disciplinary autonomy was fought with a special kind of vigour. The struggle to articulate theatre studies as its own distinct discipline went hand in hand with an urgent decolonizing mission, with efforts to proclaim a tradition of national theatre that was separate from that of the United States and Europe. For this reason, performance studies, often associated with the study of "non-theatrical" or "extra-theatrical events," has been met doubly with suspicion. It has been viewed as a threat not only to an artistically hermetic theatre studies curriculum, but also to the hard-won and hyper-nationalist field of "Canadian theatre."

But what if we were to think of performance theory not as something that leads the exodus from Canadian theatre but rather as something that leads back to it? Professing performance can give theatre back to itself, reminding theatre what it is today and what, in fact, it always has been.[15] In its expansive, interdisciplinary reach, performance helps us to see that what we are experiencing is not so much a crisis in theatre as a crisis in what people categorize *as* theatre. As Marvin Carlson notes, performance theory shifts attention from theatre as "a static work of art" to "considering it as a spatial, embodied event, thus opening the way to developing an aesthetics of the performative."[16] Focusing on the spatiality and "eventness" of theatre requires attending not only to the material conditions that surround any theatrical staging but also to the form of today's theatre productions. Many of these productions are self-consciously designed as environmental actions and interactions, spilling out of the black boxes where theatre has traditionally lived. If our architectural doppelgangers have multiplied, should not our understandings of theatre multiply as well?

Luckily, the theatre scene in many Canadian cities already illustrates the ubiquity of performance. One need look no further than Theatre Passe Muraille (TPM), long considered among the richest veins of home-grown Canadian theatre. Its entire fall 2012 season focused on staging shows that literalized the meaning of its French name – "Theatre Beyond Walls." Each show challenged the sense of enclosure implied in the hermetically sealed theatre building by opening itself up to vibrant interactions with the surrounding neighbourhood, or what performance studies likes to call "the spaces of everyday life." Examples of this site-specific approach included the Queen West Project, a play about homelessness and mental health in which audience members were paired with dancers who took them on a movement-led tour of Queen Street; the Four Corners, an audio tour of the intersection of Queen and Bathurst, featuring the voices of community residents and the sounds of the urban landscape; and TPM Everywhere, a series of pop-up theatre pieces in which stilt-walkers, clowns, and other characters snuck up on unsuspecting audiences and engaged them in public spaces.

TPM's Theatre Beyond Walls season is not a one-off or gimmick. Nor is it (only) an example of "weird-ass-shit," a phrase that circulated in Toronto recently following Soulpepper artistic director Albert Schultz's use of it to describe the new theatrical forms that are populating major theatres like Canadian Stage, under the leadership of Matthew Jocelyn, and Harbourfront World Stage, under the direction of Tina Rasmussen.[17] In fact, reactionaries like Schultz, and critics who support them, have been blasted repeatedly in the press for these very dismissals. (To quote Martin Morrow's valiant defence of the companies' avant-garde experiments, "what you call weird-ass shit today could be a classic tomorrow.")[18] TPM's recent work, like that of Canadian Stage and Harbourfront World Stage, exemplifies the kinds of gutsy performative interventions that are becoming the celebrated norm in theatres across the country and shifting our perception of what counts as theatre today.

Consider this description of Vancouver-based Neworld Theatre's show LANDLINE, a trans-provincial collaboration with Secret Theatre in Halifax (a production discussed in more detail by its co-creator Dustin Harvey in chapter 2):

LANDLINE is a shared experience for two people on opposite sides of the country. The piece uses city streets, cell phone technology and poetic suggestion to engage audience members in a game of unlikely rendezvous.

You are guided via text message to a well-chosen location for a possible meeting. You arrive and consult a journal that contains a set of directions urging you to conjure a city thousands of miles away. You imagine a person next to you. You receive a series of text messages from a person on the other side of the country guiding you on a walk through your own city – and you are doing the same for them. Finally you guide each other into a café where you each find a table set for two, 5000 km wide. You finally meet via video screen. What happens next is between you and the stranger who has been walking with you the entire time.[19]

LANDLINE, like TPM's fall 2012 season, epitomizes the growing influence of the performative turn in theatre in at least two ways. First, it casts spectators as performers and gives them a sense of agency in steering the direction of the show. This approach follows Erika Fischer-Lichte's insights about the nature of the performative turn. "Today, performance is no longer seen as the mysterious locus for an inexplicable encounter between actors and spectators," she writes.[20] Further, "the performativity proposed by the performance [is] not to be realized through conventionalized [spectatorial] actions such as clapping, jeering, and commenting."[21] Instead, it can be found in "a genuine structural redefinition" of the relationship between performer and spectator and "an open-ended result."[22] The poetic description of *LANDLINE*, in other words, could be said to define a more broadly applicable characteristic of leading-edge theatre production today, its activation of an engaged public sphere: "What happens next is between you and a stranger who has been walking with you the entire time."

Second, shows like *LANDLINE* undermine the borders that have been erected between the arts, challenging perceptions of their distinctiveness. Here, as in TPM's 2012 shows – and a large number of others presented by leading theatre companies, venues, and festivals across the country (from Vancouver's PuSh Festival, to Calgary's High Performance Rodeo, to Toronto's Videofag, to Montreal's Festival de théâtre des Amériques) – a theatre piece could easily double as relational art, as urban tour, or as the latest experiment in digital media. "Be it art, music, literature, or theatre," Fischer-Lichte proclaims, "the creative process tends to be realized in and as performance."[23] Put differently, intermedial events like *LANDLINE* are concerned less with appearing as sacred works of "art," or as part of discrete disciplinary traditions, than with creating invigorating performative experiences.

Earlier I claimed that, rather than offering theatre a set of radical "new" ideas, performance studies gives theatre back to itself. As Jill Dolan maintains, while metaphors of the performative found in performance studies bring theatre studies' privileging of humanist aesthetics into high relief, we would do well to remember that many of these metaphors were borrowed from theatre studies in the first place.[24] So too, saying that theatre is a spatial, embodied event, one that exceeds the confines of a theatre building, should ring true for any specialist in Canadian theatre who has studied the early collective creations of companies like TPM, which were often developed and presented in extra-theatrical venues (e.g., *The Farm Show*). Furthermore, the association of performativity with interdisciplinarity in fact relies on the essentially interdisciplinary nature of theatre. As any theatre-maker knows, even the most conventional stage production depends upon and enjoys a porous relationship with the other arts (visual arts for scenic design, music for sound design, dance for stage movement, and so on). In its reliance upon on multiple artistic spheres, theatre models Jackson's evocative definition of performance as "an art of 'interpublic coordination.'"[25] Too often, however, theatre's boundary issues, what Jackson calls theatre's inherent "hyper-contextuality," are disavowed by those bent on defending its autonomy and disciplinary specialization.[26]

Remembering theatre's omnivorous nature and penchant for interdisciplinary entanglements can make it indispensable in financially challenged universities looking for ways to share resources. Theatre provides a model for integrating various arts rather than choosing which discrete or stand-alone disciplines to dispense with. Thus departments of theatre, visual arts, film, and architecture could share a course on stage design, each disciplinary perspective enhancing the other. More importantly, and as it happens, relatedly, performance studies reveals theatre as an art with the flexibility to traverse multiple cultural spaces and meaningfully connect with communities beyond the confines of a black box. Performance gives theatre back to its publics.

Today's Performance Exposes the Ubiquity of Theatre

Teaching theatre as a narrow, exceptional art is a missed opportunity. If we want to make theatre more relevant to our students and stave off administrative types always looking for budgets to slash, why not embrace the importance of performance in every facet of our culture? Theatre used to describe an activity that you took time out of your everyday life to do. Now we are performing constantly for so many different audiences, and in so many different media, that it barely registers as a separate activity.

Performance studies, a field attuned to the enactment of self in the spaces of everyday life, exposes the ubiquity of theatrical paradigms in our digital age. To claim that theatre is ubiquitous, in this respect, is to go beyond performance studies' familiar argument that identity is a construct produced linguistically through speech acts and physically through gesture, movement, and vestimentary codes. This claim also goes beyond the facile proposition that there is a straightforward mimetic relationship between performances of self in virtual and non-virtual spaces. Andrew Moore, for example, argues that Facebook has "merely encourage[d] users to do online what they have been doing offline all of their lives." In effect, he believes that Facebook allows a relatively unchanged "public sphere" to "migrate onto the Internet."[27]

To say that North American culture has become *increasingly* performative is to make a different sort of argument. It is to suggest that digital technologies have fundamentally changed the ways in which we project our identities on a daily basis. They have not only opened channels through which our previously private experiences are capable of being shared; we are now also incessantly *encouraged* to do so.

We announce the big stuff like births and deaths on social media platforms like blogs, Facebook, Twitter, and Instagram. But we also divulge slight changes in mood, how we slept the night before, where we are vacationing, when we are smiling, and what colour socks we are wearing. We take sepia-toned pictures of our brunch so that other people will savour it even before it is eaten. We constantly update, exaggerate, and manicure our online personae in the hopes that our real selves will live up to the image of these digital ghosts.

Our obsession with self-disclosure affects how we view all aspects of public life. It influences the demands that we make of public figures, who must constantly feed our appetites for autobiographical minutia. Hence the Twitterization of celebrity, which allows for that holy grail of audience participation: instant access to what Sinéad O'Connor thinks about Miley Cyrus's career choices. And that Kanye West is in the market for a marble conference table. And how much (or how little) Anthony Weiner understands about the private messaging function of Twitter. Hence also the recent parade of Canadian politicians announcing, to a generally bemused public, whether or not they have smoked marijuana.[28]

And who else could countenance a figure such as former Toronto mayor Rob Ford other than a populace that has been inoculated to the shock of constant oversharing? The spectacle of Ford's mayorship is proof positive of what we might call the performative turn in politics.

We evaluate our elected officials first on how well or how poorly they manage their own public images and only thereafter on how good they are at the business of governing. The 2013 scandal surrounding allegations that a cell phone video captured Ford smoking crack cocaine with drug dealers brought this process, what performance theorist Erving Goffman calls "impression management,"[29] into sharp focus, as Canadians watched Ford staggering defensively back and forth over the public/private divide.[30] In doing so, Ford has rendered visible the very selective self-disclosures in which we all engage. He would tell Torontonians about the inanity of his weekend on the radio show he curated with his brother, but he would not answer straightforward questions from the press about whether he smokes crack. He would throw a backyard barbeque for hundreds of constituents but throw a fit when reporters got near his lawn.[31] And of course the buffoonery that defined the former mayor's daily acts was guiltily welcomed in the Twitter feeds of Ford junkies (like myself). In fact, many people I know joined Twitter just to keep up with the Ford show.

In practice, these new forms of self-exposure may be more like theatre as an art form than many theatre studies purists would want to admit. Stuart Boon and Christine Sinclair make a similar observation in their analysis of Facebook: "Our life on the screen … embodies, to one extent or another, a life on the stage, albeit a digital one. The selves we re/create on Facebook are inevitably part us – recreating ourselves in digital form – and, again to one extent or another, part who we'd like to be – the creation of something new, perhaps better, but ultimately 'other.'"[32] Anyone who creates a Facebook or Twitter account will have experienced this uncanny distancing of self from itself. In many ways, it is like assembling your identity as an artificial puppet, and doing so in such a way as to insist on its provisional realness.

When I set up my own Facebook profile, I experienced something similar to stage fright as I contemplated how my own performance of self would be received by friends and colleagues. What photo should I choose to "play" me online? What likes and dislikes should I disclose? Should I show "funny Laura," "professional Laura," "parental Laura"? And what are the consequences of each of these choices? The selection of a Twitter handle and bio can be even trickier. How does one project an image of self in a few cheeky words? Some examples from a quick trawl of Twitter users' profiles: "Author, Speaker and kind of a big deal on a fairly irrelevant soc media site which inflates my self-importance"; "Im just another teen who cant live without wifi"; "An artist, performer, and ninja ballerina. Cultural chameleon."; "Unoriginal and overdramatic"; "The real me. My work, my life, my thoughts."[33]

Here the distinctions between theatre and the broader category of performance break down in complex ways and provide an excellent opportunity for educators to discuss the relationship between the two concepts. To use Judith Butler's distinctions between the two terms,[34] theatre often suggests a self-conscious act in a delimited space; it is framed by a set of artistic conventions that, in some way, acknowledge its artifice.[35] Meanwhile, performance enjoys no such distance from "the real." It describes instead those quotidian acts by which the illusion of identity is repeatedly, mostly unconsciously, naturalized.

How else can one describe the many thousands of theatrical stagings of self that are rehearsed, filmed, and uploaded for public view on video-sharing websites like Vimeo or YouTube? These self-stagings take a wide range of forms, from the comic (a woman quitting her job through an interpretive dance), to the virtuosic (contortionists flexing their bodies), to the grotesque (staging a fake suicide on Chatroulette). Indeed the preponderance of these sometimes outlandish self-stagings have led critics to ask whether YouTube has "killed" performance art, or made performance art utterly irrelevant as a distinct artistic genre.[36] While these videos are clearly evidence of self-conscious staging – the very act of uploading one's own video verifies this deliberateness – they also illustrate how the performers are enacting models of identity that precede them and to which they may be oblivious. (The countless videos of booty-shaking women replay past performances of classed and racialized femininity that were likely far from their originators' minds.) In Butler's words, these performances uncover "the social agent as an *object* rather than the subject of constitutive acts."[37]

A comparison of YouTube videos to theatre is perhaps easily made, as many YouTubers incorporate music, dance, and other entertaining genres into their artistic creations. But how about the billions of staged exchanges that take place on Facebook? Here information about the self and its investments is carefully selected and placed on the spatially delimited stage of the "News Feed" in the form of photos, links, status updates, and other kinds of public declarations. These declarations often exceed the parameters of self-performances we would deliver offline and take exceptionally creative, even histrionic, forms. Imagine randomly saying to someone at the office, "Freedom *is* on the other side of truth-telling"; or "Sigh, ugh, gasp, breath"; or "got home soaking+power outage+one hour of fire alarm+no phone reception = chips and beer for dinner."[38] Here too, strategies at "impression management"[39] may backfire – as when the repeated posts of drunken party photos online undermine one's image as a diligent, hardworking student offline. Even where these discordant identities are not accidental, they are fascinating in their capacity to denaturalize the performance of identity, exposing the process for study.

If digital technologies have dramatically increased the frequency with which we offer our lives up for public display, and have forever altered the forms that those displays can take, they have also exploded what we have hitherto conceived of as an audience. It has taken the number of spectators that we once thought were available for a performance and multiplied them exponentially, to the point where the condition of watching and being watched no longer seems remarkable. This is David Brin's "transparent society" embodied on a micro scale, a society in which we willingly give up a sense of privacy and submit ourselves to mass surveillance.[40] Our actions are not simply a capitulation to the powers that be; they are a bargain made in exchange for the opportunity to peer into the lives of others (and, thinking of Rob Ford, into the lives of those "performance artists" who govern us). Now, this surveillance is carried out not only by the state but also, and more rigorously, by our friends, family members, and anonymous citizens of digital communities. In fact, understood properly, our digital existence is characterized not by surveillance but rather by the *spectatorship* that we court in our endless run of self-directed one-handers.

Performance theory presses theatre to seize the rich opportunities offered by this sudden ubiquity of spectators. It highlights how networked spectators can perform in tandem with one another to produce socially and politically enabling collective dramaturgies. E.J. Westlake contends that, far from simply facilitating a crass form of individualist exhibitionism, Facebook users often work together "as a team … in order to affirm each other's performances and to define the local Facebook community."[41] Westlake's insight follows from Goffman's definition of "a teammate" as "someone whose dramaturgical co-operation one is dependent upon" in order to performatively create certain perceptions of reality.[42]

This "dramaturgical co-operation" operates on a mundane level every time members of the Facebook community comment supportively on their friends' posts, thereby enabling them to shore up a particular image of self. It also, perhaps more interestingly for theatre-makers, operates when communities of spectators form networks around certain issues. Take for example the Facebook group formed to agitate for the

release of filmmaker and professor John Greyson and physician Tarek
Loubani, two Canadians held without charges in an Egyptian prison for
seven weeks from August to October 2013. The group members worked
together through posts and comments to keep each other informed
about recent developments, share activist strategies, and provide one another support. Following the pair's release, one member remarked on
how the Facebook group had transformed what was formerly a set of isolated strangers gawking at a faraway scene into an activist counterpublic:

> I feel as though we have formed a community since August 16 – Tarek's
> family and friends, John's family and friends, and thousands who know nei-
> ther man personally yet gave of themselves to work for their release. As
> truly horrific as the circumstances were that united us, we DID become a
> community. I, for one, am unwilling to give that part of this journey up. I'm
> not sure where we go from here, beyond the hugs and tears and laughter,
> but somehow I want to keep this going. There are still hundreds of inno-
> cent people in Tora prison; there are 191 detainees in Lindsay, Ontario.
> Thoughts, anyone?[43]

Theatre-makers have already begun to experiment with the participatory
and activist potential of digital media in similar ways in their live performances. In *Section 98*, Toronto's Praxis Theatre invited spectators to participate in their discussion of civil rights through live texting in the theatre.

Acknowledging the presence of multitudes in today's digital environments can also extend theatre's traditional reach. This point was hit home
by the powerful response to Suburban Beast's recent show, *rihannaboi98*
by Toronto playwright Jordan Tannahill, a live-streamed confessional You-
Tube play about a teen from the suburbs experiencing bullying at school.
Tannahill reflects on the democratizing effects of using this digital stage:
"A number of viewers, mostly adolescents living well outside the downtown
core (and beyond easy access to its theatres) wrote to the company about
how much they responded to the work and how it was, in some cases, their
first exposure to theatre."[44] This expansive understanding of a play, one
attuned to an online public that is watching, and watching more often,
holds the key to finding new audiences and creating resonant sites of contact between geographically disparate subjects.

It's Time to Kick the Ampersand Habit

When Schechner says that theatre departments have "not met the challenges presented by an increasingly performative culture" and bristles

at the "AND" which now appends performance studies to department names, he is ultimately making a plea for performance to emerge as the ascendant term.[45] Theatre, he would say, can be sheltered under the umbrella of performance studies, as one of many iterations of the broader category of performance. In this respect, his recent argument echoes the one put forward in his famous 1992 keynote at the Association for Theatre in Higher Education conference, in which he proposed performance as a "new paradigm" for teaching theatre and condescendingly referred to theatre as a "beloved but extremely limited genre, a subdivision of performance."[46]

In addressing the value of a performance studies outlook in our present moment, it is not my intention to stir up the old, played-out divisions between theatre and performance, nor do I wish to argue that one should be subsumed within the rubric of the other. As Jackson makes clear, "institutional contexts differently constitute disciplinary identity."[47] Each academic institution is a complex morass of disciplinary histories, structures, and investments, and this constellation affects how, when, and where educators can profess performance. It may be more important for a department with a strong MFA in directing, and situated in a fine arts faculty, to foreground the term "theatre" in its program name than for a communications department that rarely stages plays as an essential part of its curriculum and calling card.

In the end, I am less interested in *what we call what it is that we do* than in what the "&" or "and" can easily prevent from *getting done*. All too often, it can keep intact unhelpful divisions within a department: between faculty with training in theatre studies and those with backgrounds in performance studies, between those teaching practice and those teaching theory, between those managing undergraduates and those running graduate programs. These divisions prevent us from understanding what theatre and performance might learn from one another and how they are always already entwined in any institutional location within which they arise.[48] They also get in the way of theatre educators taking seriously the new shifts in perspective that performance studies has started to bring about, especially when it is treated as either a cosmetic for departmental branding purposes or as something exterior to the department's curricular core.

Kicking the ampersand habit does not mean getting rid of the conjunction in a program's name. There are often many good institutional reasons why this phrasing exists. Rather, it means developing innovative and context-sensitive pedagogical strategies for fulfilling the promise of the "&." It means embracing the porousness of theatre to performance and performance to theatre. It means acknowledging how, in today's performative culture, each is not so "special" after all.

NOTES

1 Susan Bennett, "(No) Performance Studies in Canada," *Canadian Theatre Review* 149 (2012): 81.
2 East Yorker, "Rob Ford's Sojourn Causes a Stir Online [Comments Section]," *BlogTO*, 12 August 2013, http://www.blogto.com/city/2013/08 /rob_fords_danforth_sojourn_causes_a_stir_online/.
3 Jody Olson, "An Argument for Eliminating the Doctorate in Theater," *Chronicle of Higher Education*, 16 January 2013, para. 14, http://chronicle .com/article/Eliminating-the-Doctorate-in/136673.
4 Jeremy Nolais, "'Difficult Decision' Made – Mount Royal University Suspends Programs, Cuts Staff Positions," *Metro News*, 27 May 2013, http://www .metronews.ca/news/calgary/686582/cuts-to-mru-arts-music-approved -by-board-of-governors/.
5 Olson, "An Argument."
6 Richard Schechner, "No More Theatre PhDs?" *TDR: The Drama Review* 57, no. 3 (2013): 7.
7 Shannon Jackson, *Professing Performance: Theatre in the Academy from Philology to Performativity* (Cambridge: Cambridge University Press, 2004), 13–14.
8 Schechner, "No More Theatre PhDs?"
9 Bennett, "(No) Performance Studies in Canada," 80.
10 Unlike University of Toronto and York University, which have "ands" in the titles of their programs (U of T's Graduate Centre for the Study of Drama, Theatre and Performance Studies; York's graduate program in Theatre & Performance Studies), University of Alberta offers a PhD in Performance Studies. While this difference is significant, and speaks to the particularities of disciplinary arrangements within Alberta's institutional context, one could also read an implicit "&" here as well since the PhD in Performance Studies is housed in a "Department of Drama" and it operates alongside an MA program in Drama. (It should also be noted that the first PhD in Performance Studies in Canada was created by University of Calgary in 2006. In addition, performance studies designations can also be found in different forms at other Canadian universities – for example, Simon Fraser University offers a BA in Art, Performance, and Cinema Studies and a Certificate in Performance Studies; and Concordia University's School of Graduate Studies includes performance studies as a cross-disciplinary research current.)

11 Schechner, "No More Theatre PhDs?"

12 Ibid., 8.

13 Janelle G. Reinelt and Joseph R. Roach, "General Introduction," in *Critical Theory and Performance*, eds. Janelle G. Reinelt and Joseph R. Roach (Ann Arbor: University of Michigan Press, 1992), 5.

14 Dolan bases this observation on remarks made by Joseph Roach at the Reconstructing Theatre/History Symposium in Austin (in April 1998). See Jill Dolan, *Geographies of Learning: Theory and Practice, Activism and Performance* (Middleton, CT: Wesleyan University Press, 2001), 69. Also see p. 62.

15 Here I am riffing on Reinelt and Roach's earlier argument about the relationship between critical theory (postmodernism, phenomenology, semiotics, revisions of Marx, etc.) and theatre: "theory gives theater back again to the body politic" (Reinelt and Roach, "General Introduction," 5).

16 Marvin Carlson, "Perspectives on Performance: Germany and America (Introduction)," in *The Transformative Power of Performance: A New Aesthetics*, ed. Erika Fischer-Lichte (Abingdon, UK: Routledge, 2008), 6.

17 See in J. Kelly Nestruck, "What's Next for Albert Schultz and Soulpepper? A Return to Classical Roots (Hopefully)," *Globe and Mail*, 27 July 2013, http://www.theglobeandmail.com/arts/theatre-and-performance/angels-and-demons/article13453085/.

18 Martin Morrow, "The Good, the Weird, and the Ugly: CanStage 2.0," *Grid TO*, 26 September 2013, para. 7, http://www.thegridto.com/culture/theatre/the-good-the-weird-and-the-ugly-canstage-2-0/ (site no longer available).

19 Neworld Theatre, "LANDLINE," *Neworld Theatre*, 2012, para. 2, http://www.neworldtheatre.com/productions-landline.html. Also see script of LANDLINE and cell phone transcript from one iteration of the show: Dustin Harvey and Adrienne Wong, "LANDLINE: Halifax to Vancouver," spec. issue on Digital Performance (ed. Peter Kuling and Laura Levin), *Canadian Theatre Review* 159 (Summer 2014): 68–80.

20 Fischer-Lichte, *Transformative Power of Performance*, 40.

21 Ibid., 22.

22 Ibid.

23 Ibid.

24 Dolan, *Geographies of Learning*, 66.

25 Shannon Jackson, *Social Works: Performing Art, Supporting Publics* (New York: Routledge, 2011), 9. In using the phrase "interpublic coordination," Jackson is drawing on Nancy Fraser's important writing on "counterpublics," spaces where marginalized groups can form and discuss identities and ideas that are often in tension with those in the official public sphere. She argues that

effective counterpublics are those that do not draw a "sharp separation" between themselves and the state and that succeed in "imagin[ing] the forms
of self-management, *interpublic coordination*, and political accountability that
are essential to a democratic and egalitarian society" (emphasis added).
Also see Nancy Fraser, "Rethinking the Public Sphere: A Contribution to the
Critique of Actually Existing Democracy," in *Habermas and the Public Sphere*,
ed. Craig Calhoun (Cambridge, MA: MIT Press, 1992), 109–42.

26 Jackson, *Professing Performance*, 6.

27 Andrew Moore, "Facebook and the Liberal Arts," *Journal of General Education*
61, no. 3 (2012): 271.

28 This could also be evidence that the public's appetite for minutiae has a
limit. It is unclear if anyone was wondering whether Kathleen Wynne has
ever smoked pot.

29 Erving Goffman, *The Presentation of Self in Everyday Life* (Garden City, NY:
Doubleday, 1959), 80.

30 On 31 October 2013, Toronto police chief Bill Blair confirmed the existence of the much talked about cell phone video; in a press conference,
he announced that the digital file had been recovered during a large-scale
investigation of drug activities in Toronto.

31 For an example of this kind of performance, see *Huffington Post Canada*,
"Rob Ford Shoves Photographers as Lisi Documents," 31 October 2013,
http://m.huffpost.com/ca/entry/4181453.

32 Stuart Boon and Christine Sinclair, "A World I Don't Inhabit: Disquiet and
Identity in Second Life and Facebook," *Educational Media International* 46,
no. 2 (2009): 103.

33 unmarketing (Scott Stratten), "Instagram profile," *Instagram*, https://
instagram.com/unmarketing (this profile appeared on Stratten's Twitter
feed in 2013 but has since been slightly modified and has been retained on
Instagram); @needy, "Twitter profile," *Twitter*, https://twitter.com/needy
/status/313042622245646336; Tequila Mockingbird@KingofQueens13,
Twitter profile, *Twitter*, https://twitter.com/kingofqueens13; Samanthaaa@
sameveleigh, "Twitter profile," *Twitter*, https://twitter.com/sameveleigh;
Kristie Kenney@Kristie Kenney, "Twitter profile," *Twitter*, https://twitter
.com/KristieKenney.

34 I am using Butler's (admittedly somewhat simplistic) distinctions to illustrate how more familiar understandings of theatre and performance
might be brought together in the study of digital culture. However, it should
be noted that these terms are defined differently by other theorists in the
theatre and performance studies field, often revealing the importance of
disciplinary context in shaping their meaning (e.g., a performance theorist
with a visual arts background will define something that happens outside

an institutional art space as "theatre" while a theatre theorist may call that "performance").

35 Judith Butler, "Performative Acts and Gender Constitution: An Essay in Phenomenology and Feminist Theory," in *Writing on the Body: Female Embodiment and Feminist Theory*, ed. Katie Conboy, Nadia Medina, and Sarah Stanbury (New York: Columbia University Press, 1997), 410.

36 *New York Times*, "Did YouTube Kill Performance Art?," 18 August 2011, http://www.nytimes.com/roomfordebate/2011/08/18/did-youtube-kill-performance-art.

37 Butler, "Performative Acts and Gender Constitution," 402.

38 Naila Keleta-Mae, "Facebook Post," *Facebook*, 28 January 2013, https://www.facebook.com/nailakeletamae/posts/10152452885865057; Renu Capelli, "Facebook Post," *Facebook*, 10 October 2013, https://www.facebook.com/renu.cappelli/posts/10152364812029572; Susan Stover, "Facebook Post," *Facebook*, 8 July 2013, https://www.facebook.com/susan.stover.710/posts/10101362968457570.

39 Goffman, *Presentation of Self in Everyday Life*, 80.

40 David Brin, *The Transparent Society* (Cambridge, MA: Perseus Press, 1998).

41 E.J. Westlake, "Friend Me If You Facebook: Generation Y and Performative Surveillance," *TDR: The Drama Review* 52, no. 4 (2008): 27.

42 Goffman, *Presentation of Self in Everyday Life*, 83.

43 Lorraine McNeil, "Free Tarek Loubani and John Greyson Group [Facebook Post]," *Facebook*, 13 October 2013, https://www.facebook.com/groups/freetarekandjohn?id=502739686475669 (page no longer available).

44 Carly Maga, "Artistic Fusion: Suburban Beast and 'rihannaboi95,'" *Canada Arts Connect Magazine*, 3 July 2013, para. 7, http://canadaartsconnect.com/magazine/2013/07/suburban-beast-and-rihannaboi95/.

45 Schechner, "No More Theatre PhDs?" 7.

46 Richard Schechner, "A New Paradigm for Theatre in the Academy," *TDR: The Drama Review* 36, no. 4 (1992): 8.

47 Jackson, *Professing Performance*, 10.

48 Taking these shifts seriously also means thinking about how to address the needs of students with backgrounds outside of theatre (art history, dance studies, etc.) who are seeking performance studies degrees but, in the new conjoined theatre and performance studies programs, end up finding themselves taking courses that are heavily loaded with theatre texts or, even more commonly, working as teaching assistants in courses in theatre history. Conversely, it means considering how to make the study of things like sporting events, religious rituals, fashion shows, and the like exciting and relevant to those grad students looking for courses on avant-garde theatre or Shakespeare.

12 Including Millennials in the Theatre of the New Millennium

NICHOLAS HANSON

In the spring of 2013, a performing arts venue opened in southern Ontario, custom-built for the populist programming of Drayton Entertainment. According to the *Globe and Mail*'s J. Kelly Nestruck, "it becomes clear pretty quickly why a retirement residence paid $1-million for the naming rights at this new theatre in Cambridge, Ont. Nearly every patron in the 500-seat theatre has gray hair."[1] Is this anecdote of an all-grey auditorium just the result of attending a weekday matinee, or is the absence of iPhones a cautionary sign that younger generations will never find their way to the theatre? This question received considerable attention during the 2013 conference for the Canadian Arts Presenting Association/l'Association canadienne des organismes artistiques (CAPA-COA), with a plethora of panels bearing evocative titles, such as "Live Performing Arts in 2020: Will We Be Ready?," "Performing Arts for All: Public Engagement and the Presenting Sector," and "Putting the YOU in Youth: Building Our Audiences of the Future."[2] Many contemporary audience development strategies specifically target members of the millennial generation, a term coined by Neil Howe and William Strauss[3] and most commonly applied to people born between 1980 and 2000.

Before conceding that all performance venues should be named after retirement homes, a brief snapshot of theatre attendance trends can provide a broader perspective than a simple headcount of grey-haired patrons might suggest. Among Canadian adults aged 25 to 74, theatre attendance in 2010 was lowest for members of the youngest 10-year range, 25 to 34, and highest for members of the oldest span, 65 to 74.[4] Similarly, a large-scale survey of Toronto audiences revealed that the average age of a theatregoer was 55.[5] Thus, the statistics verify the anecdotal observations that older adults compose the largest segment of theatre audiences. That said, this information simply reflects the demographic realities of the Canadian population; the median age in our country has increased steadily over the past 40 years, from 26.2 in 1971 all the way to 40.6 in 2011.[6] In other words, theatres are aging rapidly, but so are grocery stores, restaurants, and sidewalks. During the next decade, though, Canadian society will undergo a massive transformation: the baby boomer and Generation X cohorts will start to shrink, while the entire millennial population will reach adulthood and, bolstered by immigration, form the largest generation in Canadian history, a position they will retain over the group that immediately follows them. The future of Canada will belong to millennials – economically, politically, and culturally. But valuing millennials primarily for their *future* potential, a perspective held by too many arts administrators, overlooks their already substantial influence, particularly as members of the first digital generation. As such, a comprehensive philosophical defence of theatre's value in this millennium requires a meaningful exploration of millennials as the arts audiences and participants of *today*.

In Canada, the established professional theatre companies recognize the challenges in attracting new audience members, particularly millennials – a topic further discussed by Aaron Willis and Julie Tepperman in chapter 13 of this book. While focusing on demographics, however, arts administrators have overlooked psychographics, the "understanding of the emotional landscape of audience members and the kind of lifestyles they lead and identify with."[7] Essentially, theatre companies have conceptualized audiences as a renewable resource that will be perpetually drawn to performances by some universal (yet mostly indefinable) impulses; this approach assumes that reaching millennials only requires better communication of the reasons why *anyone in any era* should engage with theatre, and it ignores the specific behavioural motivations of why *young adults in 2016* might be interested. Some of the generational characteristics associated with millennials include confidence and an embrace of self-expression,[8] a desire for authentic encounters,[9] and an orientation towards teams and a need for belonging,[10] as well as increasing levels of narcissism[11] and declining capacities for empathy.[12] At first glance, a gravitation towards groups might appear to contradict traits like narcissism; at the core, though, both of these concepts highlight a defining aspiration of the millennial generation: genuine engagement with both relationships and experiences. Theatre provides particularly effective methods for developing empathy in individuals and fostering connectivity in communities; as such, this chapter proposes that theatre directly complements the core characteristics of millennials, offering transformative experiences that contribute to the actualization of more engaged people and societies. Moreover, theatre's inherent human interactivity augments its enriching benefits for millennials *now*, in an increasingly digital world. Canada's established theatre companies, in contrast, have overlooked the reasons why millennials need theatre today; this chapter argues that the consumerist initiatives used to lure millennials – social media campaigns, reduced ticket prices, and audience outreach programs – operate on a functionally transactional level, resulting in a fundamental disconnect with a generation that cherishes genuine engagement.

Developing Empathy

Discussions about generations, particularly younger ones, tend to evoke nostalgic recollections and trite oversimplifications. As such, this article begins with a prefatory note: though millennials exhibit a number of collective traits, any generation includes a wide spectrum of individuals; thus, they should never be considered a monolithic block with a singular set of characteristics. Relative to other generations, millennials demonstrate higher levels of narcissistic behaviour, coupled with diminished capacity for empathetic awareness. To measure individuals' positive and inflated self-perceptions within the "normal" range of the population, researchers commonly use the Narcissistic Personality Inventory, an assessment tool that includes 40 forced-choice dyads such as "I prefer to blend in with the crowd/I like to be the center of attention."[13] Twenge et al. studied American college students' responses and discovered that from 1982 to 2006, students scored "progressively higher" in terms of narcissism.[14] An epidemiological study of diagnoses for narcissistic personality disorder (NPD) indicated similar trends, noting that the prevalence of NPD among millennials was approximately 50 per cent higher than the total adult population.[15] In addition, elevated levels of narcissism are correlated with diminished levels of empathy and compassion.[16] As one example, Sara Konrath, Edward O'Brien, and Courtney Hsing observed that today's American college students, compared to those from the late 1970s and early 1980s, are "less likely to agree with statements such as 'I often have tender, concerned feelings for people less fortunate than me' and 'I sometimes try to understand my friends better by imagining how things look from their perspective.'"[17]

Scholars have not confidently explained the root causes of millennials' increase of narcissism and decline of empathy. One research stream implicates the parenting and teaching approaches of the 1980s, which sought to boost self-esteem by celebrating simple participation rather than distinguished accomplishments.[18] Investigations into the relationships between narcissism, empathy, and social media platforms like Facebook remain in the nascent phase, though Shawn Bergman remarks, "our research suggests that [social network] usage is not an indicator of narcissism, but rather a product of the times."[19] Around 2000, just as the first millennials reached adulthood, reality television occupied a dominant position in the entertainment landscape.[20] The stars of popular reality TV programs scored higher than actors, musicians, and comedians on the Narcissistic Personality Inventory.[21] Quite reasonably, one could surmise that reality TV shows and personalities have contributed to a youth culture that values expressions of individuality and also applauds self-centric behaviours.

Observations about theatre's capacity to develop empathy stretch back to Aristotle. Two contemporary scholarly concepts, from distinct disciplinary backgrounds, bolster the notion that theatre might provide some particularly fruitful means to increase the empathic abilities of its spectators and participants. In specific contexts, the reading of fiction appears to improve an individual's level of empathy. Keith Oatley theorizes that enrichment of an individual's empathic skills only occurs when the reader is "emotionally transported" within a story, usually by absorption in the actions of characters.[22] Recent empirical studies from P. Matthijs Bal and Martijn Veltkamp support the connection between reading and empathy, explaining that

[w]hen an individual reads a story, he/she predicts the actions and reactions of the characters, by inferring what they are thinking, feeling, and intending. In order to do this, the reader sympathizes with the characters in the story, through taking the perspective of the characters and to experience the events as if it is the reader's own experience. Moreover, some stories are able to make sense out of the senseless, and offer possibilities to understand other people across time and space, an opportunity which is not readily available in daily life. The sympathy a reader feels for the characters is then integrated in the self-concept of the reader, through which the reader accumulates his/her ability to take the perspective of others, and to feel empathy.[23]

David Comer Kidd and Emanuele Castano discern a richer empathic boost from reading literary fiction (typified by interpretive elements and complex characters) over popular fiction (driven by narrative tension and stock identities); according to their analysis, whereas "mundane social experiences may be scripted by convention and informed by stereotypes, those presented in literary fiction often disrupt our expectations. Readers of literary fiction must draw on more flexible interpretive resources to infer the feelings and thoughts of characters."[24] Though these studies focus on reading, many of their observations seem logically extendable to theatre. The notion of being "emotionally transported" regularly occurs in the experiences of both theatregoers and performers. Theatre's emphasis on the spoken word, along with the material conditions that frequently restrict the number of actors, encourages a dialectic method of playwriting that allows audiences to consider opposing perspectives in a more contemplative setting than personal conversations or bombastic television panels.

The connection between theatre and empathy is further reinforced by discoveries in neuroscience. As a result of the brain's mirror neuron system, observation and participation are perceived in very similar ways. In simplest terms, the human brain allows people to understand, and even experience vicariously, the actions and feelings of others.[25] Applied to theatre, an art form that is inherently simulational, this concept proposes that "the neuronal pathways that trigger certain facial expressions light up in the viewer's mind, too, upon seeing those facial expressions."[26] Furthermore, this phenomenon occurs despite the audience's (presumed) recognition that the production's events and characters are fictitious in nature. Preliminary investigations on the relationship between neuroscience and acting are already under way, for both stage[27] and screen.[28]

Suggesting that theatre offers a panacea for millennials' soaring narcissism and withering empathy would be naive, to say the least. That said, contemporary scholarship related to reading and neuroscience provides evidence that empathy can be developed, and through largely enjoyable activities. In order to attract millennials, though, theatre companies often promote the spectacular elements of their productions, as if theatre could compete on these terms with an increasingly crowded array of entertainment options. Such a framing ignores the idea that theatre delivers not merely a few hours of diversionary delight but, more importantly, the potential for a transformative experience for its audience. Theatre is needed *now* for millennials, not just because it can rival the immersive joy of playing *Angry Birds* on an iPhone, but also because it provides something larger than entertainment – a buffer for narcissism and a catalyst for empathic maturation.

Building Community

Another way that theatre can enrich the lives of millennials stems from its capacity to foster a sense of community. Over the last half century, participation in service organizations, sporting associations, and social meetings has dropped significantly, as has the frequency of visits between friends and family members.[29] This trend counters our general preference for congregating with others rather than spending time alone.[30] For millennials, social interactions are increasingly occurring through digital channels; for instance, about a third of Canadian university students send more than 200 text messages per day.[31] Pew Research Center describes millennials as history's first "always connected" generation, but what are they are really connected to, and how meaningful are those connections?[32]

In today's on-demand culture, where people can select their own content to watch on their own digital device in just about any location, theatre is often lamented as obsolete. Nevertheless, the perceived limitations of theatre – a predetermined starting time in a fixed location – actually provide the conditions for enrichment, because they compel audience members to encounter other humans in a communal experience. A theatre auditorium provides one of the few places where cell phone usage is (largely) taboo; the event features the exhibition of humans, not screens. As such, theatre provides an opportunity for people to sit in close proximity to others, while watching and listening to other people, in a live environment. The rarity of that scenario cannot be overstated, nor can the possible benefits in terms of fostering a community. In a demonstration of millennials' influence on the contemporary theatre experience, digital devices have recently infiltrated the once-sacrosanct theatre venue through the advent of "tweet seats," a section of the auditorium where patrons can use their smartphones to write online comments during the actual live performance. By attempting to capture the attention of young adults, theatre companies risk aggravating their regular supporters. Moreover, tweet seats' capability to engage people with performance is fundamentally misguided, because they provide an inferior facsimile of the theatre experience, one that diminishes human connectivity – the very element that offers the greatest benefit to millennials.

Theatre as a means to find a sense of community is not a novel idea. People attend arts events as occasions for social contact.[33] Opportunities for personal interactions are especially motivating for occasional arts patrons.[34] Younger adults, who might lack familiarity with the artistic product of a venue, may be attracted to events by the social aspect.[35] The current experience of attending theatre, on the other hand, rarely facilitates socialization, as people sit in dark silence during the performance and get herded out of the venue shortly after the final curtain. Even the intermission, an opportunity for discussing the drama on stage or in your companions' lives, appears to be on the wane, with many new productions eliminating breaks in the action.[36] A modern solution for stimulating social interactions might be found in the same way used by theatres from the Romans to the Elizabethans: food and drink. For instance, the 2013 iteration of the Edmonton Fringe Festival sold a record 117,000 tickets to its indoor performances, a number likely bolstered by the fact that the 11-day event attracted 735,435 to the fairgrounds.[37] Drawn by multiple beer tents and food vendors, a largely youthful demographic flocked to the outdoor gathering spaces of the annual festival, where circulating artists distributed promotional material and persuaded random revellers to purchase tickets to the shows. Millennials exhibit a preference for *going out* rather than attending one specific event like a play; this trend appears to have encouraged some Canadian theatre companies to revitalize the social ambience of their venues. Mirvish Productions now allows the consumption of drinks within the auditorium, Canadian Stage hosts lively block parties, and the bar at Theatre Passe Muraille remains open after performances so patrons can connect and converse. Although expanding food services might seem like a minor operating detail, such a move reimagines theatre facilities as open public spaces; as well, it echoes a shift in perception of theatre engagement from attendance at a specific performance to the sort of broader, participatory experience that boosts theatre's relevance for millennials.

Audience (Dis)Engagement

Canada's established professional theatre companies acknowledge that their current operating models are not effectively connecting with millennials. As Jacoba Knaapen, executive director of the Toronto Alliance for the Performing Arts, bluntly states, "Our industry knows it is behind. We all recognize the fact that we need to leap ahead."[38] In an effort to attract millennial patrons, theatre companies employ a number of strategies, which commonly include social media campaigns, reduced ticket prices, and audience outreach programs. At first glance, these ideas appear to foster meaningful relationships with younger adults; upon closer inspection, though, many of these programs treat millennials as a mere commodity, without understanding why they might want to connect with theatre activities. The superficial nature of contemporary audience development practices essentially limits their effectiveness in courting millennials, a cohort seeking genuine engagement with people and experiences.

Technology plays a central role in the attempt to reach prospective millennial audiences. Over the last two decades, theatre companies have slowly developed their presence on the Internet.[39] During the last few years, theatre companies have further expanded their online identities to include social media platforms, particularly Facebook and Twitter. In a Pew Research Center survey, 82 per cent of American arts institutions claimed to use social media to "Engage with audience members either prior to, during, or following an event" and 65 per cent indicated they use social media to "Learn more about [their] audience, patrons, or stakeholders."[40] Despite the perception that social media platforms facilitate relationships between arts organizations and patrons, Stephen Preece and Jennifer Wiggins Johnson observed in an examination of online profiles that "there seemed to be little audience-initiated interactions on the social media Web sites; the majority of the interactions consisted of a staff member making a post and a small group of fans or followers responding."[41] Many established theatre companies appear to understand social media platforms merely as a tool for promotion, instead of as an intrinsically dialogic form of communication. For instance, consider the following comments about Twitter from *Beyond the Curtain: How Digital Media Is Reshaping Theatre*, a report featuring contributions from the Stratford Festival and other major theatre companies:

> This new kind of "word of mouth" has opened up a whole new market. Patrons can tweet something to their followers and have it read by hundreds instead of verbally telling a select few friends. Unfortunately this development does have its disadvantages as well. Twitter is so instantaneous unofficial reviews of the performance arrive online a lot faster than the traditional reviews.[42]

Clearly, *Beyond the Curtain* propagates the concept that Twitter is a tool to expedite marketing efforts by delivering information about a production to greater numbers of people; the use of the word "unfortunately" is particularly telling, as it signals a real discomfort with the possibility of negative feedback within the realm of an online conversation.

Building true engagement through social media requires that theatre companies limit the content that serves their own interests and increase the material that adds value to the lives of their audiences, by offering entertainment, enrichment, or education. Instead of bombarding audiences with promotional materials, theatre companies might encourage discussion about a contemporary arts topic or share a humorous backstage anecdote; essentially, the online identity should mirror a core attribute of the theatre experience – fostering community. Thinking even more broadly, theatre companies should recognize that vibrant social media activity not only attracts millennials, but also migrates that deepened sense of community to the human connections at the physical theatre venue. Pre-existing relationships with peers, artists, and organizations would enhance an individual's emotional engagement with a production and thus augment theatre's capacity to provide perspectives and emotions that develop empathic skills.

In addition to social media campaigns, established theatre companies regularly attempt to attract millennials by offering discounted tickets, often at a fraction of the regular price. At the Stratford Festival, for example, the best seats for the 2013 production of the musical *Tommy* cost $144, but people aged 16–29 could purchase tickets for $25. Canadian Stage sells $15 tickets to patrons under 30, compared to a top price of $99, while Vancouver's Arts Club Theatre discounts their $70 tickets to $22 for students and the Calgary-based Alberta Theatre Projects offers student tickets for only $10.

Given millennials' nickname of "Generation Debt," the practice of offering discounts seems like an intuitive solution. In reality, though, income level barely affects arts attendance; a person's educational background and social status are far more significant factors in the decision to attend a play.[43] As Joanne Scheff explains, "for the vast majority of people, rejection has set in before price becomes a consideration, since for these people there is probably an irreversible barrier: lack of interest."[44] The most vivid example of luring millennials with discounted tickets occurred during the 2008 Labour Party conference in the United Kingdom, when Culture Secretary Andy Burnham pledged to offer a *million* free theatre tickets by the year 2011 to people under the age of 26. The program, administered by Arts Council England and cheerily titled "A Night Less Ordinary," operated from February 2009 to March 2011. The goal of a million tickets was reduced several times, and by the completion of the scheme, 400,000 tickets were used. Of that tally, though, many of the tickets were used by repeat participants who indicated that they would likely have attended the productions even without free tickets; all in all, only 6,800 young people are estimated to have visited a theatre for the first time.[45]

To be clear, ticket prices are a by-product, not the cause, of a bigger issue: the reduction of the artistic experience to a transactional exchange. On Broadway, commercial producers usually sell shows based on name recognition of the play or performers, not familiarity with a specific organization or venue; as such, they can leverage various supply-and-demand ticket-pricing strategies to maximize revenues before the production closes. In Canada, on the other hand, where the majority of professional theatre activity occurs at not-for-profit organizations programming annual seasons, crafting long-term associations with audiences is essential for sustainability. Theatre companies in this country, facing years of challenging economic conditions, have adopted a Broadway-style philosophy of selling seats instead of relationships. For instance, many Canadian theatre companies offer price reductions not only to students but also to "young" adults up to age 30 or 35. In most cases, including all of the deep discounts described in the previous paragraph, a number of restrictive conditions apply, such as limits to the quantity or location of tickets, as well as requirements to line up early in the morning or immediately before the show begins. Unsold theatre tickets possess no value the next day; economically speaking, these youth-oriented deals are designed to reap a partial admission fee for seats that would otherwise go unfilled. In other words, theatre companies that offer last-minute discounts on unsold tickets are actually no more generous than bakeries that donate day-old bread; in both cases, the full retail value of the commodity has expired.

For theatres, this practice provides the short-term benefit of additional ticket revenue but causes more significant long-term problems. By forcing young people to wait in lines and jump through hoops, theatre companies risk suggesting that theatre attendance involves an onerous procedure while also creating a negative impression of their organization before the curtain even rises. More importantly, deeply discounted tickets imply that a theatre company's productions possess limited worth, a devastating notion considering that reputational quality is one of a theatre's most valuable assets. Despite earning relatively limited incomes, millennials demonstrate comfort with paying for premium goods and experiences, especially if the brand carries social cachet among their peers, such as Apple or Lululemon. In these cases, the purchaser receives not only a physical item but also a sense of belonging. When theatre companies sell tickets with discounted prices and complicated restrictions, the financial transaction is emphasized instead of the experience of community that accompanies a live performance. Canada's established theatre companies have absorbed a consumerist model; yet they have also focused on selling something – tickets instead of experiences – that does not capture the imagination of younger adults.

Theatre administrators would likely concur with the assertion that theatre's ability to foster genuine engagement, with both experiences and relationships, plays a central role in attracting millennial audiences. Indeed, *engagement* has emerged as a buzzword in contemporary arts policy, along with the equally ubiquitous concepts of *outreach* and *audience development*. These terms convey a spectrum of ideas, describing how "[a]n institution can increase participation in three basic ways: (1) by *broadening* it – i.e., capturing a larger share of the existing market by attracting individuals who constitute a natural audience for the arts but are not currently participants; (2) by *deepening* it – i.e., intensifying its current participants' level of involvement; and (3) by *diversifying* it – i.e., attracting new markets comprising those individuals who typically would not entertain the idea of participating in the arts."[46] In the context of Canadian theatre companies, common audience development activities include pre- and post-show discussions, theatre tours, newsletters, study guides, public lectures, and open rehearsals. In theory, audience development strategies help "break down the barriers – whether physical, psychological, social or informational – that hinder people from participating in or attending the arts."[47] Despite the substantial human and financial resources required to operate audience development programs, their ability to cultivate meaningful relationships with patrons is debatable. Many of the events involve mostly passive audiences that receive information without actively contributing or participating. Arts consultant Alan Brown traces a correlation between personal arts practice and attendance at professional events; for instance, sizeable percentages of orchestra audiences play a musical instrument, gallery visitors pursue recreational arts or crafts, and theatre spectators enjoy singing, dancing, or writing.[48] Numerous theatre companies offer classes for young people or professional artists, but far fewer options exist for recreational adults. Hosting patrons for a season of weekly classes or regular workshops would encourage far closer ties to a theatre company than a question-and-answer session with actors. In essence, companies have clearly demarcated theatre as something that is delivered to, not shared with, audiences; this divide might suit the current population of regular arts attenders, but for a generational cohort whose school experiences encouraged self-expression and group collaboration, this divide between spectatorship and participation reduces potential excitement and interest.

The most pressing concern with contemporary audience development strategies stems from their relationship to revenue creation. In virtually every Canadian theatre company, audience development is housed within the marketing departments, which frames their operations in an inherently commercial context, a reality that is confirmed by the language used in a trio of 2013 job postings. The Stratford Festival's advertisement for a Director of Audience Development stated, "You will oversee the Box Office, Front of House, Food & Beverage and Retail operations, and ensure that revenue targets are met in these areas"; the post omitted any mention of relationships or engagement.[49] Roseneath Theatre, a Toronto-based Theatre for Young Audiences (TYA) company, searched for an Education and Audience Development Manager with an ad that required the incumbent to "Promote and sell shows to educational organizations."[50] A posting for the Factory Theatre connected outreach to finances in both the title and the duties; their description of an ideal Marketing and Audience Development Manager began by stating, "The classic line 'bums in seats' is your mantra," and included a responsibility "to create and execute marketing strategies to meet or surpass audience revenue goals."[51] Tethering audience development to monetary targets compels administrators to play it safe, by programming theatre productions and activities that audiences will probably appreciate, based upon their enjoyment of similar encounters in the past. Philosophically, this audience development strategy connects potential audiences to specific productions rather than to theatre as a broader art form. When aesthetic or genre trends inevitably change, theatre companies may find themselves squeezed on both ends, by alienating loyal patrons who resist the artistic shifts and by failing to have ever captivated younger cohorts with any real sense of why theatre might matter in their lives.

Concluding Thoughts

On some level, theatre companies need to place more emphasis on administrative operations in order to embrace millennials. In one simple example, enabling online transactions has been a pressing priority for performing arts organizations' websites.[52] Despite this attention, purchasing an online ticket for a theatre production remains a Byzantine task, at least from the perspective of millennials accustomed to buying a new song, movie, or app with one simple tap of a screen. Furthermore, theatre companies could explore innovations in terms of digital ticketing; in 2016, a person can flash their iPhone to board a plane headed to an international destination, yet a patron still requires a paper ticket to attend a production at the Tarragon.

More important than operational details, though, companies need to consider ways that theatre content, aesthetics, and experiences might generate a sense of purpose for millennials. Two productions that both toured across Canada in 2013–14 provide contrasting examples of ways to engage with millennial audiences. *Kim's Convenience*, written by Ins Choi and produced by Soulpepper Theatre, became the most financially successful production in the history of a company known mostly for interpretations of iconic texts from the last century.[53] With a slice-of-life view of a Korean Canadian corner store, the production shared youthful perspectives about family tensions, employment prospects, and cultural expectations. Millennials might naturally identify with the younger characters, but the emotional resonance of the show cultivates an ideal setting to consider the older characters' viewpoints, thereby developing their empathic abilities. *The God That Comes*, co-created by theatre director Christian Barry and indie music sensation Hawksley Workman, is "a wine-soaked rock & roll cabaret" inspired by *The Bacchae*.[54] The cabaret format of the production creates a welcoming social environment for the audience; the technical rider for the show speaks volumes about the intended vibe, stipulating, "We prefer the audience to be permitted alcoholic drinks in the hall."[55]

Tailoring artistic programming to millennials' interests is an important step in attracting the digital generation; the next step involves elevating the specialness of a theatre visit. As Diane Paulus, artistic director of the American Repertory Theater, exclaims, "The theater needs to be something where you feel: 'I have to experience it.' Not just read or see it. People are craving experience – they are *desperate* for experience."[56] Millennials treasure experiences more than material goods, a trait so pervasive that it is described by the acronym FOMO – fear of missing out.[57] In an extension of this idea to a theatrical context, millennials want not only to watch theatre productions but to celebrate the experience. No production encapsulates the elements that might make theatre feel *now* for millennials more than Punchdrunk's *Sleep No More.* After smaller-scale versions in London and Boston, the New York production opened in 2011, to rave critical responses and ongoing commercial success. Loosely based on *Macbeth,* the interactive theatre piece allows audience members to circulate freely throughout a series of abandoned warehouses designed to resemble a hotel; actors perform mostly wordless vignettes in a carefully choreographed circuit. The fragmented narrative arc and visually evocative staging aligns with the aesthetic preferences of millennials; moreover, the opportunity to not only participate but also execute some control over the experience dovetails with core millennial traits like group connectivity and a personal sense of specialness. From the beginning, the production included a bar; a rooftop lounge and high-end restaurant were later added. All of this adds up to a show that *Vogue* proclaims has the "sexiest young audience in New York at the moment."[58] With regular line-ups outside the theatre, *Sleep No More* provides a clear reminder that millennials are part of the audience *now,* though they might be engaging with the arts in new ways and new locations. Canada's established theatre companies should take heed of this trend; otherwise, they might find themselves looking to fund even more of their venues with the sponsorship of retirement residences.

NOTES

1   J. Kelly Nestruck, "The Future of Theatre Is Cheesy," *Globe and Mail,* 6 July 2013, R1.

2   CAPACOA, "Conference 2013 Schedule," January 2013, http://www .capacoa.ca/en/conference/past-conferences/2013-culture-of-place /schedule-2013.

3   Neil Howe and William Strauss, *Millennials Rising: The Next Great Generation* (New York: Knopf Doubleday, 2000).

4   Kelly Hill, "Factors in Canadians' Arts Attendance in 2010," *Statistical Insights on the Arts* 11, no. 1 (September 2012): 1–54, http://www.hillstrategies .com/content/factors-canadians'-arts-attendance-2010.

5   Strategic Counsel, "TAPA Audience Survey: Attendance and Engagement with Arts and Cultural Activities in Toronto," November 2013, http://tapa .ca/wp-content/uploads/2014/10/TAPA_Audience_Report_FINAL _REVISED.pdf.

6   Statistics Canada, "Population by Broad Age Groups and Sex, Counts, Including Median Age, 1921 to 2011 for Both Sexes – Canada," 19 July 2013,

http://www12.statcan.gc.ca/census-recensement/2011/dp-pd/hlt-fst/as-sa
/Pages/highlight.cfm?TabID=1&Lang=E&PRCode=01&Asc=0&OrderBy=1&
Sex=1&View=1&tableID=22.

7 András Szántó, "Marketing, Technology and Research: Keys to a New Future
in Building Arts Participation: A Conference Report" in *Proceedings from the
Wallace Foundation Arts Grantee Conference*, ed. András Szántó (New York:
The Wallace Foundation, 2008), 9, http://www.wallacefoundation.org
/knowledge-center/audience-development-for-the-arts/strategies-for-expanding
-audiences/Documents/arts-for-all-connecting-to-new-audiences.pdf.

8 Paul Taylor and Scott Keeter, eds., *Millennials: A Portrait of Generation Next*
(Washington, DC: Pew Research Center, 2010).

9 Don Tapscott, *Growing Up Digital: The Rise of the Net Generation* (New York:
McGraw-Hill, 1998).

10 See Neil Howe and Reena Nadler, "Yes We Can: The Emergence of Millennials as a Political Generation," New America Foundation, February 2009,
https://www.lifecourse.com/assets/files/yes_we_can.pdf; Patricia Martin,
Tipping the Culture: How Engaging Millennials Will Change Things (Chicago:
LitLamp Communications, 2010).

11 Jean Twenge et al., "Egos Inflating Over Time: A Cross-Temporal Meta-
Analysis of the Narcissistic Personality Inventory," *Journal of Personality* 76,
no. 4 (2008): 875–902.

12 Sara H. Konrath, Edward H. O'Brien, and Courtney Hsing, "Changes in
Dispositional Empathy in American College Students Over Time: A Meta-
Analysis," *Personality and Social Psychology Review* 15, no. 2 (2011): 180–98.

13 See Robert Raskin and Calvin S. Hall, "The Narcissistic Personality Inventory: Alternate Form Reliability and Further Evidence of Construct Validity,"
Journal of Personality Assessment 45 (1981): 159–62; Robert Raskin and Howard Terry, "A Principal-Components Analysis of the Narcissistic Personality
Inventory and Further Evidence of Its Construct Validity," *Journal of Personality and Social Psychology* 54 (1988): 890–902.

14 Twenge et al., "Egos Inflating Over Time," 882.

15 Frederick S. Stinson et al., "Prevalence, Correlates, Disability, and Comorbidity of DSM-IV Narcissistic Personality Disorder: Results from the Wave 2
National Epidemiologic Survey on Alcohol and Related Conditions," *Journal
of Clinical Psychiatry* 69 (2008): 1033–45.

16 W. Keith Campbell et al., "Do Narcissists Dislike Themselves 'Deep Down
Inside'?" *Psychological Science* 18 (2007): 227–9.

17 Konrath, O'Brien, and Hsing, "Changes in Dispositional Empathy," 187.

18 See Jean Twenge, *Generation Me: Why Today's Young Americans Are More Confident, Assertive, Entitled – and More Miserable Than Ever Before* (New York: Free

Press, 2006); Jean Twenge and W. Keith Campbell, *The Narcissism Epidemic: Living in the Age of Entitlement* (New York: Free Press/Simon & Schuster, 2009).

19 As quoted in Christen Conger, "Don't Blame Facebook for the Narcissism Epidemic," *Discovery News*, 4 August 2011, www.news.discovery.com/tech/dont-blame-facebook-narcissism-epidemic-110804.htm.

20 Susan Murray and Laurie Ouellette, *Reality TV: Remaking Television Culture* (New York: New York University Press, 2008).

21 S. Mark Young and Drew Pinsky, "Narcissism and Celebrity," *Journal of Research in Personality* 40 (2006): 463–71.

22 Keith Oatley, "Emotions and the Story World of Fiction," in *Narrative Impact: Social and Cognitive Foundations*, ed. Melanie C. Green, Jeffrey J. Strange, and Timothy C. Brock (Mahwah, NJ: Lawrence Erlbaum, 2002), 39–70.

23 P. Matthijs Bal and Martijn Veltkamp, "How Does Fiction Reading Influence Empathy? An Experimental Investigation on the Role of Emotional Transportation," *PLoS ONE* 8, no. 1 (30 January 2013): 2.

24 David Comer Kidd and Emanuele Castano, "Reading Literary Fiction Improves Theory of Mind," *Science* 342 (2013): 378.

25 Vittorio Gallese, Christian Keysers, and Giacomo Rizzolatti, "A Unifying View of the Basis of Social Cognition," *TRENDS in Cognitive Sciences* 8, no. 9 (September 2004): 396–403.

26 Erin Hurley, *Theatre and Feeling* (New York: Palgrave Macmillan, 2010), 35.

27 Rhonda Blair, *The Actor, Image, and Action* (New York: Routledge, 2008).

28 William Brown, "Is Acting a Form of Simulation or Being? Acting and Mirror Neurons," in *Theorizing Film Acting*, ed. Aaron Taylor (New York: Routledge, 2012), 120–34.

29 See Robert Putnam, *Bowling Alone: The Collapse and Revival of American Community* (New York: Simon & Schuster, 2000); Robert Putnam and Lewis Feldstein, *Better Together: Reviving the American Community* (New York: Simon & Schuster, 2004).

30 Daniel Kahneman et al., "A Survey Method for Characterizing Daily Life Experience: The Day Reconstruction Method," *Science* 306 (December 2004): 1776–80.

31 Paul Trapnell and Lisa Sinclair, "Texting Frequency and The Moral Shallowing Hypothesis" (paper presented at the annual meeting for the Society for Personality and Social Psychology, San Diego, CA, 26–8 January 2012).

32 Taylor and Keeter, *Millennials*.

33 Scott R. Swanson, J. Charlene Davis, and Yushan Zhao, "Art for Art's Sake? An Examination of Motives for Arts Performance Attendance," *Nonprofit and Voluntary Sector Quarterly* 37 (2008): 300–23.

34 Kevin F. McCarthy et al., *The Performing Arts in a New Era* (Santa Monica, CA: RAND, 2001).

35 Alan Brown, "Initiators and Responders: Leveraging Social Context to Build Audiences," *Knight Foundation Issues Brief Series* 4 (Summer 2004): 1–11.

36 Alice T. Carter, "Arts Groups Increasingly Skipping Intermission," *Pittsburgh Tribune-Review*, 30 October 2011, http://triblive.com/x/pittsburghtrib/ae/theater/s_764585.html.

37 Liz Nicholls, "Fringe Frenzy Grows Again; Rookie Director Utas Already Looking Ahead to Next Year," *Edmonton Journal*, 26 August 2013, A3.

38 As quoted in Craig Thompson and Ted Boniface, *Beyond the Curtain: How Digital Media Is Reshaping Theatre* (Stratford, ON: Avonova, 2011), 7, http://www.avonova.ca/assets/uploads/pages/image/files/Beyond_The_Curtain.pdf.

39 See Jim Royce, "Building an Online Presence for Live Theatre: Experience from the Field," *TCG Centrepiece*, August 2001, http://www.tcg.org/pdfs/publications/centerpiece/centerpiece_0801.pdf; Gregory D. Saxton, Chao Gao, and William A. Brown, "New Dimensions of Nonprofit Responsiveness: The Application and Promise of Internet-Based Technologies," *Public Performance & Management Review* 31, no. 2 (2007): 144–73; Suzanne Berman, "Performing Online: PR Through Web Gives Arts and Cultural Institutions New Power," *Public Relations Tactics* 15, no. 10 (2008): 21.

40 As quoted in Kristin Thomson, Kristen Purcell, and Lee Rainie, *Arts Organizations and Digital Technologies* (Washington, DC: Pew Research Center, 2013), 29.

41 Stephen B. Preece and Jennifer Wiggins Johnson, "Web Strategies and the Performing Arts: A Solution to Difficult Brands," *International Journal of Arts Management* 14, no. 1 (2011): 28.

42 Thompson and Boniface, *Beyond the Curtain*, 29.

43 Catherine Bunting et al., "From Indifference to Enthusiasm: Patterns of Arts Attendance in England," Arts Council England, 1 April 2008, http://www.artscouncil.org.uk/media/uploads/indifferencetoenthusiasm.pdf.

44 Joanne Scheff, "Factors Influencing Subscription and Single-Ticket Purchases at Performing Arts Organizations," *International Journal of Arts Management* 1, no. 2 (1999): 26.

45 sam culture ltd., "A Night Less Ordinary – Evaluation," *Arts Council England,* 5 April 2012, "http://www.artscouncil.org.uk/media/uploads/pdf/ANLO_FINAL_REPORT.pdf.

46 Kevin F. McCarthy and Kimberly Jinnett, *A New Framework for Building Participation in the Arts* (Santa Monica, CA: RAND, 2001), 3, http://www.rand.org/content/dam/rand/pubs/monograph_reports/2005/MR1323.pdf.

47 Rebecca Scollen, "Talking Theatre Is More Than a Test Drive: Two Audience Development Methodologies," *International Journal of Arts Management* 12, no. 1 (2009): 5.

48 Kay E. Sherwood, "Engaging Audiences: Report on The Wallace Arts Grantee Conference," in *Proceedings from the Wallace Foundation Arts Grantee Conference*, ed. Kay E. Sherwood (New York: The Wallace Foundation, 2009), 5, http://www.wallacefoundation.org/knowledge-center/audience-development-for-the-arts/strategies-for-expanding-audiences/Documents/Engaging-Audiences.pdf.

49 "Job: Director of Audience Development – The Stratford Festival (Stratford, Ontario)," *Canada Arts Connect*, 15 October 2013, http://canadaartsconnect.com/2013/09/job-director-of-audience-development-the-stratford-festival/Q2 (page no longer available).

50 "Education and Audience Development Manager," *Work in Culture*, 15 October 2013, http://www.workinculture.ca/The-Job-Board/jobs/Education-and-Audience-Development-Manager.

51 "Marketing and Audience Development Manager," *Factory Theatre*, 20 August 2013, http://www.factorytheatre.ca/admin/employment (listing no longer available).

52 Saxton, Gao, and Brown, "New Dimensions of Nonprofit Responsiveness."

53 J. Kelly Nestruck, "Angels and Demons," *Globe and Mail*, 27 July 2013, R1.

54 The God That Comes, "About: The Experience," 2013, http://thegodthatcomes.com/about/the-experience.

55 The God That Comes, "Technical Rider," 2013, http://thegodthatcomes.com/pub/TGTCTechnicalRider.pdf.

56 Craig Lambert, "The Future of Theatre: In a Digital Era, Is the Play Still the Thing?" *Harvard Magazine*, January–February 2012, http://harvardmag.com/pdf/2012/01-pdfs/0112-34.pdf.

57 Andrew K. Przybylski et al., "Motivational, Emotional, and Behavioral Correlates of Fear of Missing Out," *Computers in Human Behavior* 29, no. 4 (2013): 1841–8.

58 Adam Green, "*Macbeth* Takes Manhattan: New Stagings of the Shakespearean Classic," *Vogue*, 6 April 2011, para. 7, http://www.vogue.com/873937/macbeth-takes-manhattan-new-stagings-of-the-shakespearean-classic/.

13 Convergence Theatre: Necessary Producers

A DIALOGUE BETWEEN JULIE TEPPERMAN
AND AARON WILLIS

The two of us met while attending George Brown Theatre School's three-year acting conservatory in Toronto and were married in 2004. We co-founded and are still co-artistic directors of Convergence Theatre, a Toronto-based, artist-driven, indie theatre company. Since forming in 2006, Convergence has created and produced three original plays – *Auto-Show*, *The Gladstone Variations*, and *YICHUD (Seclusion)* – as well as co-produced the Canadian premiere of Sarah Ruhl's *Passion Play*.

With each new project, Convergence explores innovative ways to push the boundaries of intimacy between audience and performer in an effort to create unique, surprising, immersive audience experiences. Our productions to date have had large ensembles (between 25 and 40 people) and have taken place in site-specific locations (*The Gladstone Variations* had the audience following characters through Toronto's historic Gladstone Hotel), in non-traditional venues (*AutoShow* comprised seven 10-minute plays which took place in cars, and *Passion Play* was a four-and-a-half-hour epic which took place in Toronto's Withrow Park and Eastminster United Church), and in traditional theatre spaces that are completely reimagined (*YICHUD (Seclusion)* transformed Theatre Passe Muraille into a synagogue).

Convergence exists on a project-by-project basis, receives no operating funding, and we are its only staff. Having to do everything necessary to get the work up onstage makes us "necessary producers" of our own work, and we continue to face substantial obstacles. When we were asked to address the question of "Why theatre now?" it seemed natural to explore our challenges in the form of a dramatic dialogue between us – a Platonic dialogue in which we work towards asking this question of one another. At the time we crafted it, *Passion Play* – a massive production with a 40-person ensemble and a budget of $150,000, our largest yet

– had just closed after two years of work, and we were immersed in post-production tasks. We were exhausted and burnt out from seven years of non-stop creating and producing, and wondering where to go from there.

Julie: I don't think I want to create theatre anymore.

Aaron: Please elaborate.

J: Not like this. I lie awake in bed trying to answer that awful question "What's next?" and I'm remembering *all* the hours and hours of unpaid work we've put in over the last seven years. You and I, no staff, working out of our one-bedroom apartment –

A: Sometimes *in* the bedroom!

J: – always juggling a gazillion other theatre gigs at the same time.

A: Sometimes I feel like I have three full-time jobs. If only there were more hours in the day …

J: No! We can't go on like this. We will suffer, the work will suffer.

A: So what's the solution? Quit?

J: I don't know … I just … how did we get here? How did this happen?!?

A: Do you seriously want me to answer that at 3 a.m.?

J: Yes!

A: Okay, well … we started Convergence Theatre because we wanted to be more than just actors.

J: We wanted to create acting opportunities for ourselves, but in addition to that you wanted to start directing and I wanted to start writing.

A: We wanted to choose what we work on, with whom, and how. Take some control over our careers.

J: But we have *zero* control! Seven years later, what've we got? Nothing but fond memories!

A: I wouldn't say nothing … Some of the most profound and enriching relationships, both professionally and personally, have come about as a result of our starting Convergence.

J: Okay, I would agree with that.

A: All four shows have been artistically successful – two have been re-mounted, one toured –

J: I don't need our bio!

A: My point is, we're doing well! We've opened a lot of doors for ourselves in the theatre community, which has led to other professional opportunities for each of us, we've created work for over 150 people, and we've become known as really efficient, excellent producers.

J: But we never wanted to be producers! We became producers because nobody else was going to create these opportunities or mount these shows for us. We're producers by default, we're producers *by necessity.*

A: "Necessary Producers"?

J: Yes! And it's killing the artist in me.

A: Let's back up ... Convergence Theatre aside, tell me why, way back when, you decided to become a theatre artist in the first place.

J: I saw the movie *Annie* when I was five.

A: That's why you wanted to be an actor. But seriously – why make theatre?

J: Well ... theatre asks us to engage more fully with our society. It challenges us to look within ourselves, to examine the choices we make and how we treat each other. At the end of the day, people ultimately crave communal experiences. Which is what theatre is: a live, communal experience.

A: Exactly! Theatre isn't like other art forms – you need other people to create it and to witness it in a communal setting – friends and strangers, converging under the same roof and partaking in a ritual. It's about shared space. For a few hours we all agree to enter into another world together. Our experiences while in that world will differ depending on our own experiences and world views, but we do it communally, in real time, laughing collectively, crying collectively, sharing moments of recognition.

J: I think people need theatre now more than ever. We're in the middle of a technological revolution that's having a major sociological impact. On one hand we've never been more connected; on the other hand we've never been more isolated. Theatre demands that we break down those barriers of isolation; it asks us to come out from behind our screens.

A: You're not talking like someone who wants to throw in the towel.

J: You're missing the point – it's the harsh realities of creating theatre that's killing us, not our beliefs! This kind of life isn't sustainable. Look at it this way: a big show like *Passion Play* took roughly two years from start to finish to produce. Say I put in an average of 30 hours of producing work per week (recognizing that I'm also working many other theatre jobs at the same time). That's 3,120 hours of unpaid work over two years! I was also an actor in the show, so part of what I'm doing as a producer is fundraising my own salary so I can be paid as an actor for roughly 8 weeks of work.

A: A smart business person would ask, "Why not also fundraise your salary as a producer?"

J: Sure, that's always the hope, that there'll be something left for the producer in the end, but we all know that the producer's budget line is the first to go when other budget lines increase.

A: You were saying ...

J: So, 2 years = 104 weeks, 8 of which are paid acting work, which leaves 96 weeks of unpaid producing work. Those 96 weeks are sucking the desire to create theatre right out of me.

A: So that's it then? You quit?

J: That's harsh.

A: But you're maxed out?

J: Aren't you?

A: Sure, it's demoralizing. We (and so many artist-producers like us) put way more time and energy into making the work happen than actually making the work.

J: The administration vs. creation balance is waaaay off.

A: It's no wonder we're burnt out. There's no infrastructure to sustain us or support our growth. When you think that *Passion Play* cost $150,000 to put up, and we not only successfully raised that money with our partners, but created an impactful piece of theatre ... well, you'd think we'd be able to build on that somehow.

J: It's a horizontal ladder.

A: If we worked in a law firm we'd have made partner by now!

J: And after all this work, there's nothing left in Convergence Theatre's bank account to move forward with ...

A: Just you and me up in the middle of the night wondering what to do next.

J: By the way, I *hate* that – when people come up to me after a show and ask, "What are you up to next?" The dead body of the last play is still warm!

A: It makes the work seem totally disposable.

J: It's indicative of our theatre community's misplaced emphasis on quantity. Of course everyone is striving for quality, but there's this feeling that we've all gotta keep pumping out work in order to stay in the game.

A: Why?! So we can work two more years to bring yet another project to life only to have it disappear forever after what, a single three-week or four-week run? Even if a production is successful and it sells out, at the end of the run we have no way of extending the show or making it live again.

J: We just don't have the infrastructure or the funding to support longevity. The future feels bleak.

A: You're right – it's totally crazy to be doing this. Why does anyone do it? If you and I were able to make a living by being hired to act, direct, write, and teach, would we ever self-produce again?

J: I dunno ... I admit I get high on being in a position of control.

A: The original impulse was to be in a position to choose, remember? To have some control over how our careers unfold – more specifically to have control over how our projects unfold.

J: Gone are the days of waiting for the phone to ring with the offer of a gig. It's about being our own bosses.

A: But it's about more than just control, it's about being an artistic leader, a connector. Isn't that what all indie artists want, to some degree? To create, to initiate, to take risks?

J: Yes. To choose what we work on, how, and with whom is central. Also, as artistic leaders we're in a position to consider who the work is for and what the larger impact could be.

A: That's a whole conversation in itself – getting people to attend. How often do you go see an indie show and recognize more than half the audience?

J: Almost always. We're so used to putting on costumes and performing for our friends.

A: Even the granting bodies recognize the trend of low attendance and recommend budgeting for an overall average audience of 30 per cent ... that's just sad.

J: The theatre community is constantly complaining that there's "an audience problem" and that it's so hard to get "bums in seats" –

A: I hate that – it reduces people to a body part.

J: We're the problem, not the audience! On the whole, theatres still haven't found effective ways other than traditional marketing strategies to get people excited about attending live theatre. Especially young people.

A: If you build it they will come? No! One expensive ad in a newspaper does not an audience make!

J: Why do you think we've had a good track record of getting people out to see our shows?

A: In part because we don't have a season, which means we're not trying to sell five shows a year. But a big reason is that our productions tend to challenge people's perceptions and expectations of how and where theatre can take place.

J: The uniqueness of the location is a big reason why our attendance has been consistently high, I think.

A: It's never a gimmick. The location always serves the play or, in the case of *The Gladstone Variations*, is integral to the play. It's become clear that people crave a unique live experience.

J: One of the most exciting "aha" moments for me was sitting in the car during *AutoShow* and watching people's faces as they approached. I thought, "We're on to something here."

A: Which continued right on through to *Passion Play* – watching 100 people follow Queen Elizabeth across Danforth Avenue [*Figure 13.1*].

13.1 Maev Beaty as Queen Elizabeth in *Passion Play* by Sarah Ruhl (June 2013, Toronto). Photo by Keith Barker.

J: Or during the pre-show for *YICHUD* – people danced the hora and improvised with the bride and groom – it's amazing to connect with audiences on that level.

A: Yes – exploring different ways to push the boundaries of intimacy between performer and audience has always been a touchstone for us. We want our audience to feel that they're an integral part of their theatre-going experience; we invite them to be engaged participants, as opposed to simply passive observers.

J: Another reason why we've been successful at both getting people out to our shows and fundraising large amounts of money is because you and I make serious efforts to stay engaged with people. And this is by far one of the most stressful administrative burdens we've taken on, because maintaining relationships takes a lot of time and energy.

A: The Stratford Festival has whole departments devoted to donor relations – "Gifts Managers" – as well as people whose full-time jobs it is to work on audience development, group sales, and so on. At Convergence it's just you and me. Granted, we're smaller, but size is relative – what we do is still a lot for two people to manage.

J: If I've learned anything from self-producing it's that people give to us because it's *us.* They like us. They've built a relationship with us, be it socially or through doing community theatre with us or through our teaching work. They become invested in seeing us and our work succeed. Sometimes the particular project is even secondary to the fact that they're wanting to support you and I. Because we put in time with them.

A: And putting in time ... well ... takes *time!* It's good to be talking about the audience before anyone else – they're our customers, right? In one respect, they're the people we should be thinking about the most, and putting the most energy into staying connected to. If they don't keep showing up, spreading the word, the whole endeavour is pointless.

J: These "relationship values" also extends to our relationships with the artists we engage.

A: What did Mike Nichols say is the key to casting?

J: No assholes!

A: So true! And as producers it's important to show the professional artists we engage that we value them, and one way of doing that is making sure we always pay them, no matter how small an amount. Asking people to work for free means asking them to subsidize our dream with their time and energy, to care as much about our baby as we do, and that devalues them and their work.

J: And this is why our budgets are often so high – with such large ensembles, 70 per cent or so of the expenses go to paying people. That's another reason why I think we've been successful with grants and fundraising. We're not sinking money into lavish sets, we're paying *people*.

A: Yeah, just not ourselves! ... I want to get back to something you said earlier ... you used the word "burden" – is maintaining relationships, specifically with donors, really a burden to you?

J: Not necessarily the actual face time with people. Most of the donor relationships we have feel mutually enjoyable. But it's so hard to create work-life boundaries.

A: When a donor calls an artistic director they call her office number; when they call us they call our cell phone. Maybe we should pay for an office line ...

J: Out of our own pockets?!

A: So what makes it a "burden"?

J: When you have 200 donors, that's 200 thank-you notes, all with personal touches so it doesn't feel generic. It means making sure people get their incentives depending on their donor level, it means following up, checking in, taking care ... all of that is very time-consuming. The amount of time I spend on email alone makes me want to cut off my fingers!

A: You take expressing gratitude very seriously.

J: But we have to! How many times have we donated to a show and had no acknowledgment of the gift and no follow-up about the incentive? It's embarrassing!

A: This has actually been a big issue for us when we've partnered with larger institutions. We bring the donors to the project and then their staff spell their names wrong in the program! In the end it makes us look bad.

J: And how can we ever go back to those people and make future asks when we've abused their trust? I've become totally control-freaky about it because it reflects so poorly on our values. I mean, fundraising isn't about taking the money and running ... it's all about gratitude and relationship building, inviting people who give to recognize that they're an integral part of the picture. And that just takes time and constant care, there's no away around it.

A: Reminds me of that "Tent Talk" you moderated for the Fringe a few summers ago – that panel of "non-theatregoers."

J: Oh yeah ... that guy who I met randomly at a concert at SummerWorks who wasn't even aware that he was at a theatre festival! He insisted he disliked going to the theatre, and I managed to convince him to see a show that I thought he'd like based on his favourite movies. I gave him two comps, and he came and really loved it. After that I put him on our

e-list, and I wondered if he'd see our show the next summer but he
didn't. On the panel, I asked him why he didn't come, wasn't he reading our emails? He said, "Anything with the word 'theatre' in it I just
delete or it goes into my spam."

A: Amazing!

J: And I was like, "But you know who I am!" And he said, "I know who
you are, not the name of your theatre company." Even when I emailed
him to sit on that panel it took three times before he responded, and
it was the email that had his name in the subject line that finally got
his attention.

A: It just proves that the personal connection wins out every time.

J: But we have 3,000+ people on our e-list! How do we keep in touch with
3,000 people *and* pursue funding *and* keep up relations with donors
and get people to come *and* make the work???

A: It's exhausting.

J: The problem is there's no money for us to pay someone to do all the
admin work we need support doing. Because we operate on a project-
by-project basis, we can't access operating funding via grants.

A: Such is the way for artist-driven, non-incorporated, non-charitable
theatre companies like us.

J: Theatre. Company. That still doesn't quite feel like it adequately reflects who we are and what we do.

A: "Where's your theatre?" Love that question! The idea of not having
a venue puzzles some people, even though most theatre companies
across the country are non-venued.

J: Are you saying you want a venue?!

A: No! Just agreeing that the term "theatre company" has an old-school
ring to it.

J: Epiphany: If I had a T-shirt store and the T-shirts never turned a profit
and even started *costing* me money to make, I'd shut down the store,
right?!

A: Right.

J: Because businesses are meant to make money, not lose money.

A: Right. And the overall idea behind a not-for-profit is that we're only ever
meant to break even. Money comes in for a show and it gets put directly
into that show. We start at zero and finish at zero, with nothing much
left in the bank for the next project, not to mention our overhead costs.

J: We've been putting all of our energy and resources into the product –
the shows – and very few resources into the business – our company.
It's as if we've been making T-shirts for $100 but can only sell them for

$25 and have to raise the other $75 ourselves. That's the worst business model ever!

A: I just read in a Soulpepper show program that "less than half the cost of the season is covered by ticket sales with much of our mandate being non-revenue generating." They, like most theatre companies, rely on "philanthropic support," which makes up 40 per cent of their annual operating revenue.

J: That's how the arts generally work – in theatre, the expenses are almost always going to be greater than the box office revenue, and so we have to fundraise the rest ourselves.

A: Maybe we should seriously consider changing the scale of the work we do. Maybe massive-budget shows with huge ensembles aren't the smartest business model?

J: But whether the projects are small or large, the problems we face are still the same.

A: If I had a great idea for a one-person or two-person show, you'd be against that?

J: That's not the point. I won't be forced to only do small shows because they make more economic sense. We should all be doing the shows we need to do, period.

A: And our dreaming shouldn't be dictated by the flaws in the system. We should be dreaming big, all of us! And figuring out ways to make big dreams work, instead of settling.

J: There must be a way to build on all we've accomplished these past seven years ... try to flip the horizontal ladder into a vertical position.

A: Well, if operating funding would allow us to create some infrastructure and sustainability, why not bite the bullet and put together a board of directors so we can incorporate and be eligible for operating grants? Then we'd finally be able to hire someone to do all the admin work that bogs us down. Of course, there'd still be a ton of oversight, but we could hire an actual producer, not a necessary one.

J: But just because we're eligible for that kind of funding doesn't mean we're guaranteed it. The number of arts organizations has increased exponentially in the last 5–10 years, while the funding pool has substantially decreased. There's a lot of competition out there for operating funding ...

A: True, but once we're incorporated, we can apply for charitable status. We already operate like a not-for-profit, so why not take it a step further so we can provide our donors with tax receipts and increase our funding potential?

J: Do I need to remind you why "going charitable" is such a terrible idea for us?

A: Okay … let's re-cap: Our first two productions, *AutoShow* and *The Gladstone Variations*, started at the Toronto Fringe Festival and were fairly cost-effective and low-risk from a financial point of view. When we remounted *Gladstone* the budget was 20 times larger because we were no longer producing within a festival. It took us one year to raise those funds, and we were limited as to who we could ask for donations because we couldn't provide tax receipts. However, with *YICHUD* and *Passion Play* we created legitimate partnerships with theatres who are registered charities and who could provide our donors with tax receipts. This enabled us to make asks to foundations and increased the amounts that individual donors gave because of the tax receipt incentive. That said, for our next production –

J: If there is a next production –

A: – unless we create another legitimate partnership with a theatre who has charitable status, we have no way of accessing funds from the foundations with whom we've built relationships, and our individual gifts will likely decrease because we can no longer provide tax receipts. And so I ask you again, what's wrong with considering incorporation, charitable status, and establishing a board?

J: You mean a board that can hire and fire us?

A: That situation is a bit extreme …

J: Talk about management! We've acknowledged that the administration vs. art balance is already off. Why add another gigantic burden to our plate just so we can provide tax receipts? Time and time again we've seen small theatres get crushed under the administrative weight of becoming a charity because they felt it was the only way to grow but they couldn't actually sustain it.

A: I wish we had in Canada what they have in the United States – their tax laws allow for something called "fiscal sponsorships," where any non-profit can sponsor an organization or individual artist who is then permitted to use the non-profit's charitable number for the duration of the project. Canadian tax laws are much more rigid and don't allow one charitable entity to "umbrella" a non-charitable entity unless it's a legitimate partnership, such as a co-production.

J: You should read Jane Marsland's paper that she wrote as a research fellow at the Metcalf Foundation: "Shared Platforms and Charitable Venture Organizations: A Powerful Possibility for a More Resilient Arts Sector."[1] Jane, an avid arts advocate, champions the creation of a Canadian version of what you're talking about. That's the future …

A: In the States, and also in Europe, they have a much better track record for philanthropy and their tax laws reflect that.

J: Becoming a charity is totally antithetical to the mindset we need to create art. The whole concept behind not-for-profits is that they require oversight, which is why the rules for non-profits in Canada are way more stringent than they are for any for-profit small business.

A: And that level of oversight discourages risk, and risk is essential in art making.

J: I maintain that theatre is a business, not a charity! A theatre is not Run for the Cure or the United Way. When I think of those charities and then I think of theatres as charities ... that makes no sense to me.

A: So if the current model no longer reflects the ways in which we and so many artists like us are working, it's incumbent upon us not to change the art making but to change the models.

J: Exactly! Don't conform and "go charitable" just because it's the only model available to us right now ...

A: Society has this messed-up idea that art and commerce don't mix. But they absolutely do and ought to mix more often.

J: Artists often make excellent business managers.

A: Some of the most successful theatres are successful because they've placed artists at the centre of their organizations. Sure, not every artist has those skills or wants to be filling those roles, but we should remember that producing is a creative endeavour ... I don't think it's generally recognized that way.

J: And this is exactly why artist-driven companies are currently the primary incubators of new work in English Canada.

A: Artists know how to live and work on a shoestring budget. Artists know how to squeeze everything they can out of a dollar. Artists understand the value of in-kind donations, exchanges, and sharing of resources. Artists adhere to deadlines, they get "bottom lines" – there's no bottom line more unforgiving than "the audience is coming on this date and the show must go up no matter what."

J: Artists know how to collaborate, problem-solve, be flexible, adapt, improvise, and can be experts at conflict resolution.

A: And yet there continues to be this "us and them" mentality ...

J: Remember those statistics that were going around after the Harper government slashed some important arts funding for touring programs in 2008?

A: Yes! According to the Conference Board of Canada, in 2007, 1.1 million people across the country were employed in the arts and culture sector, which contributed $84.6 billion to the GDP. That's comparable to jobs in agriculture, forestry, fishing, mining, oil, and gas combined.[2]

J: I get it, I get it, the arts have value, the arts make money, the arts can and should be a central part of a society's economic well-being … you're preaching to the choir.

A: Which brings us back to theatre as a business.

J: Right, we're a small business and our product is theatre. We have three revenue streams when we're doing a show: box office, project grants, and fundraising. But what about the revenue streams when we're not in production mode? When we have no play to sell, therefore no box office.

A: And not being incorporated, we're ineligible for operating grants.

J: What if we fundraised for our operating in a grass-roots way like we do for our shows?

A: You mean "crowdsourcing"?

J: Yeah, but for our operating funding: "Give us the $25 you spend on lattes a month, and help us pay our Convergence Theatre bank fees for three months." We could approach our larger donors as well. Imagine someone funding a part-time producer for six months.

A: What's the incentive?

J: They contribute to our ability to plan our next steps, thereby becoming our "Operating Angels" and thus contributing to the health of our company and the birth of our next show.

A: Still, the larger donors will need a tax receipt …

J: What about focusing on education and outreach? Bringing theatre workshops into schools and communities.

A: These are good ideas, but the challenge remains that you and I will still spend most of our time administering these programs. We need to be able to pay someone to administer them.

J: Or we need someone who is willing to come on board for little to no money and raise their own salary via the administration of these fundraising initiatives.

A: Hmmm … or what about creating the $100 T-shirt?

J: Huh?

A: Look to the product itself. What if our next large-scale show is created with a for-profit commercial mindset? It's still high-quality theatre, but we create a product that people will pay for.

J: Why would people pay big bucks for "high-quality theatre" when they can go to the movies for $13 or just stay home and stream really good TV practically for free?

A: Why. That is the million-dollar question. What do people want and what will people pay for?

J: Can we create a product, a show, that can sustain itself over time? A show that could run indefinitely? A show that can reach beyond a typical theatre-going audience? What would attract the non-theatregoers? What will get them in the door and get them and their friends coming back for more?

A: There's a serious paradox at work here, though. We used to think that if we stayed as a small, project-to-project operation, we could just focus on the art making. We could go dormant between projects, each of us working our usual freelance jobs, and the Convergence producing machine would come to life again when we had an exciting idea.

J: That didn't happen though, mainly because we never really went dormant. We've just been working non-stop and careening towards burnout.

A: Yes – so the paradox: if we stay small, and keep going project to project, the energy and time required to get each project up is unsustainable. On the other hand, if we attempt to grow, think more long-term, and think "for-profit," we just increase the stress and workload and end up burning out anyhow.

J: Right. We can't be full-time creators and full-time administrators. Basically we need to find a way to fund and grow our small-scale business, by creating a model that serves and enhances the things we're already doing really well, as opposed to conforming to a system that would hamper us and eventually kill us.

A: We need to determine what kind of structures we need to invent in order to help artists like us grow and thrive both artistically and economically.

J: A model that allows us to be financially prudent while still allowing us to take artistic risks and explore new artistic territory.

A: We need to create the kind of organization that can live healthily somewhere between those two extremes and still authentically reflect our artistic visions and values.

J: And also a better working culture in the arts – it's not just about making the art, it's about *how* we make the art. Again, it comes down to building and maintaining healthy relationships with the groups of people who make our work possible, namely, our audience (which includes donors, sponsors, and *potential* donors and sponsors), our artistic partners, and our producing partners.

A: I'll add to that the importance of mentorship. Sure, we're all poor, but larger theatre companies can do a much better job of sharing their knowledge and resources beyond just, "Feel free to use our photocopier after hours"! Exchanges between large-scale and small-scale theatres and between senior, emerging, and mid-career artists is the only way to create a healthier arts ecology.

J: There's a quote I love that Nightwood Theatre once used in one of their brochures. It's by an American director named Anna Shapiro. She says, "I'm pretty sure the only way you get to have a life in the theatre is if somewhere in your life you come upon a group of people who, although they don't need you, make room for you."[3]

A: Yes! And we've been very fortunate – a lot of people have made room for us. But even more so, we've created our own spaces.

J: And maybe that's the key to our survival, to our sustainability and our future growth: we must make room for other people. We can no longer be just a two-person operation. We must expand and continue to put artists at the centre of Convergence Theatre, under our artistic leadership.

A: Which means sharing and expanding our core artistic and working values.

J: And making sure that we, as a smaller theatre company, don't end up replicating the problems of larger theatres.

A: Which inevitably comes down to our not conforming to current models that we know won't work for us –

J: But choosing and creating new structures that allow us to work flexibly and grow at our own pace.

A: You sound a lot more optimistic than when we started talking.

J: Don't worry, I'm not! I'm just not sure we can give up without really investigating all the questions we've raised. Where will the money come from? Can we do better than just survive? I don't know. Will we ever be able to grow in a way that reflects our working ecology?

A: Do you remember the transcript of the speech by Sean Holmes, the artistic director of the Lyric Hammersmith Theatre in the UK?

J: Yeah, it was about the launch of their "Secret Theatre" season.

A: Something he said stuck with me: "Maybe the existing structures of theatre in this country, whilst not corrupt, are corrupting … Structures forced by economic realities of course, but also by an unconscious acceptance of those structures."[4]

J: We have collectively become disillusioned with the traditions in which we are working. And so it's our prerogative, our duty, to imagine different structures for making theatre in the face of our own field's failure to provide career paths and growth for us and future generations of artists.

A: We have to empower ourselves and each other as *spaceholders*, as creators of an artistic context. Which brings us back to impact: *because we existed, something changed.* That's really what it comes down to – relationships and impact.

J: You're reminding me of the Jewish concept of *tikkun olam* – repairing the world.

A: What about it?

J: I really do believe that theatre is an integral part of repairing the world. Theatre is essentially my religion, the lens through which I see the world. When we were doing *YICHUD*, I realized that the same things that draw me to theatre draw me to Judaism: culture and community.

A: To be an active member of a larger community – I think that's a universal human desire.

J: If we can excite people about a live shared communal experience at the theatre, surprise people with what theatre is capable of, then we may just be able to create theatre-lovers for life, one theatregoer at a time.

A: We accept that the world is not in great shape. It's broken and needs more fixing than we can conceive of. The sheer amount of problems in the world, and the myriad of forces working against us as artists, as people, as citizens, makes us all feel powerless and hopeless at times.

J: Powerlessness and hopelessness – those too are communal experiences.

A: Maybe it's a little over-the-top idealistic, but why would we work ourselves to the edge of burnout for little to no money if we didn't truly believe that we are somehow contributing to building a better society? Theatre should reflect back to us what humans are capable of, help us ask ourselves how we ought to live.

J: Now more than ever, theatre can and must be a bulwark against despair.

NOTES

1 Jane Marsland, "Shared Platforms and Charitable Venture Organizations," *Metcalf Foundation*, June 2013, http://metcalffoundation.com/wp-content/uploads/2013/06/Shared-Platforms-and-CVOs.pdf.

2 Conference Board of Canada, "Positioning Canada's Culture Sector in the Global Market," in *Compendium of Research Papers: The International Forum on the Creative Economy* (Gatineau, QC: Conference Board of Canada, 2008), 46–51, http://www.sfu.ca/bcreative/files/resources/CreativeEconomy Compendium.pdf.

3 Anna Shapiro, quoted in Patricia Cohen, "Who's in Charge of This Show? She Is," *New York Times*, 24 June 2009, http://www.nytimes.com /2009/06/28/theater/28cohe.html.

4 A season launch speech given on 17 June 2013 by Sean Holmes, artistic director of the Lyric Hammersmith Theatre in London, announcing their "Secret Theatre" season. A reprint of the speech can be accessed here: Sean Holmes, "Maybe the Existing Structures of Theatre in This Country, Whilst Not Corrupt, Are Corrupting," WhatsOnStage.Com, 18 June 2013, http:// www.whatsonstage.com/london-theatre/news/06-2013/sean-holmes-maybe -the-existing-structures-of-theat_31033.html.

14 Are We There Yet? Using Theatre to Promote Positive Interdisciplinary Intercourse

JAMES MCKINNON

Why theatre now? Because it can solve problems and accomplish objectives that flummoxed scientists, sociologists, educators, and policymakers for decades. This chapter presents an answer to "Why theatre now?" that takes place in a world unaffected by the closures of playhouses or the greying of the subscription base – partly because it is a world with more urgent problems. The play I will discuss does not confront weighty metaphysical issues or challenge aesthetic frontiers; its purpose, simply put, is to help its audience make better choices about their lives. This may seem like an exceptionally ambitious project to those who think that theatre merely *reflects* reality, or a totally misguided one to those who, like Oscar Wilde, believe that the purpose of art is to conjure beautiful fantasies, not to discuss ugly truths or teach serious lessons. But this essay takes the position that theatre can and should seek to improve the lives of individuals and their communities by showing people how to make good choices and motivating them to do so. In addition, I will show how theatre can help researchers, universities, and health professionals – among others – in their missions to build better, healthier communities and improve society. Ultimately, I want to illustrate how, regardless of the apparent decline of the regional theatre model, theatre retains a vital purpose and presence as an effective medium for promoting the development and well-being of individuals and communities.

The play is *Are We There Yet?* (*AWTY*), by Edmonton playwright Jane Heather. It is a participatory play designed to equip adolescent audiences with skills, behaviours, and attitudes that help them avoid negative sexual experiences (including sexually transmitted infections and unplanned pregnancies). *Are We There Yet?* has been touring in Alberta since 1998 and has also been adapted for other communities across Canada. From 2006 to 2010, *Are We There Yet?* was the subject of a national

Community-University Research Alliance (CURA) project, funded by the Social Sciences and Humanities Research Council of Canada, which evaluated the efficacy of the play. This research project found strong evidence to suggest that *AWTY* works – in fact, it seems to be more effective than many of the better-known and more widely practised approaches to sexual health education. The CURA project reveals a way for theatre to transcend its traditional disciplinary confines and provide the impetus for innovative and effective interdisciplinary research initiatives. In chapter 11 of this book, Laura Levin argues the need for theatre to extend its "interdisciplinary reach" to consider how performance permeates many aspects of contemporary culture. In a similar spirit, *AWTY* and the CURA project illustrate how theatre can be used as an effective means of public pedagogy in other disciplines, and as I will argue, may be seen as an answer to the central question of this book.

The problem in which *Are We There Yet?* intervenes is an urgent one. Although most North American school systems have been integrating some form of sexual health education for several decades, research shows that "sex ed" has been ineffective, regardless of whether it focuses on disseminating knowledge (e.g., about reproduction and STIs) or on sending a clear message (typically either "sex before marriage is wrong" or "always use a condom"). Research shows that even though the majority of teens in North America have knowledge and values consistent with responsible sexual conduct, many are unable to translate these values into positive behaviours.[1] Adolescents are now far more likely to engage in sex before they finish high school than they were three decades ago: approximately 25 per cent of Canadians will have had sexual intercourse by the age of 16, with the majority of young Canadians initiating sexual intercourse between 16 and 19 years of age.[2] In addition, teens are engaging in sexual activities with multiple partners and are not using condoms.[3] The remainder of this essay will briefly describe the play and its special features, the research project and its findings, and how and why theatre succeeds where other methods fail. All three of these components – the play, the research alliance, and its findings about the play – offer their own answers to the question posed by this book. *Are We There Yet?* illustrates theatre's unique advantages for promoting learning, community development, and interdisciplinary research.

Are We There Yet? – The Play

Are We There Yet? uses the metaphor of learning to drive to frame a participatory dramatic examination of the beginning of sexual life. It focuses on difficult choices that adolescents must confront, often without much help – or rather, with an abundance of unhelpfully conflicting messages from popular media, peers, parents, and educators. It examines issues such as how to make decisions about sex, how to negotiate sexual comfort levels with a partner, how to navigate awkward conversations about sexual health and conversations, and so on. It also includes scenes that acknowledge the mixed messages sent by conventional sex-education content (such as a parody of a cheesy film about puberty) and popular culture (including a sequence where the participants get to construct their "ideal" male and female sex idol and then deflate them), in order to help teens "sift through all the messages that bombard them and determine safe and respectful sexual practices in their own worlds and relationships."[4] It dramatizes situations such as discussing sex with a parent; discussing sexual comfort zones with a partner and dealing with the possibility of different comfort levels; discussing topics like sexual health and condom use; and dealing with the unrealistic expectations and pressures that result from being saturated with highly sexualized popular media.

Are We There Yet? was originally produced by Concrete Theatre in Edmonton. Every year from 1998 to 2013 the company has remounted a new production, which goes on tour all over Alberta. The play has also been adapted for different regions and communities, including an urban adaptation for Vancouver, a rural adaptation for Nova Scotia, and an aboriginal adaptation for Saskatchewan. It has also been performed in Toronto. The play is typically (and ideally) delivered as part of a package including a follow-up sexual health workshop offered by a community-based partner. The Concrete Theatre production typically introduced this partner at the performance, where he or she could field technical questions during and after the performance.

Are We There Yet? alternates between scripted, realistic scenes and participatory sequences wherein the audience gives the characters suggestions and advice about how to deal with difficult situations. In other words, audience members are invited to ask the performers to test the likely outcomes of various courses of action for dealing with tense situations that they will likely encounter soon, if they have not already. In the framing prologue of the performance, the actors encourage the students to be creative and even ludicrous when they give "advice" – contrary to the accustomed practices of their classrooms – as long as it is not aggressive, offensive, or otherwise disrespectful. Within this atmosphere, participants are allowed to remain relatively anonymous, and can ask serious questions under a guise of jesting. ("Obviously I knew all along that *that* was a silly thing to suggest. I just wanted to see if the actors would do it.") In fact, the actors *will* attempt to put the participants' advice, however silly, into action. This demonstration of respect and willingness to honour their end of the bargain earns trust; and since most ludicrous courses of action end the scenario quickly and unsuccessfully, participants tend to tire of them quickly and move on to the more interesting challenge of helping the characters *succeed.* Thus the participants can experiment, by proxy, with tactics for resolving personal dilemmas and observe what works and what does not.

Unlike many, if not most, sexual health programs, the primary objective of *Are We There Yet?* is not to transmit information about how reproductive organs work or how to protect oneself from STIs and unplanned pregnancy; instead, it aims at helping participants develop and practise the skills and attitudes they need to *use* that information "to normalize sexuality in a positive way."[5] The play presumes that knowledge about sex and its implications – of which most adolescents have, if anything, an overabundance – is useless if one does not possess the confidence and self-reliance to use it effectively. Teenagers experience unplanned pregnancies and STIs not because they were ignorant of them, but more likely because they found the prospect of discussing those issues more terrifying than the possible traumatic outcomes of unprotected sex. *Are We There Yet?* uses the framing metaphor of learning to drive to allow its participants to conceive of the embarrassing aspects of the unpredictable and unstable adolescent body in familiar terms, and the participatory episodes allow them to practise putting their knowledge to use in a safe, hypothetical situation and to observe their peers doing the same.

Because the play's utility derives from its ability to meet the needs and interests of its specific audience, it has been adapted to serve audiences in different social and regional circumstances. For example, one of the participatory scenes has the actors inviting suggestions from the audience about where one might go to get condoms. When the play was performed for a rural aboriginal community in Saskatchewan, this scene was replaced, because local health services ensure that condoms are both familiar and widely available in the community. On the other hand, when it was adapted for Nova Scotia, a scene that takes place at the mall – where the characters went to buy condoms – had to be relocated because there were no malls to go to, and condoms were more difficult to acquire (particularly anonymously) in the conservative, rural communities the play visited. Each regional adaptation also has other distinctive qualities, particularly in casting. One of the central principles of this type of theatre is that the people in the audience are given opportunities to advise characters who are like themselves. The actors, therefore, must reflect the community as much as possible, so they are always young enough to represent teenagers with authenticity, and casting for local adaptations typically reflects the ethnic and cultural demographic of the community – insofar as it is possible to do so with a cast of four.

Community-University Research Alliance (CURA)

Both the objectives and constitution of the project provide a good example of how theatre can become a vital nexus for community development and interdisciplinary collaboration – and its findings offer a frank and compelling answer to the central question of this book.

Project partners included playwrights Jane Heather and Kenneth Williams (author of the Saskatchewan adaptation); theatre companies which produced and toured each of the four regional adaptations (Concrete Theatre in Edmonton, Mulgrave Road Theatre in Nova Scotia, Neworld Theatre in Vancouver, and the Saskatchewan Native Theatre Company); researchers and graduate students in theatre, sexual health, human ecology, and occupational therapy, representing three major universities (Alberta, British Columbia, and Guelph); and health services partners and schools in the communities served by each regional adaptation. The lead investigators included Jan Selman (drama), Brenda Munro (human ecology), Jim Ponzetti (social work), and Shaniff Esmail (occupational therapy).[6] For the principal investigators, the CURA created a unique opportunity for interdisciplinary research, with theatre at its hub; it also provided a valuable opportunity for graduate and postgraduate researchers to gain experience and insight into the research mission of the university.

The principal objectives of the CURA were to develop a sound method, incorporating both quantitative and qualitative research methods, to assess the impact of using participatory theatre in community and educational programming, and particularly to evaluate the impact of the *Are We There Yet?* program (AWTYP[7]) on its audiences. The CURA investigated the necessity and efficacy of regional adaptations to suit local communities, the role of "identity style" in sexual decision-making, and "culturally and socially effective community partnerships and mobilization models for health promotion and harm reduction."[8] The ultimate goal of the research project was to determine what effect the AWTYP had on the behaviours and attitudes of its audiences: did watching the play (and participating in the follow-up workshop) make young audiences more likely to make healthy, positive decisions about sex? While a full discussion of the data and analysis is beyond the scope of this chapter, in general the findings have been very positive. They also have broader implications for the future of theatre, which, for all its liabilities in an increasingly competitive entertainment market, seems to possess unique advantages in the arenas of community development and education.

The Research Process

A questionnaire developed by an interdisciplinary team with backgrounds in sociology, family studies, occupational therapy, developmental psychology, and theatre was administered to students before and after they participated in the AWTYP. Students (including a control group) also answered a follow-up questionnaire a month later. Well over 800 participants were sampled from audiences in Edmonton, Saskatchewan, and Nova Scotia. To assess the efficacy of the program on different kinds of students, the survey collected demographic information about age, gender, and identity style orientations.[9] It also asked students about their behaviours and attitudes related to sexual decision-making and about their response to the play. Since there were no extant instruments for measuring the effect of participatory theatre on spectators, the research team created one – this alone is a significant outcome of the collaboration between theatre and social science research. The survey measured five aspects of theatrical reception, determined by a review of theatre theorists dating back to Aristotle and his *Poetics* and forward to Brecht, Boal, Marvin Carlson, and others: pleasure, identification, empathy, participation, and impact.[10] The qualitative inquiry sought to flesh out the findings of the survey by giving participants an opportunity to elaborate on their responses and by exploring how they constructed their experience of the play. It also revealed impacts and outcomes that the survey alone could not, such as one student's decision to end an abusive relationship in the wake of the play, and another's realization that she was a victim of sexual assault and that she needed to seek help.[11] Focus groups and interviews also shed light on the degree to which each participant influences the content, direction, and meanings of the play and interprets its meaning within his or her own unique framework, so that no two performances, or receptions, are the same.

The research findings are positive. A large majority reported pleasure (89 per cent), identification (62 per cent), and empathy (63 per cent);

more than half (56 per cent) reported participating in the play; and 74 per cent agreed that they will use the experience to make better choices in the future.[12] Students were struck by the authenticity of the play's content and reported that they found it more engaging and preferable to either conventional classroom-based "sex ed" lessons or seeking information from their parents – although several females reported that the play led them to have "very open and deep conversations with their mothers."[13] Outcome measures were also positive when compared to the control group. After participating in the AWTYP, students reported less embarrassment and difficulty with communicating about sex, increased awareness of the importance of setting and communicating personal boundaries, and more confidence asserting their boundaries. One key finding was that theatre may have a significant impact *even on youth who claim otherwise*: the "diffuse-avoidance" group – youth characterized by a tendency to delay and defer decision-making – perceived themselves as being less affected than others, but outcome measures suggest that they may have been *more* affected than others.[14]

The research findings, in and of themselves, suggest a powerful answer to the central question of this book: theatre can have a measurable, positive impact on the real-life behaviours of the people who participate in it. Youth who participated in the AWTYP were generally more likely to make positive, safe choices about their sexuality than they were before participating and when compared to a control group. Moreover, theatre can achieve these results where *other options have failed*. Teens in all focus groups commented on the superior realism and enjoyability of *AWTY* compared to regular classroom programming. In the following section I will attempt to explain the results, both in terms of the social science theories driving the assessment and from the theoretical perspectives on theatre that motivated the creation of the play in the first place.

How Does Participatory Theatre Succeed Where "Sex Ed" Fails?

The success of the *AWTY* program contrasts sharply with the well-documented failure of the conventional models of sexual health education that it responds to, and examining the underlying causes of these failures helps shed light on why and how participatory theatre can provide a productive alternative. The first-generation of "sex ed" focused on sexual health literacy and emphasized transmitting knowledge about sexual reproduction and STIs.[15] Although evaluations of this approach showed that student knowledge increased, it did not appear to affect the behaviours leading to pregnancy and sexually transmitted diseases.

The next generation of sexual health programs, therefore, focused on transmitting a *message* rather than information. The message was usually either "intercourse before marriage is dangerous and wrong"[16] or "always use a condom." Neither of these approaches has succeeded in appreciably reducing risky sexual behaviours.[17]

The information-based model fails in its assumption that knowing abstract biological facts assists people with making immediate, personal decisions. The second model fails because its focus on a single message makes it useless to anyone in any situation to which the message does not apply. People who are already sexually active do not benefit from an "abstinence-only" message, which does not allow adolescents to take ownership of their sexuality. On the other hand, the "always use a condom" message offers little help to someone who lacks the self-efficacy and skills to decline an unwanted sexual advance. When researchers asked students themselves why they thought sexual education is not working, the participants confirmed that in their experience, sexual health programming was both dull and "unrelated to the real world."[18] In addition, the format or medium of sexual health education is often incompatible with its stated intentions: most sexual health programs extol the virtues of assertiveness, but they do so in the form of lectures and "educational" films which the students are expected to passively absorb.

The theory of learning domains helps explain both the failures of conventional sex ed and the potential of theatre-based models. Thomas Reeves points out that learning outcomes in primary and secondary education are typically defined in relation to three major domains: cognitive ("to know" or "to think"), affective ("to feel" or "to care"), and psychomotor ("skilled behaviour").[19] Sexual health education fails when it focuses exclusively on the cognitive domain (e.g., knowledge about sexual reproduction), or the affective domain (e.g., by invoking a sense of fear and shame about the consequences of risky sexual practices). Moreover, as Reeves points out, there is a fourth domain, which is frequently omitted: the conative, which is the domain of volition or *action*.

Simply put, effective sexuality education needs to focus not (or not only) on providing accurate information but on *motivating behavioural change*. To identify and assert one's sexual boundaries requires a capacity to *act*, not merely knowledge or fear about the consequences of failing to act. It also requires knowledge about which action to take; in regard to the psychomotor domain, the "skilled behaviour" in question must be correctly identified, and in safeguarding sexual health, the ability to communicate one's sexual boundaries and interests is more important (and more difficult) than the ability to use a condom. It is not simply a lack of information (or manual dexterity) that leads to negative outcomes from sexual activity, but a combination of not knowing which action to take and/or not believing that it will work.[20]

Pleasure and Empathy

Theatre is not merely a discipline to be learned – it is, critically, a *medium of learning*, as many of its practitioners and theorists dating back to Aristotle have noted.[21] Several key factors make theatre – particularly *participatory* theatre – an ideal medium for effective sexual health education. First, theatre creates *pleasure*; indeed, even Brecht, one of the most stridently didactic theatre artists, claims that pleasure "is the noblest function that we have found for theatre."[22] Although many students do not associate pleasure with "being taught," it is most certainly associated with powerful learning experiences. As noted earlier, if the purpose of a lesson is (as in this case) to motivate behavioural change, it must target the affective domain as well as the cognitive. Pleasure includes, but is not limited to, the experience of "delight," says *AWTY-CURA* investigator Jan Selman. "When considering pleasure, we need to think about it in the plural – the pleasures of humour, arousal of emotions, empathy, or a moment's reflection, of recognition, insight, of being transported to a new or strange place, of being endowed with intelligence, of taking power. All these and more are parts of this phenomena."[23] *Are We There Yet?* offers a variety of pleasures, perhaps beginning with the pleasure of catching on to the driving/sexuality metaphor presented in the first part of the play:

INSTRUCTOR: Lesson One: Know your vehicle. What you need to know before you start the car.
   Mechanics and Equipment

ACTORS hold up two cartoon diagrams of the human body, one male and one female. INSTRUCTOR uses a pointer to point to different parts of the body through the demonstration.

   The engine *[points to head]*: the control centre, everything is routed through here including the gas pedal and the brake pedal.
   Signal lights *[mouth]*: to signal to others when you want to slow down, stop or change direction.
   The windows and mirrors *[ears and eyes]*: must be kept clear to hear and see incoming messages and signals.

Other standard equipment includes headlights *[breasts]*, gearshift lever *[boy parts]*, glove compartment *[girl parts]*, and various other knobs, buttons, dials, gauges, etc. scattered through the vehicle *[whole body sweep]*.[24]

AWTY scored very highly in the category of pleasure, with over 90 per cent of audiences indicating that they enjoyed the play, a finding confirmed by qualitative data. In addition, analysis of the data shows that the level of pleasure correlates positively with positive outcomes for spectators: the more they enjoy, the more they learn.[25]

Theatre also reinforces learning through *identification* and *empathy*, by building emotional involvement with characters. "Make a character worthy of our concern, we care more. Make a character attractive, we engage. Add a foible, they are human, so more like us. Put them at risk, we get emotionally involved."[26] Jeanne Klein posits a correlation between the spectator's capacity for identification and their learning outcomes: when spectators strongly identify with a character and the situations he or she confronts, they "may likely adopt the character's prosocial and/or antisocial behaviors in similar situations."[27] For one spectator this identification caused her to realize that she was in a bad situation and had to take action:

I saw the play and then I saw a couple of things he did to me in the play and that was pretty much what ended the relationship, I couldn't stay in it after that ... [B]efore I saw it, I think I knew what was going on. I just didn't want to admit it and it was a little bit hard to ignore after I saw the play.[28]

As with pleasure, the researchers found that the spectators' reported level of identification and empathy corresponded positively with learning outcomes: the more strongly students identified with and empathized with the characters, the more able they were to communicate about sexual issues and boundaries. Identification and empathy also motivated participation – students reported that they gave advice to make the play "entertaining and fun," but also because "they wanted to guide the characters to make better decisions"[29] – and participation levels, in turn, correspond with more powerful learning, as outlined in the next section.

Participation and Critical Distance

Theatre creates immersion and empathy but also enables the "critical social reflection leading to social change that Brecht sees as central to theater."[30] *AWTY* uses "characters like me" to create empathy and a variety of formal and theatrical devices to interrupt emotional immersion in the story and create critical distance, including "the juxtaposition of theatrical styles and points of view, the use of multiple characters and actor/character transformations, actors' informal interaction with the audience as themselves before and after the show, and direct audience address."[31] In a moment of crisis, the character turns to the audience for help. In one scene, Mac tries to convince the audience that he doesn't need to use a condom: "[E]verybody knows it's just not as good for the guy. Like it reduces the sensation, that's what my brother says. And we don't have diseases so maybe we don't need them."[32] The audience sees right through his feeble objections because although they may empathize with his crisis, they see it from a critical distance. The real issue, as they soon reveal, is that he's embarrassed and overwhelmed by the prospect of selecting and buying condoms. Mac gathers feedback from the audience but spars with them: rather than accepting their advice immediately, he blocks and parries, forcing participants to work harder and develop stronger arguments.[33]

These participatory elements of *AWTY* align with both social learning theory (SLT) and constructionist learning theory. Theatre encourages learning through observing others and modelling their behaviour, which, according to SLT (and Aristotle's theory of mimesis[34]) is one of the most powerful ways people learn how to negotiate the world and has also proved effective in other sexuality education contexts.[35] In addition, constructionist learning theory proposes that learning experiences are more powerful when they involve opportunities for learners to transform the world around them and have productive impacts on their environment. Both kinds of learning take place in sections of *AWTY* which invite participants to give advice that will influence the outcome of a story. During the scene with Mac, the active participants are practising, by proxy, precisely the skills and motivations *AWTY* wants them to develop. By helping Mac confront his fears, they are confronting their own. Meanwhile, the students who observe rather than directly participating are absorbing information about the social norms in their community and comparing their classmates' behaviours to their own. Similarly, in "Lesson Two," the characters Marcel and Delphi, who have been dating for a few weeks, discover that they have different levels of comfort with sex, and the audience is asked to diagnose the problem and propose a remedy. Students are encouraged to toss out suggestions spontaneously and simultaneously – there is no "raise your hand" rule, so they can speak with relative anonymity. Those who offer suggestions get an opportunity to see how they play out in a simulation of reality and exert a productive influence on the world; those who choose to watch learn by observing the actions of both their peers and the characters. Importantly, everyone gets to see the consequences of "bad" choices as well as good ones. Often, students suggest a "compromise," which is an effective resolution strategy in other circumstances but not in this case. When the actors explore the implications of "compromise," the students realize that this would actually force one party to go farther than he/she is comfortable with, and this allows all the participants to revise their beliefs without facing the stigma of giving a wrong answer.

Participatory theatre enables student-centred learning by allowing the audience to actively influence the content and direction of the performance. Active discussion and participation sections pitch the content of each performance to the specific and eclectic needs of the spectators, because their needs and interests drive the discussion. Students can influence the content and the field and level of discourse, which helps them integrate and synthesize knowledge into their current levels of experience.[36] Their suggestions are discussed, debated, and put into action, and the possible consequences of suggested actions are also explored. This active discussion is fruitful for students with different needs: those for whom the first sexual experience is still on the horizon may leave the session feeling more confident about their ability to deal with awkward situations when they arise, while those who are already sexually active may reconsider their behaviour in light of what they have discussed and observed.

Participatory theatre is an ideal medium for encouraging active, engaged learning because – as scholarship on teaching and learning frequently argue – the method of delivery and the environment in which the content is delivered are as important as the content itself. To create a positive, productive, safe environment, the play and the actors deploy humour to release tension, dispel anxiety, and signal their acceptance of the spectators. Humour also arouses affective interest, thus motivating participation. By treating the audience as a collective and encouraging the spectators to yell out suggestions as they please without asking permission or raising their hands, the actors signal that different rules apply here. Participatory theatre creates a safe yet engaging atmosphere which encourages the spectators to talk about the situations on stage and, by proxy, in their lives.

As a vehicle for content, participatory theatre activities are more engaging than knowledge transmission activities and better at accommodating individual needs than static media like films and textbooks.

Increasingly, as we age, learning becomes associated with cognitive activities, and thus it becomes, for most people, more boring and less transformative. Role playing, which has been proven effective in other studies as well,[37] is particularly helpful when encouraging the discussion of personal boundaries. *Are We There Yet?* shifts the focus away from passively absorbing information and instead tasks participants with directing the characters through challenging situations. When they do so, they experience agency, success, and the self-efficacy and confidence noted as necessary for making healthy choices regarding sexuality.[38] To the extent that the participants empathize and identify with the characters, the affective domain is engaged; and the act of intervening in and helping solve a difficult situation for the characters involves both the conative domain (the capacity to act) and the psychomotor domain – because the "skilled behaviour" in this case is precisely the ability to use communication to intervene in and defuse a tense situation.

Conclusion

The *Are We There Yet?* program and Community-University Research Alliance present some compelling answers to the question "Why theatre now?" For one thing, the research findings serve as a strong reminder that theatre is not simply a discipline or subject to be learned but – and rather uniquely among the subjects encountered in a university course catalogue – a *medium* of teaching and learning, and an exceptionally powerful one at that. This lesson is reiterated again and again in both theatre theory and practice, from Aristotle to Brecht to Boal, and confirmed by the various theories of teaching and learning mentioned earlier.[39] In principle and in practice, participatory theatre is one of the most effective means yet seen for promoting sexual health – and thereby, healthy communities. It should be considered more often as a means for teaching and learning, particularly when the "lesson" entails the internalization of attitudes and behaviours, as opposed to the transmission or absorption of facts. In addition, the interdisciplinary *AWTY*-CURA model shows how theatre can play a vital role in the social mission of universities in Canada and worldwide. Although the public has increasingly come to view universities in terms of "post-secondary education," their primary role remains the production and dissemination of knowledge that benefits society. *Are We There Yet?* performs this role in several ways. First, the play puts advanced knowledge about sexual health into practice, effectively and broadly applying the findings of social science and sexual health research. Few grade nine students benefit directly from peer-reviewed journal publications, but many have benefited from participatory theatre. Second, the CURA shows how theatre can advance its own cause by seeking productive and mutually beneficial connections with other disciplines. In many universities, theatre and drama are formally associated with literary studies, but it may have much more to gain from – and much more to offer to – alliances with other disciplines, particularly those that share the desire to transform society through direct intervention and those that share its collaborative working models and speculative, experimental outlook. These alliances are critical to the survival of theatre, because if the general public comes to see theatre only as a moribund art form, its viability as a field of post-secondary studies will be seriously jeopardized. Emile Zola warned over a century ago that theatre must align itself with the modern scientific revolution, or perish;[40] while his faith in positivism (and naturalism) may now seem naively optimistic, his fantasy of an alliance between theatre and social science still has much to offer – to both parties.

NOTES

1 F. Scott Christopher and Rodney M. Cate, "Factors Involved in Premarital Sexual Decision-making," *Journal of Sex Research* 20 (1984): 363–76; Marita McCabe and Eoin J. Killackey, "Sexual Decision Making in Young Women," *Sexual and Relationship Therapy* 19, no. 1 (2004): 15–27; and Laurie Zabin et al., "Adolescent Sexual Attitudes and Behavior: Are They Consistent?" *Family Planning Perspectives* 16, no. 4 (1984): 181–5b.

2 Alexander McKay, "Prevention of Sexually Transmitted Infections in Different Populations: A Review of Behaviourally Effective and Cost-effective Interventions," *Canadian Journal of Human Sexuality* 9 (2000): 95–120.

3 Eleanor Maticka-Tyndale, "Reducing the Incidence of Sexually Transmitted Disease through Behavioural and Social Change," *Canadian Journal of Human Sexuality* 6, no. 2 (1997): 89–104. For reviews see Lisa Crockett, Marcela Raffaelli, and Kristin L. Moilanen, "Adolescent Sexuality: Behavior and Meaning," in *Blackwell Handbook of Adolescence*, ed. Gerald R. Adams and Michael D. Berzonsky (Malden, MA: Blackwell, 2003), 371–92; Brent C. Miller et al., "Adolescent Pregnancy and Childbearing," in *Blackwell Handbook of Adolescence*, ed. Gerald R. Adams and Michael D. Berzonsky (Malden, MA: Blackwell, 2003), 415–49. Also see Loretta E. Gavin et al., "A Review of Positive Youth Development Programs that Promote Adolescent Sexual and Reproductive Health," *Journal of Adolescent Health* 46, no. 3 (2010): S75–S91.

4 Jim Ponzetti et al., "The Effectiveness of Participatory Theatre with Early Adolescents in School-based Sexuality Education," *Sex Education* 9, no. 1 (2009): 96, doi:10.1080/14681810802639905.

5 Ibid.

6 Jan Selman, "Research," *Are We There Yet?* (*University of Alberta*, 17 October 2013), http://www.ualberta.ca/AWTY/research.html.

7 The "*Are We There Yet?* program" refers to both the play and the accompanying follow-up workshop run by the sexual health professional who travelled with the actors. Not all schools opted to include the workshop, but all were encouraged to.

8 Selman, "Research."

9 Brenda Munro et al., "Identity: Is Theatre an Asset in Dealing with Hard-to-Reach Youth?" *International Journal of Learning* 16, no. 6 (2009): 101–15.

10 See Aristotle, *Poetics*, ed. and trans. Richard Janko (Indianapolis: Hackett, 1987); Bertolt Brecht, "Theatre for Pleasure or Theatre for Instruction," in *Brecht on Theatre*, trans. John Willett (New York: Hill and Wang, 1964), 69–76; Augusto Boal, *Theater of the Oppressed* (New York: Urizen, 1979); and Marvin Carlson, *Theories of the Theatre* (Ithaca, NY: Cornell University Press, 1993).

11 Shaniff Esmail, James McKinnon, and Brenda Munro, "Internal Combustion: Sexual Health Education: Urgency and Strategies for Change," in *Theatre, Teens, Sex Ed: Are We There Yet?*, ed. Jan Selman and Jane Heather, (Edmonton: University of Alberta Press, 2015), 21–45.

12 Ibid.

13 Ibid.

14 Munro et al., "Identity."

15 Betty M. Hubbard, Mark L. Giese, and Jacquie Rainey, "A Replication Study of 'Reducing the Risk,' A Theory-based Sexuality Curriculum for Adolescents," *Journal of School Health* 68, no. 6 (1998): 243–7.

16 Ibid.

17 Ibid. Also see Ingela Lundin Kvalem et al., "The Effect of Sex Education on Adolescents' Use of Condoms: Applying the Solomon Four-group Design," *Health Education & Behavior* 23, no. 1 (1996): 34–47, doi:10.1177/109019819602300103.

18 Donald B. Langille et al., "So Many Bricks in the Wall: Young Women in Nova Scotia Speak About the Barriers to School-Based Sexual Health Education," *Sex Education* 1, no. 3 (2001): 245–57.

19 Thomas Reeves, "How Do You Know They Are Learning? The Importance of Alignment in Higher Education," *International Journal of Learning Technology* 2, no. 4 (2006): 294–309.

20 This model is consistent with others, such as the information motivation
behaviour (IMB) model, which proposes that learning activities need to
motivate behavioural change as well as providing information, and the
health belief model, which states that individuals will act to protect their
health when (a) they perceive their vulnerability to a specific threat and
(b) they believe that they can reduce their vulnerability by taking a single,
specific action. See Jeffrey D. Fisher and William A. Fisher, "Theoretical
Approaches to Individual-level Change in HIV Risk Behavior," in *Handbook
of HIV Prevention*, ed. John L. Peterson and Ralph J. DiClements (New York:
Kluwer Academic, 2000), 3–55; William A. Fisher and Jeffrey D. Fisher,
"Understanding and Promoting Sexual and Reproductive Health Behavior:
Theory and Method," *Annual Review of Sex Research* 9 (1998): 39–76.

21 Even theatre's enemies and detractors acknowledge that it is a powerful tool
for learning – indeed this is what makes theatre so dangerous to commen-
tators like Stephen Gosson, who called theatre the "School of Abuse." See
Stephen Gosson, *Schoole of Abuse, Containing a Pleasant Invective Against Poets,
Pipers, Plaiers, Jesters and Such Like Caterpillars of the Commonwealth* (London,
1579).

22 Brecht, *Brecht on Theatre*, 180.

23 Jan Selman, "It's the Wheel Thing: What Can Theatre Do? And How Do We
Know?" in *Theatre, Teens, Sex Ed: Are We There Yet?*, ed. Jan Selman and Jane
Heather (Edmonton: University of Alberta Press, 2015), 412. See also Anne
Ubersfeld, "The Pleasure of the Spectator," *Modern Drama* 25, no. 1 (1982):
27–39.

24 Jane Heather, "Are We There Yet?" (unpublished play script, University of
Alberta, 1998; rev. ed., 2006), 5, http://www.ualberta.ca/AWTY.

25 Selman, "It's the Wheel Thing."

26 Ibid.

27 Jeanne Klein, "From Children's Perspectives: A Model of Aesthetic Processing in Theatre," *Journal of Aesthetic Education* 39, no. 4 (2005): 49–50.

28 Audience member quoted in Selman, "It's the Wheel Thing."

29 Selman, "It's the Wheel Thing," 423.

30 Angela Curran, "Brecht's Criticisms of Aristotle's Aesthetics of Tragedy,"
Journal of Aesthetics and Art Criticism 59, no. 2 (2001): 171. See also Brecht,
Brecht on Theatre.

31 Selman, "It's the Wheel Thing," 425.

32 Ibid., 428.

33 Ibid., 430.

34 See Aristotle, *Poetics*.

35 See Marvin Eisen, Gail L. Zellman, and Alfred L. McAlister, "Evaluating the
Impact of a Theory-based Sexuality and Contraceptive Education Program,"

Family Planning Perspectives 22 (1990): 261–71; Wayne Weiten, *Psychology: Themes and Variations*, 5th ed. (Belmont, CA: Wadsworth Thompson Learning, 2001).

36 Esmail, Munro, and McKinnon, "Sexual Health Education."

37 Ibid.

38 "Health Canada, Population and Public Health Branch," in *Canadian Guidelines for Sexual Health Education* (Ottawa: Health Canada, 2003).

39 See Aristotle, *Poetics*; Brecht, *Brecht on Theatre*; Boal, *Theater of the Oppressed*.

40 Emile Zola, "Naturalism on the Stage," in *Dramatic Theory and Criticism: Greeks to Grotowski*, ed. Bernard Dukore and trans. Belle M. Sherman (New York: Holt Rinehart & Winston, 1974), 692–719.

15 Thinking Beyond the Boundaries of Theatre, Math, and Reality

JOHN MIGHTON IN CONVERSATION WITH
KATHLEEN GALLAGHER

On 18 October 2013, Kathleen Gallagher conducted an interview with mathematician and Siminovitch Prize–winning playwright John Mighton, in front of an audience at Hart House Theatre. The interview, staged as a lead-up event to the announcement of the 2013 Siminovitch Prize, addressed issues to do with education and theatre, and it demonstrated John's unique interdisciplinary perspective on the role of theatre today.

John: I think one of the reasons we struggle in theatre, why theatre struggles to find audiences now, is because we have a population that's not really been educated according to their full potential. Consequently, many, many people start to lose their sense of curiosity, their sense of wonder, their sense of engagement, empathy, all those things. I think children are born with this infinite sense of curiosity and wonder, and over and over they're told that they can't do certain things that aren't important to adults, and that is their experience through school. So they're lucky to survive leaving with one interest by the end of high school. I think we'll never have a flourishing theatre or artistic community until we start to address these problems.

Kathleen: So maybe one of the problems that you're talking about is this idea that one either has talent in the arts or talent in sciences and math and technology, but can't be gifted in both those areas.

John: Yeah, it's as if you're using one half of your brain, you have to leave the other half empty for storage ... Less than 50 years ago, people thought women couldn't do mathematics. We had slaves less than a hundred years ago. We see differences between people or things people can't do and we just assume they're genetic or natural or inborn, and we still haven't really gotten very far beyond that, otherwise people would be protesting the state of education now. They would be; they would recognize it as probably the most serious issue facing us. I hope one day we'll look back on this as a kind of dark age, that we'll recognize how little we actually did to educate children. I mean we've made a lot of progress, we've made enormous progress on every front, but we really haven't even begun to tap into a fraction of the potential that children have. Not just for academic success but for joy, a sense of wonder, a sense of self-efficacy, and motivation.

Kathleen: But there are many reasons why we hold onto that kind of thinking; it serves many interests. It's not that we're just unenlightened, it actually serves the labour market. It serves many interests.

John: Yeah, that's a really difficult issue. It certainly produces people who accept low wages and will work in very terrible conditions. But in the long run it doesn't really service our economy at all, if you take a wider view. We'd have a much more productive economy with a well-educated population. There's even deeper losses that come from failing to educate people. We think, if our government put walls around our national parks and said only certain people can come in here, that only certain people have the talent to come in here and appreciate this beauty, we'd think that was insane. But that's what we've done in the arts, in both the arts and the sciences. For instance, we'd think children were stunted if they didn't see any beauty in the visible world, in a mountain or a star, but we think it's natural for them to see no beauty in the invisible world, the incredible patterns and connections that extend through time and space and connect everything in the universe. We think it's natural that they have no appreciation of the absolutely awe-inspiring elegance of the universe. Whether you believe there's a creator or not, constantly it outstrips our imagination. We think it's natural for them to have no sense of that, so there's a loss there.

Kathleen: I know that you've talked about this before but I think the idea of talent in the arts or in any area, and the idea of giftedness in education, are at odds a little bit with this better educated utopia that you're imagining. How do you think about those ideas, given that they are very ubiquitous and I presume problematic in your view of things?

John: There's research that shows, as early as kindergarten, that kids start to compare themselves and decide who's talented and who's not in any given subject, and we allow those comparisons to exist because we think they're natural and innocent. But what if every kid could do well in any subject? The kids that decide they're not in the talented group, their brains stop working efficiently, they stop engaging, taking risks, listening, and they get more and more anxious as they fail. So I think the hierarchies produce themselves. That's not to say that every kid is the same, but we could raise the standard in every subject so that kids could experience the wonder of any subject.

I never felt I had a gift for theatre; it took me years. What changed my life was reading Sylvia Plath's *Letters to Her Mother* when I was around 21. And it was clear from the letters that she taught herself to be a writer by sheer determination. She set out as a teenager to become a poet; she read everything she could about poetry, she memorized poems, she did something we'd never tell young writers to do now. She wrote imitations of the poems she loved, and you could see her early poems are very derivative but gradually as she developed her craft, she began to capture her experience. And that was a revelation to me, at age 21, that I could actually follow a path to develop a talent for something. Until then I thought you just had to be born with a gift. So I started imitating her poems and those of other poets and, by a series of accidents, ended up in theatre. I think that there are only two things that have kept me going in theatre. One is, I think I've been lucky enough to maintain a sense of wonder I had as a child, that came partially from reading science fiction. That's what gave me a sense that math was a potentially magical subject. And this idea that if you persevered, you could learn something. And maybe a third thing is that I recognized that I would only be able to write if I used a lot of found material. So I would copy down conversations I heard, or things I'd read in journals or articles, and then try and place those things next to each other and see what would happen in the space between. And I think that gradually developed some skills as a kind of editor of the things I was hearing and seeing. So I think for young writers that's something I think they don't know they can draw on. The world is constantly producing things that will surpass your imagination and are often more rich and interesting than anything you could create sitting in front of a blank piece of paper. And so you can draw on that.

Kathleen: In your writing and thinking you talk a lot about this idea of practice, and I think you have quite specific ideas about how you practise other than in that sort of drilled, monotonous way that many of us have had in math education. So I was wondering, what does that practice look like in theatre? What does that practice look like in the arts?

John: It started off very mechanically, trying to find out how a writer would write. I remember reading once that Hemingway set out to write one good sentence a day at one point in his career. So I just tried to write one good sentence or to write a line like some other writer and gradually realized that I could use my own experience. I remember in New York once I heard someone in the street, a woman yelling, and in the middle of a fight the woman yelled at her boyfriend, "You just don't know what you don't want," and I thought that was a great line, a great double negative. And that's when I began to realize that all I had to do was listen.

Kathleen: Right. That reminds me of when I first read Kenneth Branagh's biography. He says he's often asked, How do you become a great actor? And I remember this line, he said, "You want to become a great actor, go to the gallery and look at great art." His answer was, perceive the world; open yourself up to all kinds of experiences and different kinds of arts.

John: And the other thing I think I realized as a mathematician and a playwright is that there are a lot of similarities between what I do in both areas because in both you're looking for patterns, and connections, and resonances, analogies. I think I was inspired by writers like Beckett and Chekhov, who were just amazing at finding a formal structure for their plays that would allow all of the things they experienced to fall into place. I first started to understand that in theatre when in the 1980s I read that apparently people didn't call each other long distance very often, or enough, from the point of view of Bell Canada. And so that's why Bell started their "Reach Out and Touch Someone" campaign, to really tell people they needed to connect with people in distant places. So in one of my first plays, *Scientific Americans*, there was this psychologist working for the military, talking about how they had started the "Reach Out and Touch Someone Campaign," and then that was juxtaposed with a son calling his mother and he hadn't called his mother in a long time. So I realized you could have ideas that float above and frame the action and then all the mundane things that are happening in people's everyday life would be juxtaposed against them. So that's when I started realizing the formal structure of the play was very important for me. And I think it really came to a head with plays like *Half Life*. My mother was in a nursing home for quite a while and had had a stroke and couldn't feed herself, and so she needed to be in the home. I spent a lot of hours waiting there and often had the experience of conversations being interrupted and I remember being at a party once and telling a story and someone had come up and interrupted the story, and when the person went away I decided I wouldn't continue telling the story. And the person I was talking to completely forgot that I was telling the story, even though it was a few seconds earlier and I thought it was a pretty important story!

Kathleen: That sounds like a lot of parties I've been to.

John: Yeah. So then I started watching at parties, and seeing how often that happens. And so the opening monologue of *Half Life* the character talks about that and says that about 60 per cent of the time people are not listening to the story they're being told. That monologue sets up that structure of the play and a lot of the scenes of the play are interrupted. Actions constantly interrupted, characters disappear or are forgotten because that felt like the experience in the home. I learned from writers like Beckett and Chekhov how to take the things I was hearing in everyday life, the richness of that experience, and then frame it and give it a structure. That partially also came from my mathematical training, always looking for that structure.

Kathleen: Structure. That's a fabulous example. So I want to ask a question about *The Little Years*, which was at the Tarragon last season. I loved your thoughts in the program notes and I was fantasizing about the opportunity to ask you this question from a year ago. So, aha! Here I am now!

John: I hope I have a good answer!

Kathleen: That's right. You better not have just made this up, because now I'm holding you accountable! You said, "I wrote *The Little Years* because I wanted to explore, through the characters of the play, the way a person's beliefs about time, talent, and the value of art play out in their daily lives." Fine, that was acceptable. Then you went on to say, "New and almost paradoxical ways of thinking about time and space have emerged in contemporary mathematics and physics. One day, we may be forced to re-imagine, re-examine our unconscious beliefs about art because of these ideas." What does this mean? I've been waiting a year to ask you this question!

John: I was hoping you wouldn't ask me that! So, well, you know I think artists are really insecure, playwrights particularly, are really insecure because if you imagine a playwright in the 1930s, who was very popular at the time and moved thousands of people, but their work is forgotten, we tend to think of them as failures. And that idea that the value of a work of art is tied to how long it lasts really started to become pressing for artists around the time of Newton, when there was an idea that time went on forever, with every moment indistinguishable from the last, forever and ever. Before that, people thought time was circular, and they often created works of art anonymously. I mean, there was a huge commodification of time and artists began to think that their value depended on how long their work lasted. I've always been really depressed by that, because you have no control over the fate of your work. Your work might be completely valueless if it doesn't last or if it isn't seen by enough people. So I got some relief when I started thinking about these new ideas about time. For instance with relativity – this is something a character mentions in the play – but if you had a painting and it was put on a rocket ship and sent away from Earth, and people continued to write about it for thousands of years in Earth time but it only lasted two years in rocket ship time, how long has the painting actually existed? With different frames of reference, time flows at different rates; there is no meaning of absolute time. It becomes hard to even date things, which calls into question whether time can really confer value on things when there is no absolute standard of time. And then there are even worse paradoxes which I really can't get into, but I'll just tell you there's a German mathematician called Cantor who went mad because he discovered that there were different kinds of infinity.

Kathleen: Oh no. I have enough trouble with the one kind of infinity!

John: Yeah, most people do! One kind of infinity is pretty much enough, but there are many, there are infinitely many infinities, as it turns out. So, if you match your fingers on two hands, you know there is the same number of fingers on both hands because I can pair them up. So he said, that's how we should compare the size of infinite sets and then he actually proved that there are some infinite sets you can't pair up with others. They're actually bigger in a well-defined sense.

So the other most mind-boggling discovery or breakthrough in the twentieth century was quantum mechanics, and in quantum mechanics, some people think that when we make measurements, the universe actually splits into different versions of itself. And these aren't quacks, these are people who developed a whole branch of computing that will have a huge impact on us one day called quantum computing. They're actually building computers based on very strange properties of electrons. So the people who think there might be multiple universes aren't quacks. And so I just figured, you can show very easily that if the universe branched in two every second, that that interval, that universe that's branching has a bigger order of infinity than straightforward Newtonian time where you just have a linear series of instances. So if you're an artist, you really prefer to live in the branching universe because you'd have a much higher order of immortality!

Kathleen: Yes, and because the people in that other universe saw my play for years, it was packed every night!

John: Yeah, so there's a very well-defined mathematical sense in which you'd have more immortality in that branching universe, even though they're both infinite. So I wrote a philosophy paper on this, just to kind of relieve myself from this idea that we know what time is, and that we know what immortality is and so on, and I think we've moved away from a sense of time that maybe some ancient cultures had. And that's what I tried to capture in *The Little Years* was that maybe there's another way that our work persists or affects people that's much smaller that may be more valuable in a way. Just through the people you touch in your lives. There's a great American philosopher, Thomas Nagel, who wrote a book called *Mortal Questions*, which is a beautiful series of essays. And he said in it that you know the things that happen to a person can extend beyond the boundaries of their body and even beyond the boundaries of their life. So our lives can be affected by what people say about us, by what our children do, things like that, we're kind of corporate entities that live well beyond ourselves and I wanted to try and capture that feeling too in *The Little Years*. So that's why there's a character in the play you never see, you just get a portrait of their life from what people say about them. And then you see a character whose life is deeply affected by a woman who's growing up in the 1950s who is discouraged from going into the arts and sciences – whose life is deeply affected by what people say about her. But in the end it's her niece that has a deeper impact on her than her famous brother.

Kathleen: Culturally it's true; we're sort of impact-obsessed. It's the age of measurement in some ways. And I was thinking about the writers in the field of theatre and education, like Michael Balfour, who talks about "a theatre of little changes"; I think it's a similar kind of counter-narrative to this idea that art has to solve all the problems and have enormous impact and make these great changes, otherwise it has no value.

John: And this comes full circle back to education. Because I remember once teaching a grade three class in Parkdale about fractions. And I taught them for about five weeks and taught them stuff that grade seven kids would struggle with. And at the end of that time they all wrote this test that would've been about a grade seven level and they all sat there, including kids who couldn't formerly sit still, and they all got over 90 on it and the most exciting thing was that the kids who missed it begged to write the test because they knew it wouldn't be punishment or a ranking – which are the two things we use tests for – or a threat because they knew it was a chance to show off. And they felt safe and secure and they would do well. And the atmosphere in that class was really magical because the kids were no longer competing against themselves; they were competing against the problem. They were solving the problem for the thrill of surmounting a series of challenges and also for the sheer beauty of seeing a pattern or seeing a connection. I mean I even broke up a fight once by telling a bully to apologize to the other kid or I wouldn't give him his bonus question. And he apologized to get the bonus question. So that's the kind of sense of joy that kids have at succeeding and exploring these deep things, and imagine what society would look like if instead of competing for scraps of praise or success, they constantly have the experience of discovering new things, exercising their imaginations, roaming the universe with their minds. If they had that experience all the way through without that kind of unhealthy competition, then I think we would have a different approach to art. People would create art because it's a spiritual experience, a way of communing with the beauty of the universe, I think. They would of course care what people thought but in a much healthier way.

Kathleen: I want to ask you a philosophical question because you have lectured in philosophy as well. I'm interested in your sense of the place of conceptual versus applied knowledge in math, in the arts, and in life for that matter. And my thinking about this is that there is a lot of instrumentalism in education now, a lot of celebration of the applied nature of things, and I sometimes think that our thinking and our learning about big concepts and ideas and conceptual thinking about art or life falls to the wayside in this kind of educational context.

John: That's another great question, very complex, and I think there are a lot of false dichotomies around concepts and applications and so on. So I'll talk about two examples maybe, one in the arts and one in the sciences.

One of the reasons I think kids have struggled so much in mathematics is because we keep mistaking the ends of education for the means to get kids there. We want kids to be creative, to be innovative, to use intuition, all these things. So we start with big, rich problems, highly conceptual. What does conceptual mean now in mathematics, or what does problem-solving mean in any area? It means rich, complex, usually highly relevant or contextualized, something that kids would be interested in. That was a huge push in education, and it's a positive push because you don't just want the kids understanding things in a rote way. But there's also some potential negative side effects to that approach because rich and conceptual also means more complex than most kids can handle. So what cognitive scientists are finding now is that you build the concepts, the end goal is concepts and learning, but you actually build them through smaller challenges. For instance, they found that chess players don't learn the game, they don't learn to play chess well just by playing chess. They play mini games with one or two pieces over and over again until they figure out that position. They memorize positions, they study moves of master players. None of those things look very creative or like they're going to produce a genius, but actually those are the things that produce genius and creativity. So the end looks very different from the means to get someone there. And we make that mistake over and over again. We even make it in really innocuous ways like unfortunately in education people began to call practice "drill and kill." There's a famous cognitive scientist, Herb Simon, who said that's one of the worst ideas in education because all the research on how kids become good at things shows that they need a lot of practice. The challenge in education is how you make the practice interesting. And we found in JUMP[1] that if you just raise the bar incrementally and have a well-scaffolded lesson kids will practise forever. They love reaching higher and higher levels so you can make practice interesting but it's gotten to the point where kids were even discouraged from learning their times tables because that was just a rote drill that would discourage them. Well now cognitive scientists are finding that we have very poor working memories, and if you haven't committed the basic facts to long-term memory then your working memory is constantly overwhelmed trying to remember those facts. And you can't actually solve problems or reach a high conceptual level, so out of these things that look very mechanical or rote, they're actually fundamental to high-level conceptual thinking. There's a false dichotomy there. Also a kid who doesn't know their times tables is never going to see a pattern, or make a prediction or an estimate; every day is a new day. So they're never going to generalize or think conceptually.

And it's the same in the arts with basic skills, basic training skills that true talent doesn't come, well for a few people it seems to emerge out of nowhere, but the vast majority of people get there through practice and building up incrementally. So I think the other dichotomy in the arts is this idea that you either have a deeply emotional or engaging piece of work, or an intellectual piece of work or a conceptual piece of work. T.S. Eliot said once that Shakespeare and the metaphysical poets managed to make people feel what it was to have a thought. That those things weren't separated, and that, I think, should be a goal of theatre because there's no other place than on stage where you can make people feel what it is to have a thought.

Kathleen: That's a perfect segue to my final question: Why theatre now? And, for that matter, why math now?

John: I'll quote one more philosopher, Richard Rorty, who said that great literature – he may also have been talking about philosophy – makes us feel what it is to be another person. And I think that that's something that's really essential in this age when we have such divisive politics. So many issues we can't solve because we lack empathy or understanding of the other side. I think that's really a role for theatre now, to make people understand the multiple perspectives on an issue. And understand the importance of issues viscerally.

To give an example, one of the nominees for the Siminovitch Award, Chris Abraham,[2] who I was lucky enough to work with, created a play called *Seeds* about genetic engineering, which is incredibly powerful but incredibly complex, and opened my eyes to all kinds of issues. Daniel Brooks has done similar work; his latest play, *Civility*, is about city politics. People need to see those things. My partner Pamela Sinha has written a play about trauma, partially about post-traumatic stress; it's running now and has had a profound effect on audiences. There's no better area for helping people understand those issues and to begin to understand multiple perspectives on those issues. And in mathematics, I mean, there's a simple answer. Everybody understands economic loss: there's a huge economic loss from having a population that's not fully numerate. But there are those deeper losses I talked about, an inability to connect with the natural world on a deep level or understand the consequences of our actions. An inability to see the profound beauty of the world that keeps mathematicians working on these puzzles and problems endlessly, because it's just so satisfying. And surprisingly, for children, there is new research that shows that math is a much better predictor for long-term success for elementary school students than reading even. It's the number one predictor of long-term success; math becomes a gateway for so many people, particularly disadvantaged students. And so it's extraordinary, it's a matter of equity; it's extremely important that we start to eliminate these hierarchies and allow all students to succeed in math regardless of what adults think of math, that it's got to be boring or it's not that important. I believe kids have a right to develop all of their potential in every subject and that we won't really have a fully realized society until we do that.

A Question from the Audience: I just wanted to make a point, actually answering partly your question about "Why theatre now." One of the things I also see in the unity in the arts and particularly between theatre and science is really the bottom line in those fields is the search for the truth. And that's something I see in current society that is so missing from every aspect of our society, not just through politics, actually even in academic life and education. The truth gets obscured. It gets obscured for many reasons, including a political correctness, which has really seeped through our society. I wonder if you could just comment on that, because to me, that's why we need theatre so badly. It really illuminates the truth that we sort of are missing around us.

John: Yeah, I hadn't really thought of that. It's a great question. I think there's a growing and frightening disregard for scientific evidence. I mean science isn't certain and one of the stupid arguments is, "Oh, you're not certain global warming's happening, so why should we do something about it?" But the people who say that would never buy a car from someone who wasn't an expert in that area or that wasn't manufactured by experts in that area, and if 99 per cent of engineers on earth said that that car's brakes are likely to fail, you wouldn't buy it. So why would we do the same thing with global warming? It's just insane disregard, and our politicians get away with that. And so it's very important to re-establish a respect for truth, even if it's not certain, you know there's no such thing as certainty. In theatre, truth is much more difficult and I think, you know, that plays that appear to be profound and discover truths can look dated 10 years later. Truth is harder to gauge in theatre, but I think that theatre sparks debates about the truth and, quite often, helps people progress or see new truths. I was profoundly affected by Rorty's statement that art can help you experience what it feels to be someone else. Because I think theatre and particularly film have done more to create tolerance and open up discussion in the world than almost any other media. So that's a very good point that theatre is essential for some sort of exploration of the truth.

NOTES

1 John Mighton founded the JUMP Math program. JUMP Math is a registered charity working to promote a numerate society. JUMP Math's mission is to enhance the potential in children by encouraging an understanding and a love of math in students and educators.

2 Chris Abraham won the 2013 Siminovitch Prize for directing one week after this conversation.

PART V

Why Theatre Always

16 From Epidaurus to the BackSpace at Passe Muraille: Hard Seats, Real Theatre

JUDITH THOMPSON

"Why theatre now" feels like a trick question, the kind we were asked in theatre school, by glowering and leering instructors, when there was a right answer and a wrong answer. Give the wrong answer, and you might end up playing the maid in the theatre school production of *Hedda Gabler*, or you might even be "asked to leave" at the end of term. It also feels like an impudent question, a question one might be asked by a radio host who finds theatre tedious but needs to fill up another half an hour in a meandering Sunday afternoon interview. However, in the last seven or eight years, while scanning the audience at Stratford, in downtown Toronto theatres, in theatres in New York and London, as well as outside in parks, and in closets and churches for Fringe productions, while reading hateful and ignorant reviews of productions I have loved, or raves of plays or productions that have baffled me, and naturally, hearing about more vicious reviews of my own work ('twas ever thus), always in contrast to the extraordinary embrace by the audience, I have indeed asked myself that question. It has become a voice, shouting in my head, like the voices a psychotic hears, always screeching, never letting me alone. As a friend with psychosis who hears scolding voices told me recently, "Even when it snows, and when I lock myself in the bathroom and hide under the sink, the volume does not go down. The voices persist."

"Why theatre now? Why, why, why? What the hell are you doing?"

In my own productions, I love to sit in the booth and watch the audience watching the play. Sometimes, as in the production of my last collaborative play, *Rare*, with nine performers with Down Syndrome, I fall in love with the audience as I watch them fall in love with the performers, with the play. They are riveted and emotionally present. And that answers the question. There. This is what it is for, the surging adrenaline, the feeling of absolute presence, that nothing else and nowhere else matters, absolute focus, absolute *now*, absolutely alive.

I asked my Facebook friends what they thought. One of my favourite answers was from Seana McKenna, the brilliant actress who was one of my National Theatre School classmates. She wrote, "why theatre now? Because theatre is ONLY now." I really, really liked that. My other favourite response is from one of my first-year students at the University of Guelph: he said he believes theatre is far more powerful than film or television because theatre does not *date*. I jumped up and down when he made that observation: yes! Even the best movies made just 15 or 20 years ago make me queasy because of the hairstyles and the shoulder pads and the makeup – and the way they talk, it's just not *now*. Even when theatre is *not* now, it *is* now. I love that definition, those reasons, and they almost satisfy me. But not quite.

So in the summer of 2012 I went to the source, the real thing: Epidaurus, the 20,000-seat limestone theatre in the country where (recorded) theatre began. Yes, I experienced a transcendent *Oedipus Rex* from those hard, incredibly uncomfortable cold limestone benches. Sitting on them brought back my adolescence in Kingston, Ontario, limestone city, where I would sit with my friends in what I still consider the most beautiful spot in Ontario – on the great flat slabs of limestone by the Kingston Psychiatric Hospital, overlooking the rough emerald and sapphire Lake Ontario, where we would smoke menthol cigarettes and talk for the whole afternoon about our crushes, looking out at Snake Island and, beyond it, America. And just as we could hear conversations on the farthest end of the shore, I heard every word of *Oedipus Rex* perfectly, though I didn't understand a single one, as it was in Greek. Though I counted about 40 busloads of tourists, the theatre, of course, was less than a third full. I could imagine it packed with human beings who were spiritually ravenous for what it is that only the theatre can give. In an era with no television, radio, film, Netflix, Facebook, or smartphones, theatre was the only form of full engagement with the joy and the horror of being human. There was sport, of course, which engages with the capacity of the human body to move beyond seeming limitation and become god-like, and religion – our relationship to eternity – both are part of theatre, which is so much more than the sum of those parts.

Maybe, sometimes, an act of theatre can show that human life matters. That human action matters. It can be wretched, it can be evil, and it can be sacred. Or does it show, as in *Oedipus*, that human life doesn't really matter. That despite our belief that we are somehow important, we are no different than mushrooms; the gods can pick us up and eat us, or just kick us away.

There is also the notion of theatre as a force for social change, for the greater good. I like this reason. I do believe, fiercely, that we must make the invisible visible; that is what I do best, to reveal ugly hidden truths – my mother might call it "muckraking" – to provoke acts of kindness and compassion and, yes, revolution. All that is true, and more and more is my only reason for making theatre, as it is my form of revolution, the form I understand; but no matter how noble our defined reasons for making theatre may be, doesn't it all begin with the self: the hungry, quivering self, clamouring for recognition, for validation? For friends? Okay, let's get personal here. I admit, I often have felt invisible – not because I am ignored, not because I am quiet and still and downcast and dress only in greys and browns, but just because. I often feel that I am turning to vapour. Okay, I know it's strange, but there it is: unless I am engaged with my family, my dogs, or in a rehearsal room, I am like someone on the Starship Enterprise in that machine, the transporter, grainy, half there and half not. Making theatre has always lurched me into life. When I was 11 years old and played Helen Keller, blind, deaf, and mute, I could suddenly see, hear, and speak! This was what being really alive really was, oh yes, and it sustains my life 58 years later.

If I am doing this, my life matters. Maybe it's an illusion, a delusion, wishful thinking, but that is how I feel. And how much of the audience feels, isn't it? Isn't that why they come to the theatre? But the more pressing question is, why *don't* they come?

Sometimes, even at strong productions of great plays, I see, in some cases, next to no audience, as on a snowy Saturday night a few winters ago for Tara Beagan's wondrous *Desire Under the Elms* adaptation; wonderful text, beautiful design, amazing acting – and about nine people in the audience. Where was everyone? Or there is a house crammed with people but I see a good portion of the audience asleep and others on their cell phones; I hear them open candies and cough as if we are in a tuberculosis epidemic. I hear them laugh in a robotic, reflexive way, mostly out of goodwill, because they feel the actors and the play begging for a laugh, sometimes because a situation in the play has triggered their snobbery, or their expectations of a stock character or situation, and this enrages me – not at the audience, never at the audience, but at the play, and the producers – isn't our mandate to *awaken*? To awaken ourselves in the writing and the acting, which will in turn awaken the audience? Why affirm all that keeps most of us semi-comatose? All that perpetuates violence and corruption? Isn't that what there are movies and sitcoms for? The audience comes to the theatre to be awakened, the way skiing down a steep hill awakens us. They come to be moved, to experience language, and voices, and the exquisite concentration of a whole life in an hour, to receive the great gift of the actor's interior life channelled through the characters, to have the beautiful dragon that sleeps within aroused to life.

I love the audience. They come with hope. I am grateful for their presence and their goodwill, for without them, there is no theatre! They are spending their hard-earned money, they are leaving their cozy homes, and they are getting their coats on and going out into the cold or the heat and sitting in hard seats for up to three hours. And sometimes, they will see naked guys in yoga positions lighting their farts (as in a Sky Gilbert play I took my mother to about 20 years ago!). Sometimes they will be utterly confused or are not rewarded for their efforts with an engaging piece of theatre. Sometimes, they are bored senseless, or just bewildered, or worse, insulted. And that is not right. That is a violation of the audience. But sometimes they are probed in private places and something is stirred up that has long been dormant and sometimes they are ready and sometimes they are not, and that can make them angry. *Furious.* That is good theatre, theatre that makes them *fume*, but when theatre is bad and boring we must ask ourselves why. Was the company blinded by the erotic love spell that seems to fog up most rehearsal processes? Did nobody step in and say, "Hey guys, I am seeing clearly. I know you all love each other, but this is really, really terrible." Disasters happen frequently, which makes me love the audience even more, for having faith, for coming out, for believing that something great, ineffable, unspeakably beautiful and meaningful, something that will give their lives more muchness is going to happen. Thank you, audience, for your faith. You seem to understand "Why theatre?" Even more than we do.

Theatre, it has been said over and over, is like church. The ceremony. The spirituality. The story. The faith it requires. The potential for boredom, repetition, and absolute emptiness. The decline in audience. The numbers, especially in North America, are seriously declining; churches are closing up. There are many of us who are deeply dismayed by the rampant sexual abuse, the corruption of the clergy, the wealth, and the lies, and we just don't believe in Santa or the Easter Bunny or that Christ is God and his mother was a virgin, or that the holy host *is* the body of God, and the wine *is* his actual blood ... transubstantiation is very theatrical and wonderfully ghoulish, but it is not real, and nobody actually believes it is. The bleeding heart of Jesus is Jacobean, wild, and not appropriate for children. It is good strong theatre, the main difference being that religion tells us how to be and commands us to have blind faith. To not ask questions. Whereas the best theatre never answers questions but always asks deeper questions. More complicated questions ... some might argue that Judaism does that, maybe the Quakers. But the big difference is that in church, we hear the same story, over and over and over and over, and many people find great succour from that story. When my son was about four and his favourite toy car was dropped onto the road as we were crossing and was smashed by cars, we went to fetch the pieces, and he was so devastated he begged me to tell the story of how the toy car was smashed – not once, not twice, but the rest of the day and the day after. After two days of continuous repetition of the story, he was sated.

He needed to hear the details, to have the scene conjured again and again, so that he could file it where it needed to be filed in his brain. So a religious service tells the same story over and over, but audiences will see *Hamlet* or *King Lear* or *Midsummer Night's Dream* countless times and claim they get more out of it every time. Church is sort of like amateur theatre. More often than not, the pastors or priests or rabbis are terrible actors with reedy voices, though there are, of course, outstanding exceptions. Religious service seems to give those who attend strength and community, and best of all, when it ignites our interior lives – our longing for grace, truth, unconditional love, meaning, and redemption – it relumes the spiritual, and *that* is our task, isn't it? In the theatre? To reignite the flame that is flickering or even dead, so that the flame flares up into a bonfire.

So that question which for so long we would not dignify with an answer, a question that has been asked since the advent of radio, television, and film, and even more so in the last 20 years or so with the Internet – that question: not just "is the theatre dead?" but "should we let it die?" This is an "unspeakable conversation."[1] I borrow that glorious phrase from Harriet McBryde Johnson, the late renowned disability activist, who went to battle with Peter Singer, the scary bioethicist. She called this debate an unspeakable conversation because Peter Singer had declared that parents should have the right to terminate the lives of their disabled babes; she protested his appearance and so he invited her to his class at Princeton. She accepted. She went and did win over his class, but she called it an unspeakable conversation, because she felt she was there defending her right to exist. She insisted on existing. On asserting herself.

That assertion is how my career as a playwright began. In 1979, I was writing what was to become *The Crackwalker* – doodling really, with voices and scenes, and suddenly, without any planning, the killing of the baby was written. I did not know that I would include this dreadful and tragic episode from my summer as an intern at Community and Social Services in Kingston, Ontario – I thought I was writing a comedy about the welfare class, the permanently unemployable set in Kingston. I had an ear for dialogue and a gift for mimicry – but as I wrote, the play led me down, down, down to the truth, and I could not pull away. I followed my instincts, the story that needed to be told was told, and *The Crackwalker* was born. This happened again in *Lion in the Streets*, in which the character of Isobel, the girl who had been murdered years before and wandered as a ghost through the neighbourhood, asserted herself. I had written it as a kind of neighbourhood relay race, but suddenly, there was Isobel. "You know me, you know me very hard. I live next house to you." There had been several young girls kidnapped and murdered in Toronto over the years; one, Sharon Morningstar, from a park just up the street from where I lived with my husband, on Brunswick Avenue. We heard the police van driving up and down the street, giving her description over the loudspeaker, hour after hour. We knew that at that moment, she was fighting for her life. It was unbearable. Intolerable to carry on, knowing what we knew. And that is how Isobel asserted herself in *Lion in the Streets*. She ends the play: "I want you all to have your life." Every play of mine has such an "assertion."

In 2006, I was called by Brenda Surminski, who at the time was working for Ogilvy and Mather; she wondered if I might be interested in creating a play with a cast of non-actress women about beauty and aging. I found this compelling. I had been listening to my students tell their true stories for years and always found them transformative and perfect in every way. I also had been directing Shakespeare at my kid's schools for over nine years: I would find an amazing, willing, and highly organized mom to stage manage, and we would cast up to 70 kids from aged 7 to 12, with at least three playing all the main roles; we would find another mom (in one case a leading psychiatrist) who loved to sew, and maybe an artist or architect to design the set. The kids often couldn't even read the Shakespeare aloud without help at the beginning. The meetings were excruciating to any outsider, but I loved it. I thrive on this amazing journey, which I know always ends in glory for all. To guide these students through Shakespeare – not ever by reducing the plays to their plots, which I feel are just hangers, but word by word – was a privilege. And I would always find an extraordinary composer/musician who happened to be a parent of one of the kids in the show. I would ask them to set all the most potent speeches to music, and of course there were always at least 20 kids who could really sing. The shows were life-changing events for all. The lighting was makeshift, the acoustics just dreadful – we were in school gyms – but the shows were sheer magic. That theatre was as important to me as any I have ever done. And interestingly, when those kids studied Shakespeare in high school, they said they still remembered every word.

So when Brenda posed this possibility, I said yes, yes, and yes, as long as no advertising whatsoever was involved. We gathered a diverse group of women from all over Canada, and I created a play I called *body and soul*, using their words, their stories, and their bodies on the stage. I brought in music and dance and I sculpted a real play with real women: real people, real lives, the idea of *real* had asserted itself. It was hard for me to imagine writing an old-fashioned drama with made-up characters in a made-up situation. Who cares? Any of us could make up a story. It's the real stories that count. And real is *always* more interesting than made-up.

So my next project was the Grace Project or *Sick*, which I threw together in a few weeks for the Next Stage Festival in 2010: one of my children has a chronic illness and I realized that there must be many children bearing this burden, so I put out a call for auditions: we cast 14 young people between the ages of 14 and 25, all with self-defined chronic conditions, ranging from diabetes to Crohn's to Down Syndrome to depression to cancer. The show was beautiful and stunned the audience. After it closed, my performer with Down Syndrome, Krystal Nusbaum, was hungry for more theatre work. I suggested to her mother, Madeleine, that if she could organize a Fringe show, I would be happy to create a play with a large cast of performers with Down Syndrome. Madeleine said yes, and we got into the Fringe, and we were launched. We auditioned about 45 performers with Down Syndrome and chose nine. I hate auditions as an actor and even more as a director – to reject anyone is beyond dreadful. But theatre is often cruel. I have learned to never mix friends and theatre, never write for friends or with friends, and try not to cast friends. So we had a beautiful cast. Over the next six months we met several times a week and we began to create *Rare* together. I would ask a simple question – such as "What do you hope for?" – and volunteers would transcribe the answers. Nicholas Hutcheson had been my student at the University of Guelph, and I fortuitously ran into him at the opening of Hannah Moscovitch's *The Children's Republic* and begged him to help me on *Rare*. He became my assistant director and main transcriber; he is now one of four partners in our new rare theatre. I brought in the masks that I have used for teaching for the last 20 years, because I wanted to explore the mask of Down Syndrome and what is beneath. There were many moments and journeys that answered the question "Why theatre now?" For example, James, who had the most trouble communicating verbally, would often tear up the script and throw himself on the floor crying because he could not say the words, and also sometimes because one of the pretty assistants had spoken too harshly from his perspective, or because he was frightened of his mask. And though others thought maybe we should let him go, I always had faith in James, and slowly he rewarded that faith. He *rose* to our expectations. His father was amazed. He worked and worked on his lines, the lines *he* wrote – for example, "sexy is being yourself" – until they were clear. His eloquence had always been in his movement. He is brilliantly physically articulate, and discovering that, and how to use his physical language in the play, *that* was theatre practice at its best. The moment in mid-June when I shared with them the reality that 98 per cent of women choose to terminate their pregnancies when they find out their baby will have Down Syndrome, they sat on the floor, and though some of them were clearly just thinking about lunch time (a major event), Nick, who was the clearest communicator and a sort of cast leader, looked up at me and said, "But that's discrimination. It's against our right to be who we are, what we are. We are unique. We're *rare*. And we stand together!" *That*, I thought, is the core of our show. *That* is why theatre *now*. When he said that, they all cheered and hugged each other. This community does not want to be vanished because of a society that worships perfection. I was not going to silence them because I might offend some people in the audience. And though I am sure there were those in the audience who had chosen to terminate for that reason, they understood that they were not being condemned. It is clearly the lack of education, exposure, and resources that frighten people, and the doctors often guide them to make that choice, to make way for a "healthy" baby. The moment when Krystal says, "I hope to raise a child one day," we do not know what to think. We are sympathetic with her wish but unsure if it would be a wise or even possible choice. This is theatre that ties itself around your mind and pulls, gets the brain troubled and working. Glorious. Sarah would sob every time she spoke about her grandmother's death. She couldn't get through it, and though I would reassure her that she did not have to talk about her grandmother, she would insist. And finally she *was* able to get through it with a cry, yes, but an acceptable stage cry. By July, we had created a play, and we opened in the Tarragon Main Space to wild, standing ovation and tears and hoorahs. We were sold out every performance, people were waiting on blankets on the sidewalk, and the cast were superstars. Albert Shultz of Soulpepper invited us to partner at the Young Centre, over several years, to create three or four new plays with the same mandate: to make the invisible visible, to give voice to marginalized communities. So we had to become a theatre company! I know that there are hundreds of 20-something young artists starting theatre companies, but for me, this was epic. It was I having true agency as a theatre artist. I am now the artistic director of the rare theatre. No more begging at the table. I will produce my own works and continue to create these collaborative pieces, and we will produce the work of emerging theatre artists who others do not recognize, continuing our mandate – bringing them out of the dark and into the light!

We remounted *Rare* and extended the run three times. Then came another magic day: my neighbour Gillian works for Spinal Injury Ontario, and one day she knocked on my door, and when I answered she said that she had seen *Rare* and was blown away and would I ever consider creating a play with a cast of people with spinal injuries. This is another example of the serendipity that governs so much creative work – some in our community call it the theatre gods – I am calling it *assertion*; I responded that I would love to do that if she could come up with some funding so that I could pay the actors and the assistants up-front this time. She said she thought she could and *BORNE* was born: a cast of 12 exceptional artists, 8 with paraplegia and 4 with quadriplegia (see *Figures 16.1* and *16.2*). Spinal Injury Ontario recruited people with spinal injuries to come out and audition. We all knew a couple of people who were "born with"; for example, I knew that a wonderful young actress I had worked with at Ryerson Theatre School had a severely disabled sister; I emailed Maayor and she put me in touch with Maayan, who became one of the stars of our show. The interviews (I hate to call them auditions) were extensive, and it was such an honour to be in the room. In fact, Nick and I, and Lois Fine – who had been in *body and soul* and now was a company partner – looked at each other and agreed that there was nowhere in the world where we would rather be. *Nowhere.* It was such a privilege to hear these incredible stories. To be in the same *room* with these people, who hated, of course, being called brave or heroic, the whole "supercrip" narrative. At the time of this writing, we are about to go into our second workshop, in which I will coax and gather stories and continue to move the piece. One of our performers is a brilliant pianist; it seems I like to have live music now in all my pieces.

So you might be thinking that reality theatre has asserted itself. Or docu-drama. No, it is that every human being is a storyteller and a performer, and sadly, theatre school tends to homogenize young actors, so

16.1 Dan Harvey, David Shannon, and Joshua Dvorkin (from left to right) in *BORNE* (rare theatre in association with Soulpepper). Photo by Cylla von Tiedemann.

that no matter how talented, there is sameness to them. As if vanilla frosting was spread over top of them. Some of them break free of that (I hope I am one!), but I realized I needed to look to the raw, unpolished performers – for if they came to the audition that meant to me that they were performers, just untrained and unfrosted. And they don't *look* like actors, who by necessity, for their bread and butter, have to look as close to American movie stars as possible. These were new and original voices. Brilliantly exciting.

So I have a new path. Real voices creating real theatre, giving big voice to quiet communities. Uncovering those who are hidden. But the other path is very much there – I adapted *Electra* for the Women and War project – I set it in Bosnia, during the massacres of the 1990s – and Electra kills Clytemnestra on stage. Matricide asserted itself. The furies, the destroyers, the wise ones, those who take revenge on all who hurt women, they were my feminism, my rage at injustice against women, theatricalized and played in a tiny version of Epidaurus on the Greek Island of Hydra. Unforgettable.

In the spring of 2012 my dramaturge, Iris Turcott, suggested I write a one-woman play for myself to perform. The last time I had performed on a stage in front of actual people in an actual play was in 1979 at the Manitoba Theatre Centre in front of 900 people in an Alan Ayckbourn Christmas farce. My father had just died and the temperature was 40 below zero and I was despondent. I remember walking off stage and saying to my fellow actor that this was the last play I would ever perform in. I had no desire to say someone else's words ever again. I no longer felt I belonged on a stage. The playwright was asserting herself. The plays were howling to be written. On New Year's Eve right before our performance, I received a big box of amazing goodies from Gregor Campbell, the man who was to be my husband: a story called "the left-handed woman" (which I was) by Peter Handke, a fruitcake from his lovely mother, several books, and a beautiful letter, and the box read: "here come the eighties!" The world was about to change. My life was about to change: I returned to Toronto and dove back into writing *The Crackwalker* and never looked back. I withdrew from the marathon race that is an acting career: from the breathless lines of hungry young actresses, from the competition with my friends, from the starvation diets, and contentedly lived on writing grants and love, on Brunswick Avenue with Gregor Campbell. My first professional rehearsal of a play of mine was agonizing – the director, Clarke Rogers, and I were in conflict – he was on drugs and abusive, but he needed me there to show him the play. I developed cystic acne and sties and cried a lot, but we got through it, and it seemed to change theatre history somehow, despite the eviscerating reviews. Now, although I cherish the play, I cringe when it is the first play people mention with my name, or the only play. The monologues are overdone and done badly in so many auditions – and many of my "fans" have only read that play. There are 20 others, and at least 12 of them are just as powerful. So, some 30 years later, Iris Turcott was pushing me back onto the stage. The time was right. She knew how busy I was, so she insisted that I come to her office at the Factory and lock myself in there for three hours a day. I did that, and then would rush to St Michael's Hospital where my daughter was recovering from hip surgery, and there I would be for the rest of the day and most of the night. I think it may have had something to do with the terror I felt for my daughter, the guilt at not being there 24 hours a day, but the writing flowed. I wrote from my outrage, at the death of 18-year-old

16.2 From left to right, David Shannon, Nancy Xia, Russell Winklear, Joshua
Dvorkin, Dan Harvey, and Harley Nott (centre) in *BORNE* (rare theatre in
association with Soulpepper). Photo by Cylla von Tiedemann.

Ashley Smith, her suicide by ligature, choking herself to death with
strips of her gown while six correctional officers watched, having been
ordered not to go in and revive her. When she was blue, they entered:
"Ashley? Ashley? Stop this right now." And they handcuffed her while
she was already dead. Shame, shame. *Shame.* This is a girl who was ar-
rested for throwing crab apples at a postman. This was a girl who had
no sense of consequence, and thus kept digging herself further down
into the pit – every time she swore, or pushed an officer, or banged
her head against the wall, or threw her lunch on the floor, she would
be sent to the hole, to segregation, which drove her into madness
and rage. The officers would enter her cell in full riot gear. They would
not allow her mother to visit her. When she was treated as a human
being, as the people from Elizabeth Fry Society treated her, she would
respond like a human being. But when she was treated like a crazed
bull, that is exactly how she behaved. They drugged her, they tied her

up, and they tormented her. I needed to bring Ashley Smith back to life so she could *howl*, so we could all howl, and I knew I could do that with the power of theatre. Ashley Smith is asserting herself just as, in *The Crackwalker*, the baby who had been killed asserted himself, just as Isobel in *Lion in the Streets* did, and Marie and Patsy in *Perfect Pie*, and Jabber in *Enoch Arden*, and the older women in *body and soul* asserted themselves, and the sick youth in *Sick*, and Electra in *Sirens*, just as the Down Syndrome community asserted itself and now the community of people who use wheelchairs; what I do as a playwright and director and actor is surrender to this assertion, this howl from beyond.

I think the most telling and spellbinding moment in *Rare* was when Nicholas Herd danced the Dying Swan. Nicholas is the cast member who responded to my question about termination so eloquently: "It's against our right to be who we are!" I had just heard Tchaikovsky's music for *The Dying Swan* in my dance class, and I brought it in and asked Nick if he would like to dance to it. I had found Nick's dancing ability remarkable, so I wanted to take a chance. Nick embraced the idea and began work on the dance. He studied the many YouTube videos of ballet dancers in their finest moments; after months of work there he was, under the blue light Andre du Toit designed for him, the cast watching, the audience enthralled as he danced the Dying Swan with such grace, such loaded emotion that one could hear the audience breathe, through their gasps and their sobs of joy. The great Veronica Tennant sat beside me, on fire as she watched Nick dance the choreography she had danced with such passion so many times. Nick, at that moment, gave us all the answer to "Why theatre now?" His dance was the physical howl of assertion, the yearning of a vanishing community for recognition, for the right to simply be; he was representing this and every beautiful and complex community that is threatened by our demand for physical perfection. The rest of the ensemble were witness, on the stage, as were we in the audience, to this sacred moment, one four-minute dance that brought the past, the present, and the future into one sacred event, the now of why theatre.

NOTE

1 Harriet McBryde Johnson, "Unspeakable Conversations," *New York Times*, 16 February 2003, http://www.nytimes.com/2003/02/16/magazine /unspeakable-conversations.html.

17 Sequencing the Shattered Narratives of the Now

ANN-MARIE MACDONALD IN CONVERSATION WITH KATHLEEN GALLAGHER

This interview with Ann-Marie MacDonald took place in spring 2013, in the garden of Kathleen Gallagher's home in Toronto.

Kathleen: How would you characterize your work in the theatre?

Ann-Marie: My work in theatre has always shared, or has come to share, space with my work in fiction. My work in theatre is about writing and acting and creating – those three things – and they often overlap. And the theatre work all centres around acting and actors, right? As a playwright, I'm inspired by the worlds actors can create. And I want to be in the centre of those worlds, instigating the world for the actor to inhabit, so there's a very strong connection between the two. And I get a lot of energy and inspiration as a writer from actors; they really are a circuit for me. The playwriting and the acting is an electrical current. It helps make me go. I can't imagine doing one without the other. You know, I'm working on a creation inspired by *Hamlet*. This is very early days. And it's exciting and already exceedingly hard because I've had to go away and spend time with myself doing what I do as a writer, which is taking something out of the air: taking nothing and making something out of nothing. That's how it feels to me. And returning with it to a rehearsal hall where the actors are ready to catch this scrap of something that I've made out of nothing.

Kathleen: I want to ask you about the idea of the collective with theatre that's different from other arts and most certainly different from your fiction writing. So you're describing the relationship between you as a writer and the actors who breathe life into something you've created, but the audience has a piece in that too.

Ann-Marie: Well the audience is the ... final creative partner, as is the reader, to become whole and to exist. Otherwise it's an artefact or a memory; it's history. I remember when audience feedback forms were introduced. It became very important to include the audience's opinion. And I remember thinking at the time, "why would you do that to them?" And then I thought, "Oh, okay, there's an ethos at work which is inclusion and respect. Okay ... great, great." Personally, I just know that the idea that I'm going to get something out of it [audience feedback forms] that's going to be definitive or really helpful is really, really unlikely! And I feel like that is actually undervaluing what the audience brings, which is themselves, in the room, breathing and responding in a way that I pick up on. And the fact of them witnessing is extremely powerful, and someday some psycho- or neurobiologist is going to measure the quantifiable effects and the witnessing, that there is actually measurable energy and measurable change occurring in the universe because of witnessing. And that's what an audience does. They make it one whole thing and a great deal of information goes back and forth. And, you know, it can be very easy if you're gauging laughter. That's a very important and clear sign. But it's only one obvious thing. But honestly, I can feel if they're getting it. And I can feel if they're bored. And I can feel if they're engaged and why, because they are witnessing. I am able to harness that witnessing like a current.

I do respect that everybody has the capacity to witness. Whether they're going to like it or not is a whole other thing. But they're going to witness and I'm going to get a huge amount from that. The same thing with fiction. And I recently experienced this. I have a manuscript which is a rewrite and just shy of being finished, and I gave that big raw manuscript to two friends who, by virtue of the kinds of things they do in film, television, and theatre, and their knowledge of me, I thought were going to give me some really good feedback, which they did! They gave me fantastic and helpful notes, and I am grateful. But more important was the fact that their eyeballs were on the story, so suddenly I could see the story because someone else was reading it.

Kathleen: How much do you think artists in the performing arts, or even in fiction as you've described it here, how much do you think the act of witnessing has been historically understood as part of that alchemy?

Ann-Marie: I think there was a reaction against it. Broadly speaking, you know, the developed Western post-war world where it became a kind of anti-elitist elitism. The idea that if you're an artist, you're probably going to be, very broadly speaking, a middle-class boomer. And somewhere, someone has put out there an idea, this kind of ethical arrow in a quiver, that "don't pander to an audience, don't sell out. Don't do anything entertaining. Fuck the audience. That's not who we're doing this for! You've got to do this for yourself." It's individualism run amok, which is "do it for you!"

That has never made sense to me. Also, I think I have too much of a performative drive and I need the partner, I need the audience. "I was here! We were here! We were here! Here's what it was like, for me, for us!" I think a kind of snobby anti-elitist elitism infected theatre as it did many other things, and there was a faux kind of pose of truculence and hatred for the audience. I always think, "Oh my God! These people are here. They've carved out the evening. They've, they've probably paid a babysitter, they're putting their bum on the seat." And I just have compassion for them. I have compassion for their hope, for their yearning, for their openness. They have arrived; they have come. That is a beautiful, quivering, hopeful human act of optimism.

Kathleen: I have so many questions, but one of them is that this kind of thinking really flies in the face of current pressures; theatre artists are constantly being asked to account for the impact of what it is that they do.

Ann-Marie: You mean account for it economically? Justify it? Yeah, I think it's just the wrong question over and over again. It is a ridiculous question. I think it's irrelevant. I think we should just say – here's a factoid – 101: "The arts contribute to the economy enormously and in ways that aren't even measurable. A lot of jobs, a lot of economic impact." And how we add extraordinary amounts of value to a city and how that translates into concrete economic value. Can we just say that?

Kathleen: Yes. We can. You're making me think that we should talk a little bit about narrative and about story because that's the thread through many of these ideas you have about making art and being in the world, I think. I want to ask a specific question about how stories have functioned or did function historically in the theatre. How are they operating differently now, or are new stories happening, or do we need new stories?

Ann-Marie: Everything always has a historical antecedent; we didn't really invent any of this stuff whole-cloth. But that non-linear, imagistic, multidisciplinary stuff that exploded in the eighties is very interesting because it is mainstreamed now. People ingest shattered narrative all the time. And it started to go really mainstream with rock videos back in the nineties. And now, the way we watch the news, the way we download something, the way we watch television, the way we communicate, the way we go online, the way we Facebook each other – that is all shattered narrative, all non-linear narrative. It's all imagistic, multidisciplinary, and ordinary. It's mainstream. And it's all doing the same thing, which is making sense of our world, trying to make our world whole. And with the digital age comes the acceleration of trying to make my world whole. I'm trying so hard to have so many pieces and to fit them in so fast and to make my world whole over and over again. It's an acceleration of the process, and it seems like the bits get more numerous and smaller and making the world whole seems to be something people have to do over and over and over again and it seems exhausting. At worst, it becomes superficial and exhausting. So maybe what's going to be happening in terms of theatre, and certainly I think it is happening in theatre, it's happening when you look at mini-series – HBO, case in point. The stuff that people are eating up and want-ing are narratives, long arcs, intelligible arcs, and character arcs. A mode of like, "This happens. I get to know this person, and then that happens, and there is a surprising reversal, a revelation, an ambiguous ending, a resumption, a cliffhanger." So what was formerly so sophisticated and challenging, that required radical practitioners and forward-thinking aca-demics to actually explain what was going on is now everybody's job, on their iPhone and everybody is just living that way. The thing that doesn't change is sequencing. As you very rightly pointed out, invoked by your question, sequencing, timeline, pattern, wholeness, identity – that's what consciousness is made of.

Kathleen: Are the forces of globalization – and that's a vague term – are they working with us? Against us? Both with and against us?

Ann-Marie: More and more people are feeling more and more connect-ed to one another and we're extrapolating across all kinds of, what used to be, un-crossable boundaries to make connections.

Kathleen: Are people *feeling* connected or feeling that connection is possible?

Ann-Marie: I don't know if it's a question of degree or kind. Is there a shift in kind or is it just a shift in degree or is it the shift in degree created a shift in kind? I suppose it kind of works like that. But it does seem as though we're entering a new mass age.

Kathleen: And you see that on a communicative plane?

Ann-Marie: Yes, on a communicative plane, on a plane of connection: "Here's what's happening to me!" and someone else going, "That's happening to me too," in a completely different context. "Let's change this!" You know, there are fewer secrets now. We depend more and more on wilful blindness and denial because everything is known. And you know people can make theatre anywhere anytime. Mass communica-tion is amazing and it gives rise to all kinds of good things and all kinds of terrible things. But here's the thing: children can take a really long time before they can watch movies with even a basic level of jeopardy, whereas with books they can read stuff with lots of jeopardy, lots of risk.

Kathleen: Why is that?

Ann-Marie: It's because they're in control of their own inner world and imagination when they're reading, unlike when they are being assaulted by an array of images on the Internet. They're not being assaulted from without when they read a book. What's the place of an image? Why are they powerful? When are they appropriate? When do they in fact co-opt your own inner space and replace what you would understand in your own soul with what someone else wants to call it and with what someone else wants to imprint on you, in you, and have power over you because they've imprinted an image in you, before you articulated one and formulated one yourself? It's an assault!

Kathleen: So information is power and now it's also dead. Information is dead!

Ann-Marie: Yeah! Because if you put it all in the same place and let it go past your eyes extremely rapidly with no patterning and no sequencing, it's junk! It's events, unconnected, non-narrative. And it makes no sense.

Kathleen: Belle Moral ...

Ann-Marie: There we go!

Kathleen: You were just quoting your play.

Ann-Marie: Oh ... wow ... see ... we only ever do one thing! And that's why the Internet can be amoral. "Oh ... a child being raped in this ... ," "cute dog video ... ," "bomb going off ... ," "Oh my God ... a dog riding a bicycle!" (Ha ha.) "Brazilian rainforest?" (No one ever even thinks about that anymore.) "Hey ... how are we not worried about the rainforests anymore? What happened to that?" "Next!" "Beached whale." Oh my God ... you'd never believe there's this video of this guy eating spaghetti in the dark!

Kathleen: And the theatre must –

Ann-Marie: We are story-makers. As human beings, we are story-makers. And we will desensitize and scramble ourselves and deconstruct ourselves back to pre-consciousness, to post-consciousness. We will destroy our consciousness, and that's called insanity, with an unfiltered barrage of unconnected images and so-called information. And that's what artists do: we organize it. That's what our brain does. That's what culture does and artists do. Sequencing is very important, right? One of the features of trauma is the inability to sequence an event and that's why post-traumatic stress disorder is going back to a state disconnected from narrative and the present moment. It's mental illness, an affliction. And the inability to sequence and remember is an affliction and it is a feature of trauma. But artists? We've got to return. Sequence events. What was there? I know ... It's Colombo – "There's something there. I got to go back. There's something there!"

Kathleen: Okay so one of the questions of this book is that we're asking "Why theatre now?" And the "why" part matters as well as the "now" part.

What we found in talking to a lot of artists like yourself, there was a reluctance to bracket off "the now" from history. And yet there are lots of signs, even in Canadian theatre, that, to me, would make this seem to be a time worth naming in some way. But I also have a tension about that because I'm caught up in your trans-historical accounts of what the arts do and what artists do and that's why we ended up with a section in this book that we weren't anticipating which is "Why Theatre Always." It's a tension, "now" and "always" being interchangeable in this way.

Ann-Marie: I don't really see that there's a contradiction between the two, because the "now" quite rightly implies that we're in a new age. Something is different now. It's like before the car and after the car. Some things are different. Now, we're talking about the digital age. We're talking about mass communication, we're talking about the Internet. And that is different. That is "I did not grow up with this. And this is what people are growing up with now." Just as I said, people are very relaxed with the shattered narrative; all the things that were really cool and hip and confusing and "wow" are just really ordinary now. And now we're going, "Okay, what are the arcs? Let's make sense of this. Let's make deeper, slower, sense of this!" And that's why there is such an appetite for narrative and it crosses over into theatre as well. I can't speak authoritatively because I don't see everything and I don't see enough, but my sense is that narrative is experiencing a resurgence in theatre.

Kathleen: Can you point to anything that makes you believe that?

Ann-Marie: I can't point to specific things. It's just my own sense. It's the kind of writing that I do, which seems to appeal to people across a great range. That tells me something. It tells me something when kids and old people and middle-aged people and people from diverse backgrounds are feeling implied in the story that I've told. See, that's where I don't have a big wide perspective of literary criticism or dramatic criticism. I just have intuitive things and anecdotal observations and the view from where I am. But I do think that because people now, especially younger people, who are much more adept, can make their own films, can publish their own books, can express themselves, can sequence their lives, can manipulate reality in all kinds of ways and share that, that they're very sophisticated and very relaxed with all of it.

And then there is the barrage of information I've already talked about, and the indebted life and also indebted in terms of time. There's money debt we all live with as normal, and there's time debt because kids have to be in 12 different places and we have to be in 15 different places and our lives have become more fragmented and pressured. People are getting sick of fractured narrative. These things are novelties. There's an aspect of novelty and of eye candy. And then there's an exhaustion with that. There's a sugar overload and you go, "That's just not getting me through the journey!" And with every new technological innovation there is something really valuable, something really exciting. And then there's a whole lot of people who really feel it confers upon them a kind of, you know, hip sense of "Now I really belong" or "I'm the first one to get this!" And at a certain point, if everybody has it and everybody can do it, it's like, "Is that all there is?" It's Peggy Lee. It's time to sing, "Is that all there is?" to a smartphone. "Is that all there is?" to Facebook. Like "these aren't really my friends, it's not the centre anymore. What was it? What was it that I needed?" And sequencing and patterning are very, very deep within us, and fractured images and accelerated image-making can't feed that, can't answer that hunger and that need.

Kathleen: So we need narrative wholeness because of the "now" moment that we're in?

Ann-Marie: Exactly. You know, when movies came, people asked, "Oh, is theatre dead?" And every 12 years, someone asks, "Is the book dead?" Is the novel dead? No! You know what? God's not dead! The novel is not dead! Theatre is not dead! It's not dead. None of it is dead. Movies didn't kill theatre. Movies changed theatre and there was a cross-contagion. Movies made it possible for theatre to be more naturalistic, in many ways, and also, at the other end of the spectrum, more imagistic, less narrative. What can we do in theatre that they're not doing in movies? Why does this have to be a piece of theatre? Why could this not be a movie became a very important question I remember back in the eighties.

I think they are different because I think we don't have to justify it so much. I think we got a little bit allergic to narrative in the eighties and into the nineties because isn't that what movies do? And shouldn't I be making a movie? And am I just a poor cousin of the film-makers? Now I sort of think we're past that. Now just tell me a story! My children, for example, will watch a piece of theatre, a very adult piece of theatre, and they'll get the story, and they'll be there. If it was a movie they wouldn't watch it. They'd be bored because they know it's not for them. But if they're in the room witnessing and experiencing, they're getting full nutrients. Whereas a movie they'll say, "Ohhhhh, I don't want to watch that. Let's watch Harry Potter!" Great! It's the difference between eating an orange and taking a vitamin C pill. The movie is the vitamin C pill and the theatre is the orange.

You're not going to forget it. You have had a DNA exchange, literally. Something is different in the world because you were there. And that doesn't excuse the boring theatre. Boring theatre should be against the law except then we'd live in a dictatorship and I'm very pro-democracy.

My world includes boring theatre. Okay, my democracy includes boring theatre.

Kathleen: My son Liam said to me this morning – I don't know what precipitated the comment – but he said, "Oh! Remember mummy, that's just like the play we saw about freedom!" And I said, "What play about freedom?"

Ann-Marie: The medium is the message! He got the message because it was theatre. He could probably watch umpteen movies but he got it! He got the direct nutrition. But also, why theatre now? Because we can. It is the most egalitarian, unmediated, direct form of telling stories and of making connections and patterns. Yes, do a piece of theatre and then YouTube it. And share it that way. Great! Do it, do it! Make sure everybody knows that it happened. And maybe they'll come again, you know, when it happens next time. But it is radical in that way. It's just about the least elitist thing in the world.

Kathleen: That's interesting! So what is Canadian theatre now and does it matter? Does Canadian-ness matter, if we can think locally for a minute?

Ann-Marie: I think it is very hard to take any single play and say, "Why is this Canadian?" but when you look at a body of work – and we now have a body of work – I think it is possible to observe some major motifs and themes and I think that we would probably also observe something about the point of view of these pieces of theatre. And I think we would observe something about a readiness to self-question, a readiness to question, a readiness to accommodate multiple perspectives, a readiness to tackle moral questions while inviting in all the annoying gnats and buzzing flies of other voices, other perspectives. And a struggle between taking moral responsibility, articulating a moral stand out of a pluralistic place so that you don't drown in relativism and opt out morally. How do you take a moral stand in a pluralistic society? How do you not slide into relativism or right-wing oversimplifications, fundamentalist oversimplifications? I think there's something very Canadian about that, about making it as hard as possible to see clearly morally but being determined to do so and take a stand. And with Canadian work as a whole, we might see the same kind of morality coming through very, very, very different-looking packages. And saying, "I belong too! I'm going to claim a heritage. I'm going to say that this tradition is mine! This tradition that has excluded me. I'm going to put myself at the head of it. I'm going to haul it forward. I'm going to haul that cart forward. I'm going to say that it's me doing that and I'm part of it. I don't look like I'm part of it. Maybe you didn't want me at this feast. I'm queer, I'm black, I'm this, I'm that. This actually is my tradition. I might begin by trashing it, but I'm going to thrive by pushing my way into the centre of it and aren't you glad I came?"

Kathleen: Are you seeing it this way because there is a body of work you can now look back on? Or is this something that you think has been, in some way, driving Canadian theatre always?

Ann-Marie: It's hard to say because that certainly is my story. But I also connect my story to a larger one, and I do think I'm representative of it, that I'm part of something like that. I'm not the only one. I think I'm really part of the movement, of something that happened and is happening. And I think that it's also very easy to say, "Well, what does it matter anymore?" And you know, "there are no borders." Well, go to Yemen and then tell me there's no Canada!

I think it's a temporary thing. The whole obsession with digital communication. I think these things are fantastic, big, but they don't change the underlying truth. The story doesn't change. Sequencing, the need to sequence, does not change. The need to create pattern does not change. We become more sophisticated in our ability to perceive pattern and certainly the digital age is part of that, movies are part of that, imagistic multidisciplinary theatre is like that. But it's just saying we can do it this way too.

And I also like those highly seductive, site-specific shows. I always find that just really exciting and seductive. Some people, it really bugs them, where they think it's facile or something. I just go, "Yeah man, you just waved a magic wand over my brain! I'm running with you into the back kitchen of the summer house! What's going to happen? Wow!" Yeah, I love that stuff. Because I'm right in it. And we want to be in something. We want to forget ourselves so that we can make deeper contact with ourselves. I think it's what happens when people are really engaged. And it can happen just as pure escapist entertainment, and it can also happen as a profound encounter with something very deeply true that you understand about yourself and about the condition of being alive and conscious. And there's different ways of getting to that; some of it looks like art and some of it doesn't.

Kathleen: Yup! Do you have any thoughts or questions that we haven't touched on?

Ann-Marie: The only other thing I'd say, and I've said this to you before, is that when I'm writing, I do ultimately very consciously address the reader. And I'm probably at that point right now with my novel where that's the last layer for me to read and rework with that in mind such that the reader feels that it's addressed to them intimately, personally, it's for them. And I don't know if I've got that going on yet in a way that I want it to be in this book – yet! But that's the point. "This is for you! I'm telling you this!" I don't see a particular person or a particular kind of person. I just see someone who is wanting to privately encounter something that might speak to them of a kind of universal truth.

That they will feel implicated, that they will be in the current of it just like I am when the audience comes. I'm in the current that runs around between the audience and the actors. I'm in that current. I get so much nourishment out of that. And so I want them to have that with the book in a very private experience. But they're tapping into something communal but quiet, private. We all know it's there except we're not all at the theatre together. But there's a communication that happens. And that's the final alchemy. It's not the book I wrote, it's the book they read. Everybody is going to read it in a different way. And the same thing with theatre, they're all seeing it a different way. Not everyone is looking at the same person, the same part of that person. Everybody is seeing a different show. And the beauty of it is that with this, we are this huge compound eye and somehow we all … You know, Liam saw that play about freedom; we're going to get it, you know, all in our different ways.

Kathleen: When I went to see a piece of theatre a year or so ago with the co-editor of this book, my colleague and friend, Barry, he said something at the end. We both didn't like what we saw and at the end he said it didn't matter that we were there. They never took in who we were. And he didn't mean us individually or that this was somehow a sophisticated audience and we'd been pandered to; that's not what he was saying. He was saying whoever the imagined other was, it wasn't us! And because we were out there and were not at liberty to change that, we had to be uncomfortable for an hour and a half.

Ann-Marie: And to be somewhere where you weren't included and weren't welcome.

Kathleen: Right! And it wasn't us! I think it wasn't even someone else. I guess we were the foil. I think that can happen in theatre. The audience has an expectation, even though this is a performance, whether you believe it or not, which is that you are looking for that kind of connection, even if you're looking only to laugh.

Ann-Marie: It's got to matter that you're there.

Kathleen: Yeah. And it didn't matter. I feel like this is somehow seriously connected to the "now" not just because of the digital age but also because of the breakdown of certain kinds of relationships we've taken as unshakeable.

Ann-Marie: You know, we don't get together in ways that we used to. We don't stay together in ways that we used to. The theatre is a constant in that way. It becomes more important. It has a bigger job to do now.

Kathleen: That's a good note to end on.

18 A Small Essay on the Largeness of Light

DANIEL DAVID MOSES

Introduction

A scientist, I once read, set an infrared camera up backstage to investigate the response of an audience watching a play in performance. How does a play work on people, he must have wondered, in a material way?

That reflected heat revealed to the questioner that, when the play had them in its thrall, almost all the individuals in the dark were blinking their eyes in unison, almost as one. Yes, there were a few, one or two ahead or lagging behind the crowd, the joker who laughs just before everyone else, the innocent who finally makes a gasped but late connection ...

The blink, our scientist must have remembered and other scientists had discovered, is the body's punctuation mark, its period or exclamation, its question mark to the consecutive sentences of the mind's real-time ideation processes; so this play, behind its lifelike or larger distractions, might be evidence of a shared or at least simultaneous sort of thinking. We, the audience, function apparently as one mind.

It must be, I still imagine he thought, in the new world of global concerns, a way of working out of that crowd's common hopes and values, working them over, embodied by virtual events, working them through and having them witnessed in the individual breathing bodies of what is, in that time, a community. The process is often cathartic but sometimes merely an articulating – or re-articulating in other, non-cliché words – if we're lucky, of an understanding, new or old, shared among the members of the audience.

This scientist, in what seems a materialist, post-Christian Canada, reminds himself to call the play, if only to himself, behind its fashionable surface distractions, an enduring ceremony, and its material effect, common meaning or spirit.

A Small Essay on the Largeness of Light
A Poem by Daniel David Moses

We spend so much of our lives in darkness,
   We're comfortable there, kids under covers.
Even more so in the kind we create
   For the audience. And though lights may rise

And discover actors stepping onto
   The stage or there already in a scene,
We're not surprised by their brightness, only
   And still after all these years by their size.

Only the moon at dusk above a dark
   Horizon shows such magnification.
It's a quality that can only be part
   Of a dream, we explain, or illusion.

Look at that actor, the way he turns with
   His prop telescope toward the pinprick stars
In the backdrop sky, a gesture so huge
   Up there on the stage, it has to be true

He's the Galileo we learned about
   In school, it has to be now he's about
To divine the shape of the cosmos. Why
   Else would he be taking so much time? You

Don't suppose he just forgot his next line?
   Too cool, too comfortable, that magnified
Actor, that magnificent player is,
   For that to be fact. Oh the way he holds

The stage is a lesson in beautiful.
   It's all about star quality, he's sure,
Though like the moon, he shines by reflection.
   Looking for his light, he turns, about to

Monologue, and his Galileo gaze
   Falls through the fourth wall onto the people
Out there in the hall. His Galileo
   Eyes let him see us here as we've never

Seemed before. It's all, he's certain, about
   Vision, but for more than that, he doesn't
Quite have words, except those the play allows
   And they pull him now toward catharsis and

Conclusion. Only a spirit, let's say
   Galileo himself, proprietor
Of that lens, having been roused from his rest
   By an actor's performance – Did I not

Tell you the guy was good? – looks into
   The black auditorium (the dead do
See in the infrared) and finds – even
   More of a surprise – the sky we are, oh

The retina shine of eyes looking back.
   Indifferent night never shook him as
Much as our eyes do, rapidly shifting
   Through a waking dream, illusion in lieu

Of disbelief. These eyes gape and even
   He finds himself reminded of the flesh.
They're closing, opening in unison,
   Taking in the action up here on stage,

The true Galileo hearing a song
   In the night. Oh how unfamiliar
Eyes have become since his death. Was ever
   He at ease with these pinprick lights, crimson

Hunger's nightmare glare piercing the backdrop
   Those bodies are? All these legions, all these
Mouths so alive in the darkness. The ghost
   Pulls the covers back up over his head.

Collective Works Cited

Alvarez, Natalie. "Empathy, Doubt, and the Simulated Encounter." *Performance Studies (Canada) Project,* April 2012. http://performancecanada .com/?post_type=portfolio&p=545.

Arendt, Hannah. *The Human Condition.* Chicago: University of Chicago Press, 1958.

Aristotle. *Poetics.* Edited and translated by Richard Janko. Indianapolis: Hackett, 1987.

Attarian, Hourig, and Rachael Van Fossen. "Stories Scorched from the Desert Sun: Testimony as Process." In *Remembering Mass Violence: Oral History, New Media, and Performance,* edited by Steven High, Edward Little, and Thi Ry Duong, 111–27. Toronto: University of Toronto Press, 2013.

Attarian, Hourig, and Hermig Yogurtian. "Survivor Stories, Surviving Narratives: Autobiography, Memory, and Trauma across Generations." In *Girlhood: Redefining the Limits,* edited by Yasmin Jiwani, Candis Steenbergen, and Claudia Mitchell, 13–34. Montreal: Black Rose Books, 2006.

Bal, P. Matthijs, and Martijn Veltkamp. "How Does Fiction Reading Influence Empathy? An Experimental Investigation on the Role of Emotional Transportation." *PLoS ONE* 8, no. 1 (30 January 2013): 1–12. doi:10.1371/journal .pone.0055341.

Barker, Howard. *Arguments for a Theatre.* London: J. Calder, 1989.

– *Arguments for a Theatre.* Manchester: Manchester University Press, 1997.

Bauman, Zygmunt. *Does Ethics Have a Chance in a World of Consumers?* Vienna Lecture Series. Cambridge, MA: Harvard University Press, 2008.

Benjamin, Walter. *Illuminations.* London: Pimlico, 1999.

Bennett, Susan. "(No) Performance Studies in Canada." *Canadian Theatre Review* 149 (2012): 79–81.

– *Theatre Audiences: A Theory of Production and Reception.* New York: Routledge, 1990.

– *Theatre Audiences: A Theory of Production and Reception.* Abingdon, UK: Routledge, 1997.

Berman, Suzanne. "Performing Online: PR Through Web Gives Arts and Cultural Institutions New Power." *Public Relations Tactics* 15, no. 10 (2008): 21.

Bernstein, Mark. "10 Tips on Writing the Living Web." *A List Apart: For People Who Make Websites* 149 (16 August 2002). http://www.alistapart.com/articles/writeliving.

Bhagwati, Sandeep. "Lamentations: A Gestural Theatre in the Realm of Shadows." In *Remembering Mass Violence: Oral History, New Media, and Performance,* edited by Steven High, Edward Little, and Thi Ry Duong, 77–90. Toronto: University of Toronto Press, 2013.

Billington, James H. "Humanizing the Information Revolution." Library of Congress, 2001. http://www.loc.gov/loc/lcib/0110/digital.html.

Blair, Rhonda. *The Actor, Image, and Action.* New York: Routledge, 2008.

Boal, Augusto. *The Rainbow of Desire: The Boal Method of Theatre and Therapy.* Translated by Adrian Jackson. New York: Routledge, 1995.

– *Theater of the Oppressed.* New York: Urizen Books, 1979.

Bollen, Wim. "Technology and the Problem of Alienation." Paper presented at the 4S & EASST Conference, Paris, France, 25–8 August 2004. http://www.csi.ensmp.fr/WebCSI/4S/search/search_P/search_P.php.

Bond, Edward. *The John Tusa Interviews.* By John Tusa. BBC Radio 3, 7 January 2001. http://www.bbc.co.uk/programmes/p00nc42q.

– "Symposium – Edward Bond Festival." Symposium presented at Toronto, Canada, 17 June 2012.

Boon, Stuart, and Christine Sinclair. "A World I Don't Inhabit: Disquiet and Identity in Second Life and Facebook." *Educational Media International* 46, no. 2 (2009): 99–110.

Brecht, Bertolt. *Brecht on Theatre: The Development of an Aesthetic.* Edited and translated by John Willett. London: Methuen, 1964.

– "A Short Organum for the Theatre." In *Brecht on Theatre: The Development of an Aesthetic,* edited and translated by John Willett, 179–207. London: Methuen, 1964.

– "Theatre for Education, Theatre for Entertainment." Translated by John Willett. In *Anthology of Drama,* edited by William B. Worthen, 602–7. London: Heinle, 2003.

– "Theatre for Pleasure or Theatre for Instruction." In *Brecht on Theatre,* translated by John Willett, 69–76. New York: Hill and Wang, 1964.

Brin, David. *The Transparent Society.* Cambridge, MA: Perseus Press, 1998.

Brown, Alan. "Initiators and Responders: Leveraging Social Context to Build Audiences." *Knight Foundation Issues Brief Series* 4 (Summer 2004): 1–11.

Brown, William. "Is Acting a Form of Simulation or Being? Acting and Mirror Neurons." In *Theorizing Film Acting*, edited by Aaron Taylor, 120–34. New York: Routledge, 2012.

Bryant, Julian. "The Power of Metaphor." *Creating Theatre*, 27 October 2008. http://creatingtheatre.com/?p=36.

Bunting, Catherine, Tak Wing Chan, John Goldthorpe, Emily Keaney, and Anni Oskala. "From Indifference to Enthusiasm: Patterns of Arts Attendance in England." Arts Council England, 1 April 2008. http://www.artscouncil.org .uk/media/uploads/indifferencetoenthusiasm.pdf.

Burtynsky, Edward. "Artist Statement." EdwardBurtynsky.com, 2013. http:// www.edwardburtynsky.com/site_contents/About/introAbout.html.

Butler, Judith. "Performative Acts and Gender Constitution: An Essay in Phenomenology and Feminist Theory." In *Writing on the Body: Female Embodiment and Feminist Theory*, edited by Katie Conboy, Nadia Medina, and Sarah Stanbury, 401–17. New York: Columbia University Press, 1997.

Campbell, W. Keith, Jennifer K. Bosson, Thomas W. Goheen, Chad E. Lakey, and Michael H. Kernis. "Do Narcissists Dislike Themselves 'Deep Down Inside'?" *Psychological Science* 18 (2007): 227–9.

CAPACOA. "Conference 2013 Schedule." January 2013. http://www .capacoa.ca/en/conference/past-conferences/2013-culture-of-place /schedule-2013.

Carlson, Marvin A. "Perspectives on Performance: Germany and America (Introduction)." In *The Transformative Power of Performance: A New Aesthetics*, edited by Erika Fischer-Lichte, 1–10. Abingdon, UK: Routledge, 2008.

– *Theories of the Theatre*. Ithaca, NY: Cornell University Press, 1993.

Carter, Alice T. "Arts Groups Increasingly Skipping Intermission." *Pittsburgh Tribune-Review*, 30 October 2011. http://triblive.com/x/pittsburghtrib/ae /theater/s_764585.html.

Cazdyn, Eric M., and Imre Szeman. *After Globalization*. Malden, MA: Wiley-Blackwell, 2011.

Christopher, F. Scott, and Rodney M. Cate. "Factors Involved in Premarital Sexual Decision-making." *Journal of Sex Research* 20 (1984): 363–76.

Clements, Marie Humber. *Burning Vision*. Burnaby, BC: Talonbooks, 2003.

Clough, Patricia Ticineto, with Jean O'Malley Halley, eds. *The Affective Turn: Theorizing the Social*. Durham, NC: Duke University Press, 2007.

Cohen, Patricia. "Who's in Charge of This Show? She Is." *New York Times*, 24 June 2009. http://www.nytimes.com/2009/06/28/theater/28cohe.html.

Comer Kidd, David, and Emanuele Castano. "Reading Literary Fiction Improves Theory of Mind." *Science* 342 (2013): 377–80.

Conference Board of Canada. "Positioning Canada's Culture Sector in the Global Market." In *Compendium of Research Papers: The International Forum on the Creative Economy*, 46–51. Gatineau, QC: Conference Board of Canada, 2008.

Conger, Cristin. "Don't Blame Facebook for the Narcissism Epidemic." *Discovery News*, 4 August 2011. http://news.discovery.com/tech/dont-blame-facebook-narcissism-epidemic-110804.htm.

Cooper, Afua. *The Hanging of Angélique: The Untold Story of Canadian Slavery and the Burning of Old Montreal.* Toronto: HarperCollins, 2006.

Crockett, Lisa J., Marcela Raffaelli, and Kristin L. Moilanen. "Adolescent Sexuality: Behavior and Meaning." In *Blackwell Handbook of Adolescence*, edited by Gerald R. Adams and Michael D. Berzonsky, 371–92. Malden, MA: Blackwell, 2003.

Croggon, Alison. "The Irresponsible Mr. Barker." *Theatre Notes*, 22 June 2004. http://theatrenotes.blogspot.ca/2004/06/irresponsible-mr-barker.html.

Crouch, Tim. "The Theatre of Reality ... and Avoiding the Stage's Kiss of Death." *Guardian*, 18 June 2014. http://www.theguardian.com/stage/2014/jun/18/theatre-reality-adler-and-gibb-tim-crouch-playwright.

Curran, Angela. "Brecht's Criticisms of Aristotle's Aesthetics of Tragedy." *Journal of Aesthetics and Art Criticism* 59, no. 2 (2001): 165–84.

Davis, Andrea. "Sex and the Nation: Performing Black Female Sexuality in Canadian Theatre." In *Critical Perspectives on Canadian Theatre in English*, vol. 2, *African-Canadian Theatre*, edited by Maureen Moynagh, 107–21. Toronto: Playwrights Canada Press, 2005.

Davis, Karen D., and Brian McKee. "Women in the Military: Facing the Warrior Framework." In *Challenge and Change in the Military: Gender and Diversity Issues*, edited by Franklin C. Pinch, Allister T. MacIntyre, Phyllis Browne, and Alan C. Ikros, 52–75. Kingston, ON: Canadian Defence Academic Press, 2004.

Davis, Tracy C., and Thomas Postlewait, eds. *Theatricality.* Cambridge: Cambridge University Press, 2003.

Davoine, Francoise, and Jean-Max Gaudilliere. *History Beyond Trauma: Whereof One Cannot Speak, Thereof One Cannot Stay Silent.* Translated by Susan Fairfield. New York: Other Press, 2004.

Debord, Guy-Ernest. "Introduction to a Critique of Urban Geography." Translated by Ken Knabb. *Les Lèvres Nues* 6 (1955). http://library.nothingness.org/articles/SI/en/display/2.

Del-Mei, Sue, Dustin Garrett, Kylie Gilmour, Smita Misra, and Lauren Weinberg. "Fracture." Unpublished manuscript, 2011.

Dewey, John. *How We Think: A Restatement of the Relation of Reflective Thinking to the Educative Process.* Chicago: Regnery, 1971.

Dixon, Joan, and Barb Howard. *Embedded on the Home Front: Where Military and Civilian Lives Converge.* Victoria, BC: Heritage House Publishing, 2012.

Dolan, Julie. *Geographies of Learning: Theory and Practice, Activism and Performance.* Middleton, CT: Wesleyan University Press, 2001.

Eagleton, Terry. "The Death of Universities." *Guardian,* 17 December 2014. http://www.theguardian.com/commentisfree/2010/dec/17/death-universities-malaise-tuition-fees.

East Yorker. "Rob Ford's Sojourn Causes a Stir Online [Comments Section]." *BlogTO,* 10 August 2013. http://www.blogto.com/city/2013/08/rob_fords_danforth_sojourn_causes_a_stir_online/.

Eisen, Marvin, Gail L. Zellman, and Alfred L. McAlister. "Evaluating the Impact of a Theory-based Sexuality and Contraceptive Education Program." *Family Planning Perspectives* 22 (1990): 261–71.

Emunah, Renee. *Acting for Real: Drama Therapy Process, Technique, and Performance.* New York: Brunner/Masel, 1994.

Esmail, Shaniff, James McKinnon, and Brenda Munro. "Internal Combustion: Sexual Health Education: Urgency and Strategies for Change." In *Theatre, Teens, Sex Ed: Are We There Yet?,* edited by Jan Selman and Jane Heather, 21–45. Edmonton: University of Alberta Press, 2015.

Esteva, Gustavo, and Madhu Suri Prakash. *Grassroots Post-Modernism: Remaking the Soil of Cultures.* London: Zed Books, 1998.

Fancy, David, and Diana Belshaw. "Introduction: Why Acting Training?" *Canadian Theatre Review* 160 (Fall 2014): 5–7.

Filewod, Alan. *Collective Encounters: Documentary Theatre in English Canada.* Toronto: University of Toronto Press, 1987.

– *Committing Theatre: Theatre Radicalism and Political Intervention in Canada.* Toronto: Between the Lines, 2011.

– "'From Twisted History': Reading Angélique." In *Critical Perspectives on Canadian Theatre in English,* vol. 2, *African-Canadian Theatre,* edited by Maureen Moynagh, 29–39. Toronto: Playwrights Canada Press, 2005.

Fischer-Lichte, Erika. *The Transformative Power of Performance: A New Aesthetics.* New York: Routledge, 2008.

Fisher, Jeffrey D., and William A. Fisher. "Theoretical Approaches to Individual-level Change in HIV Risk Behavior." In *Handbook of HIV Prevention,* edited by John L. Peterson and Ralph J. DiClements, 3–55. New York: Kluwer Academic, 2000.

Fisher, William A., and Jeffrey D. Fisher. "Understanding and Promoting Sexual and Reproductive Health Behavior: Theory and Method." *Annual Review of Sex Research* 9 (1998): 39–76.

Fraser, Nancy. "Rethinking the Public Sphere: A Contribution to the Critique of Actually Existing Democracy." In *Habermas and the Public Sphere,* edited by Craig Calhoun, 109–42. Cambridge, MA: MIT Press, 1992.

Fraser, Patricia A. "Postcards to the Beloved: An Inquiry into Our Shared Worldliness through the Practice of a Story Mentor." PhD thesis, University of British Columbia, 2012.

Freeman, Barry, Alex McLean, Daniel Mroz, Sonia Norris, Ker Wells, Maiko Bae Yamamoto. "Aesthetic Diversities in Acting Training," *Canadian Theatre Review* 160 (Fall 2014): 15–20.

Friends of the Common. "Appendix 1: Overview: Halifax Common." Public invitation for artist proposals, Halifax, 2013.

Frisch, Michael. "Sharing Authority: Oral History and the Collaborative Process." *Oral History Review* 30, no. 1 (2003): 111–13.

Gale, Lorena. *Angélique*. In *Testifyin': Contemporary African Canadian Drama*, vol. 1, edited by Djanet Sears, 8–71. Toronto: Playwrights Canada Press, 2003.

Gallese, Vittorio, Christian Keysers, and Giacomo Rizzolatti. "A Unifying View of the Basis of Social Cognition." *TRENDS in Cognitive Sciences* 8, no. 9 (September 2004): 396–403.

Gavin, Loretta E., Richard F. Catalano, Corinne David-Ferdon, Kari M. Gloppen, and Christine M. Markham. "A Review of Positive Youth Development Programs that Promote Adolescent Sexual and Reproductive Health." *Journal of Adolescent Health* 46, no. 3 (2010): S75–S91.

Geary, James. *I Is an Other*. New York: HarperCollins, 2011.

Goffman, Erving. *Asylums: Essays on the Social Situation of Mental Patients and Other Inmates*. London: Penguin Books, 1961.

– *The Presentation of Self in Everyday Life*. Garden City, NY: Doubleday, 1959.

Gosson, S. "Schoole of Abuse, Containing a Pleasant Invective Against Poets, Pipers, Plaiers, Jesters and Such Like Caterpillars of the Commonwealth." Play script, London, 1579.

Green, Adam. "*Macbeth* Takes Manhattan: New Stagings of the Shakespearean Classic." *Vogue*, 6 April 2011. http://www.vogue.com/873937/macbeth-takes-manhattan-new-stagings-of-the-shakespearean-classic/.

Greenspan, Henry. "Voices, Places, Spaces." In *Remembering Mass Violence: Oral History, New Media, and Performance*, edited by Steven High, Edward Little, and Thi Ry Duong, 35–48. Toronto: University of Toronto Press, 2013.

Gumbrecht, Hans Ulrich. *Production of Presence: What Meaning Cannot Convey*. Stanford, CA: Stanford University Press, 2004.

Gutting, Gary. "The Real Humanities Crisis." *Opinionator: New York Times*, 20 November 2013. http://opinionator.blogs.nytimes.com/2013/11/30/the-real-humanities-crisis.

Habermas, Jurgen. *Legitimation Crisis*. Translated by Thomas McCarthy. Boston, MA: Beacon Press, 1975.

Haidt, Jonathan. *The Righteous Mind: Why Good People Are Divided by Politics and Religion*. New York: Pantheon, 2012.

Hammond, Will, and Dan Steward, eds. *Verbatim Verbatim: Techniques in Contemporary Documentary Theatre.* London: Oberon, 2008.

Handke, Peter. *Kaspar and Other Plays.* Translated by Michael Roloff. New York: Farrar, Straus, and Giroux, 1969.

Hare, David. *Obedience, Struggle & Revolt.* London: Faber, 2005.

Hart, Joseph. "A New Way of Walking." *UTNE Reader,* July/August 2004. http://www.utne.com/community/a-new-way-of-walking.aspx.

Harvie, Jen. *Fair Play: Art, Performance and Neoliberalism.* Performance Interventions Series. Houndmills, UK: Palgrave Macmillan, 2013.

"Health Canada, Population and Public Health Branch." In *Canadian Guidelines for Sexual Health Education.* Ottawa: Health Canada, 2003.

Heather, Jane. "Are We There Yet?" Unpublished play script, University of Alberta, 1998; rev. ed., 2006. http://www.ualberta.ca/AWTY.

Hedges, Chris. "The War on Language." *Truthdig,* 28 September 2009. http://www.truthdig.com/report/item/20090928_the_war_on_language.

Hengen, Shannon. *Where Stories Meet: An Oral History of De-Ba-Jeh-Mu-Jig Theatre.* Toronto: Playwrights Canada Press, 2007.

Hill, Kelly. "Factors in Canadians' Arts Attendance in 2010." *Statistical Insights on the Arts* 11, no. 1 (September 2012): 1–54. http://www.hillstrategies.com/content/factors-canadians'-arts-attendance-2010.

Hillman, James. *Re-visioning Psychology.* New York: HarperCollins, 1975.

Hobsbawm, Eric. *The Age of Extremes: The Short Twentieth Century, 1914–1991.* London: Michael Joseph, 1994.

Holmes, Sean. "Maybe the Existing Structures of Theatre in This Country, Whilst Not Corrupt, Are Corrupting." WhatsOnStage.Com, 18 June 2013. http://www.whatsonstage.com/london-theatre/news/06-2013/sean-holmes-maybe-the-existing-structures-of-theat_31033.html.

Howe, Neil, and Reena Nadler. "Yes We Can: The Emergence of Millennials as a Political Generation." *New America Foundation,* 2009. https://www.lifecourse.com/assets/files/yes_we_can.pdf.

Howe, Neil, and William Strauss. *Millennials Rising: The Next Great Generation.* New York: Knopf Doubleday, 2000.

Hubbard, Betty M., Mark L. Giese, and Jacquie Rainey. "A Replication Study of 'Reducing the Risk,' a Theory-based Sexuality Curriculum for Adolescents." *Journal of School Health* 68, no. 6 (1998): 243–7.

Huffington Post Canada. "Rob Ford Shoves Photographers as Lisi Documents Drop." 31 October 2013. http://www.huffingtonpost.ca/2013/10/31/rob-ford-house-journalists-photos_n_4181453.html.

Hughes, Jenny. "Theatre, Performance, and the 'War on Terror.'" *Contemporary Theatre Review* 17, no. 2 (2007): 149–64.

Hurley, Erin. *Theatre and Feeling.* New York: Palgrave Macmillan, 2010.

– *Theatres of Affect: New Essays on Canadian Theatre.* Toronto: Playwrights Canada Press, 2014.

Hurston, Zora Neale. "How It Feels to Be Colored Me." In *I Love Myself When I Am Laughing ... And Then Again When I Am Looking Mean and Impressive: A Zora Neale Hurston Reader,* edited by Alice Walker, 152–5. Old Westbury, NY: The Feminist Press, 1979.

Jackson, Shannon. *Professing Performance: Theatre in the Academy from Philology to Performativity.* Cambridge: Cambridge University Press, 2004.

– *Social Works: Performing Art, Supporting Publics.* New York: Routledge, 2011.

Jestrovic, Silvija. *Theatre of Estrangement Theory, Practice, Ideology.* Toronto: University of Toronto Press, 2006.

Jewkes, Yvonne. *Captive Audience: Media, Masculinity, and Power in Prisons.* Devon, UK: Willan Publishing, 2002.

Johnson, Harriet McBryde. "Unspeakable Conversations." *New York Times,* 16 February 2003. http://www.nytimes.com/2003/02/16/magazine/unspeakable-conversations.html.

Jolly, Rosemary. *Cultured Violence: Narrative, Social Suffering, and Engendering Human Rights in Contemporary South Africa.* Liverpool: Liverpool University Press, 2010.

Kahneman, Daniel, Alan B. Krueger, David A. Schkade, Norbert Schwarz, and Arthur A. Stone. "A Survey Method for Characterizing Daily Life Experience: The Day Reconstruction Method." *Science* 306 (December 2004): 1776–80.

Keen, Andrew. "Against You: A Manifesto in Favor of Audience." *ChangeThis,* 2007. http://changethis.com/manifesto/show/35.03.AgainstYou.

Klein, Jeanne. "From Children's Perspectives: A Model of Aesthetic Processing in Theatre." *Journal of Aesthetic Education* 39, no. 4 (2005): 40–57.

Konrath, Sara H., Edward H. O'Brien, and Courtney Hsing. "Changes in Dispositional Empathy in American College Students Over Time: A Meta-Analysis." *Personality and Social Psychology Review* 15, no. 2 (2011): 180–98.

Künzle, Caroline. "Ssh! Listen ..." *alt.theatre: cultural diversity and the stage* 9, no. 1 (2011): 33.

Kushner, Tony. *Angels in America, Part Two: Perestroika.* New York: Theatre Communications Group, 1994.

Kushnir, Andrew. *The Middle Place.* Unpublished script, 2011.

Kvalem, Ingela Lundin, Jon Martin Sundet, Kate I. Rivø, Dag Erik Eilertsen, and Leiv S. Bakketeig. "The Effect of Sex Education on Adolescents' Use of Condoms: Applying the Solomon Four-group Design." *Health Education & Behavior* 23, no. 1 (1996): 34–47. doi:10.1177/109019819602300103.

Lambert, Craig. "The Future of Theatre: In a Digital Era, Is the Play Still the Thing?" *Harvard Magazine,* January–February 2012. http://harvardmagazine.com/2012/01/the-future-of-theater.

Langille, Donald B., David MacKinnon, Emily Marshall, and Janice Graham. "So Many Bricks in the Wall: Young Women in Nova Scotia Speak About the Barriers to School-Based Sexual Health Education." *Sex Education* 1, no. 3 (2001): 245–57.

Lehmann, Hans-Thies. *Postdramatic Theatre.* Translated by Karen Jürs-Munby. Abingdon, UK: Routledge, 2006.

Little, Edward. "Cultural Mediation." *alt.theatre: cultural diversity and the stage* 6, no. 2 (2008): 4–7.

– "The Iconoclastic Imperative." *alt.theatre: cultural diversity and the stage* 6, no. 3 (2009): 4–7.

Little, Edward, and Richard Paul Knowles. "The Spirit of Shivaree and the Community Play in Canada; Or The Unity in Community." In *Community Engaged Theatre and Performance*, edited by Julie Salverson, 20–34. Toronto: Playwrights Canada Press, 2011.

Loy, David R. *The Great Awakening.* Somerville, MA: Wisdom Publications, 2003.

– "Lack and Liberation in Self and Society: An Interview with David Loy." *Holos Forum*, 2005. www.holosforum.org/davidloy.html.

– *Money, Sex, War, Karma.* Somerville, MA: Wisdom Publications, 2008.

– *The World Is Made of Stories.* Somerville, MA: Wisdom Publications, 2010.

Luscombe, Belinda. "10 Questions for Robert Caro." *Time.com*, 21 May 2012. http://content.time.com/time/magazine/article/0,9171,2114437,00.html.

Mackey, Clarke. *Random Acts of Culture: Reclaiming Art and Community in the 21st Century.* Toronto: Between the Lines, 2010.

Maga, Carly. "Artistic Fusion: Suburban Beast and 'rihannaboi95.'" *Canada Arts Connect Magazine*, 3 July 2013. http://canadaartsconnect.com/magazine/.

Malabou, Catherine. *The New Wounded.* New York: Fordham University Press, 2012.

Mann, Arshy. "War in the Mind Puts Focus on the UBC Veterans Transition Program." *Ubyssey*, 16 November 2011. http://ubyssey.ca/culture/film-follows-veterans-in-ubc-transition-program6230/.

Marsland, Jane. "Shared Platforms and Charitable Venture Organizations." *Metcalf Foundation*, June 2013. http://metcalffoundation.com/wp-content/uploads/2013/06/Shared-Platforms-and-CVOs.pdf.

Martin, Patricia. *Tipping the Culture: How Engaging Millennials Will Change Things.* Chicago: LitLamp Communications, 2010.

Massey, Doreen B. *World City.* Cambridge: Polity Press, 2007.

Massumi, Brian. *A Shock to Thought: Expression After Deleuze and Guattari.* London: Routledge, 2002.

Maticka-Tyndale, Eleanor. "Reducing the Incidence of Sexually Transmitted Disease through Behavioural and Social Change." *Canadian Journal of Human Sexuality* 6, no. 2 (1997): 89–104.

McCabe, Marita P., and Eoin J. Killackey. "Sexual Decision Making in Young Women." *Sexual and Relationship Therapy* 19, no. 1 (2004): 15–27.

McCarthy, Kevin F., Arthur Brooks, Julia Lowell, and Laura Zakaras. *The Performing Arts in a New Era.* Santa Monica, CA: RAND, 2001.

McCarthy, Kevin F., and Kimberly Jinnett. *A New Framework for Building Participation in the Arts.* Santa Monica, CA: RAND, 2001. http://www.rand.org /content/dam/rand/pubs/monograph_reports/2005/MR1323.pdf.

McConachie, Bruce. *Engaging Audiences: A Cognitive Approach to Spectating in the Field.* New York: Palgrave Macmillan, 2008.

McKay, Alexander. "Prevention of Sexually Transmitted Infections in Different Populations: A Review of Behaviourally Effective and Cost-effective Interventions." *Canadian Journal of Human Sexuality* 9 (2000): 95–120.

– "Research Supports Broadly-based Sex Education." *Canadian Journal of Human Sexuality* 2, no. 2 (1993): 89–98.

McKittrick, Katherine. *Demonic Grounds: Black Women and the Cartographies of Struggle.* Minneapolis: University of Minnesota Press, 2006.

McKinnie, Michael. *City Stages: Theatre and Urban Space in a Global City, Cultural Spaces.* Toronto: University of Toronto Press, 2007.

McNeil, Lorraine. "Free Tarek Loubani and John Greyson Group [Facebook Post]." *Facebook*, 13 October 2013. https://www.facebook.com/groups/31083 7169062242/?fref=ts.

McQuaig, Linda. "CCPA Connections Newsletter." *Canadian Counseling and Psychotherapy Association*, February 2011.

Miller, Brent C., Bruce K. Bayley, Mathew Christensen, Spencer C. Leavitt, and Diana D. Coyl. "Adolescent Pregnancy and Childbearing." In *Blackwell Handbook of Adolescence*, edited by Gerald R. Adams and Michael D. Berzonsky, 415–49. Malden, MA: Blackwell, 2003.

Montelle, Yann-Pierre. *Palaeoperformance: The Emergence of Theatricality as Social Practice.* London: Seagull Books, 2009.

Moore, Andrew. "Facebook and the Liberal Arts." *Journal of General Education* 61, no. 3 (2012): 264–76.

Morrow, Martin. "The Good, the Weird, and the Ugly: CanStage 2.0." *Grid TO*, 26 September 2013. http://www.thegridto.com/culture/theatre /the-good-the-weird-and-the-ugly-canstage-2-0/.

Moynagh, Maureen. "African-Canadian Theatre: An Introduction." In *Critical Perspectives on Canadian Theatre in English*, vol. 2, *African-Canadian Theatre*, edited by Maureen Moynagh, vii–xxii. Toronto: Playwrights Canada Press, 2005.

Munro, Brenda E., Jan Selman, Shaniff Esmail, and Jane Heather. "Identity: Is Theatre an Asset in Dealing with Hard-to-Reach Youth?" *International Journal of Learning* 16, no. 6 (2009): 101–15.

Murphy, Ciara. "Playing Soldier? Combining Theatre and Theory to Explore the Experiences of Women in the Military." Master's thesis, Queen's University, 2011.

Murray, Susan, and Laurie Ouellette. *Reality TV: Remaking Television Culture.* New York: New York University Press, 2008.

Nestruck, J. Kelly. "Angels and Demons." *Globe and Mail,* 27 July 2013.

– "The Future of Theatre Is Cheesy." *Globe and Mail,* 6 July 2013.

– "Now Showing at Stratford: Falling Numbers and a Bit of Stage Fright." *Globe and Mail,* 9 March 2013. http://www.theglobeandmail.com/arts /theatre-and-performance/now-showing-at-stratford-falling-numbers- and-a-bit-of-stage-fright/article9517866/.

– "What's Next for Albert Schultz and Soulpepper? A Return to Classical Roots (Hopefully)." *Globe and Mail,* 27 July 2013. http://www.theglobeandmail .com/arts/theatre-and-performance/angels-and-demons/article13453085/.

Neworld Theatre. "LANDLINE." *Neworld Theatre,* 2012. http://www.neworld theatre.com/productions-landline.html.

New York Times. "Did YouTube Kill Performance Art?" 18 August 2011. http://www.nytimes.com/roomfordebate/2011/08/18/did-youtube-kill -performance-art.

Nicholls, Liz. "Fringe Frenzy Grows Again; Rookie Director Utas Already Looking Ahead to Next Year." *Edmonton Journal,* 26 August 2013.

Nicholson, Helen. *Theatre, Education and Performance: The Map and the Story.* Houndmills, UK: Palgrave Macmillan, 2011.

Nolais, Jeremy. "'Difficult Decision' Made – Mount Royal University Suspends Programs, Cuts Staff Positions." *Metro News,* 27 May 2013. http://metronews.ca/news /calgary/686582/cuts-to-mru-arts-music-approved-by-board-of-governors/.

OAC Arts Engagement Study. "Results of a 2011 Province Wide Study of the Arts Engagement Patterns of Ontario Adults." Ontario Arts Council, 2011.

Oatley, Keith. "Emotions and the Story World of Fiction." In *Narrative Impact: Social and Cognitive Foundations,* edited by Melanie C. Green, Jeffrey J. Strange, and Timothy C. Brock, 39–70. Mahwah, NJ: Lawrence Erlbaum, 2002.

Olson, Jody. "An Argument for Eliminating the Doctorate in Theater." *Chronicle of Higher Education,* 16 January 2013. http://chronicle.com/article /Eliminating-the-Doctorate-in/136673/.

Onstad, Katrina. "Love to Hate Angelina Jolie." *Globe and Mail,* 16 May 2013. http://www.theglobeandmail.com/life/celebrity-news/love -to-hate-angelina-jolie-maybe-not-after-her-mastectomy-disclosure /article11968519/.

Paget, Derek. "Acts of Commitment: Activist Arts, the Rehearsed Reading, and Documentary Theatre." *New Theatre Quarterly* 26, no. 2 (2010): 173–93.

Panic Manual. "SummerWorks Review: The Middle Place (Project: Humanity)." 13 August 2009. http://www.panicmanual.com/2009/08/13/summerworks-review-the-middle-place-project-humanity.

Ponzetti, James J., Jan Selman, Brenda Munro, Shaniff Esmail, and Gerald Adams. "The Effectiveness of Participatory Theatre with Early Adolescents in School-based Sexuality Education." Sex Education 9, no. 1 (2009): 93–103. doi:10.1080/14681810802639905.

Preece, Stephen B., and Jennifer Wiggins Johnson. "Web Strategies and the Performing Arts: A Solution to Difficult Brands." International Journal of Arts Management 14, no. 1 (2011): 19–32.

Prentki, Tim, and Jan Selman. Popular Theatre in Political Culture: Britain and Canada in Focus. Bristol, UK: Intellect, 2000.

Przybylski, Andrew K., Kou Murayama, Cody R. DeHaan, and Valerie Gladwell. "Motivational, Emotional, and Behavioral Correlates of Fear of Missing Out." Computers in Human Behavior 29, no. 4 (2013): 1841–8.

Putnam, Robert. Bowling Alone: The Collapse and Revival of American Community. New York: Simon & Schuster, 2000.

Putnam, Robert, and Lewis Feldstein. Better Together: Reviving the American Community. New York: Simon & Schuster, 2004.

Rabey, David Ian. Howard Barker: Politics and Desire: An Expository Study of His Drama and Poetry, 1969–87. Houndmills, UK: Palgrave Macmillan, 1989.

Rae, Paul. "Where Is the Cosmopolitan Stage?" Contemporary Theatre Review 16, no. 1 (2006): 8–22.

Raskin, Robert, and Calvin S. Hall. "The Narcissistic Personality Inventory: Alternate Form Reliability and Further Evidence of Construct Validity." Journal of Personality Assessment 45 (1981): 159–62.

Raskin, Robert, and Howard Terry. "A Principle Components Analysis of the Narcissistic Personality Inventory and Further Evidence of Its Construct Validity." Journal of Personality and Social Psychology 54 (1988): 890–902.

Ravenhill, Mark. "Mark Ravenhill's Edinburgh Festival Speech: 'We Need to Have a Plan B.'" Guardian, 3 August 2013. http://www.theguardian.com/culture/2013/aug/03/mark-ravenhill-edinburgh-festival-speech-full-text.

Razack, Sherene H. Looking White People in the Eye: Gender, Race, and Culture in Courtrooms and Classrooms. Toronto: University of Toronto Press, 1998.

Read, Alan. Theatre, Intimacy and Engagement: The Last Human Venue. Houndmills, UK: Palgrave Macmillan, 2009.

Reeves, Thomas C. "How Do You Know They Are Learning? The Importance of Alignment in Higher Education." International Journal of Learning Technology 2, no. 4 (2006): 294–309.

Reinelt, Janelle G. "Three Thoughts toward a Global Poetics." Contemporary Theatre Review 16, no. 1 (2006): 150–2.

Reinelt, Janelle G., and Joseph R. Roach. "General Introduction." In *Critical Theory and Performance*, edited by Janelle G. Reinelt and Joseph R. Roach, 1–6. Ann Arbor: University of Michigan Press, 1992.

Royce, Jim. "Building an Online Presence for Live Theatre: Experience from the Field." *TCG Centrepiece*, August 2001. http://www.tcg.org/pdfs/publications/centerpiece/centerpiece_0801.pdf.

Sajnani, Nisha, Warren Linds, Alan Wong, and Lisa Ndejuru. "Turning Together: Playback Theatre, Oral History, Trauma, and Arts-based Research in the Montreal Life Stories Project." In *Remembering Mass Violence: Oral History, New Media, and Performance*, edited by Steven High, Edward Little, and Thi Ry Duong, 91–110. Toronto: University of Toronto Press, 2013.

Salverson, Julie. "Change on Whose Terms? Testimony and an Erotics of Injury." *Theatre* 31, no. 3 (2001): 119–25.

– "Imagination and Art in Community Arts." In *Community Engaged Theatre and Performance*, edited by Julie Salverson. Vol. 19 of *Critical Perspectives on Canadian Theatre in English*, 123–9. Toronto: Playwrights Canada Press, 2011.

– "Social Suffering in the Military and Possible Uses for the Creative Arts." Paper presented at the Military Veterans Health Research Conference, Kingston, ON, 14–16 November 2011.

– "Transgressive Storytelling or an Aesthetic of Injury: Performance, Pedagogy and Ethics." 2nd ed. *Theatre Research in Canada* 20, no. 1 (1999): 35–51. https://journals.lib.unb.ca/index.php/tric/article/view/7096/8155.

sam culture ltd. *A Night Less Ordinary – Evaluation*. Arts Council England, 5 April 2012. http://www.artscouncil.org.uk/media/uploads/pdf/ANLO_FINAL_REPORT.pdf.

Sanders, Leslie, and Rinaldo Walcott. "At the Full and Change of CanLit: An Interview with Dionne Brand." *Canadian Woman Studies* 20, no. 2 (2000): 22–6.

Saxton, Gregory D., Chao Gao, and William A. Brown. "New Dimensions of Nonprofit Responsiveness: The Application and Promise of Internet-based Technologies." *Public Performance & Management Review* 31, no. 2 (2007): 144–73.

Scarry, Elaine. *On Beauty and Being Just*. London: Duckbacks, 1999.

Schaffer, Kay, and Sidonie Smith. *Human Rights and Narrated Lives: The Ethics of Recognition*. New York: Palgrave Macmillan, 2004.

Schechner, Richard. "A New Paradigm for Theatre in the Academy." *TDR: The Drama Review* 36, no. 4 (1992): 7–10.

– "No More Theatre PhDs?" *TDR: The Drama Review* 57, no. 3 (2013): 7–8.

Scheff, Joanne. "Factors Influencing Subscription and Single-Ticket Purchases at Performing Arts Organizations." *International Journal of Arts Management* 1, no. 2 (1999): 16–27.

Schneller, Johanna. "The Gift of Feeling." *Globe and Mail*, 5 October 2013.

Scollen, Rebecca. "Talking Theatre Is More Than a Test Drive: Two Audience Development Methodologies." *International Journal of Arts Management* 12, no. 1 (2009): 4–13.

Sears, Djanet. "Introduction." In *Testifyin': Contemporary African Canadian Drama*, vol. 1, edited by Djanet Sears, i–xiii. Toronto: Playwrights Canada Press, 2000.

Selman, Jan. "Research." *Are We There Yet?* University of Alberta, 17 October 2013. http://www.ualberta.ca/AWTY/research.html.

– "It's the Wheel Thing: What Can Theatre Do? And How Do We Know?" In *Theatre, Teens, Sex Ed: Are We There Yet?*, edited by Jan Selman and Jane Heather, 407–33. Edmonton: University of Alberta Press, 2015.

Selman, Jan, Kate Nunn, Evelyn Derus, Shaniff Esmail, Brenda E. Munro, and James Ponzetti. "Are We There Yet?" CURA Edmonton Public School Board 2008 Report, University of Alberta, 2008. http://www.ualberta.ca/AWTY/EPSB%202008%20Report%20-%20Final.doc.

Sennett, Richard. *The Fall of Public Man*. Cambridge: Cambridge University Press, 1977.

– *Together: The Rituals, Pleasures and Politics of Cooperation*. New Haven, CT: Yale University Press, 2012.

Sherwood, Kay E., ed. *Proceedings from the Wallace Foundation Arts Grantee Conference*. New York: The Wallace Foundation, 2009. http://www.wallace foundation.org/knowledge-center/audience-development-for-the-arts /strategies-for-expanding-audiences/Documents/Engaging-Audiences.pdf.

Shirinian, Lorne. "So Far From Home." In *Remembering Mass Violence: Oral History, New Media, and Performance*, edited by Steven High, Edward Little, and Thi Ry Duong, 49–59. Toronto: University of Toronto Press, 2013.

Singh, J.P. *Globalized Arts: The Entertainment Economy and Cultural Identity*. New York: Columbia University Press, 2011.

Skloot, Robert. "The Theatre and the Crisis of Language." *Journal of Aesthetic Education* 6, no. 4 (1972): 63–75.

Sontag, Susan. *Against Interpretation*. London: Vintage, 2001.

Stanislavski, Constantin. *An Actor Prepares*. Translated by Elizabeth Reynolds Hapgood. New York: Routledge, 1989.

Statistics Canada. "Population by Broad Age Groups and Sex, Counts, Including Median Age, 1921 to 2011 for Both Sexes – Canada." 19 July 2013. http:// www12.statcan.gc.ca/census-recensement/2011/dp-pd/hlt-fst/as-sa/Pages /highlight.cfm?TabID=1&Lang=E&PRCode=01&Asc=0&OrderBy=1&Sex= 1&View=1&tableID=22.

Stephenson, Jenn. *Performing Autobiography: Contemporary Canadian Drama*. Toronto: University of Toronto Press, 2014.

Stinson, Frederick S., Deborah A. Dawson, Risë B. Goldstein, S. Patricia Chou, Boji Huang, Sharon Mand Smith, W. June Ruan, Attila J. Pulay, Tulshi D. Saha, Roger P. Pickering, and Bridget F. Grant. "Prevalence, Correlates, Disability, and Comorbidity of DSM-IV Narcissistic Personality Disorder: Results from the Wave 2 National Epidemiologic Survey on Alcohol and Related Conditions." *Journal of Clinical Psychiatry* 69 (2008): 1033–45.

Strategic Counsel. "TAPA Audience Survey: Attendance and Engagement with Arts and Cultural Activities in Toronto." Toronto: TAPA, November 2013. http://tapa.ca/wp-content/uploads/2014/10/TAPA_Audience_Report_FINAL_REVISED.pdf.

Swanson, Scott R., J. Charlene Davis, and Yushan Zhao. "Art for Art's Sake? An Examination of Motives for Arts Performance Attendance." *Nonprofit and Voluntary Sector Quarterly* 37 (2008): 300–23.

Szántó, András, ed. *Proceedings from the Wallace Foundation Arts Grantee Conference.* New York: The Wallace Foundation, 2008. http://www.wallacefoundation.org/knowledge-center/audience-development-for-the-arts/strategies-for-expanding-audiences/Documents/arts-for-all-connecting-to-new-audiences.pdf.

Tapscott, Don. *Growing Up Digital: The Rise of the Net Generation.* New York: McGraw-Hill, 1998.

Taylor, Paul, and Scott Keeter, eds. *Millennials: A Portrait of Generation Next.* Washington, DC: Pew Research Center, 2010.

The God That Comes. "About: The Experience." 2013. http://thegodthatcomes.com/about/the-experience.

– "Technical Rider." 2013. http://thegodthatcomes.com/pub/TGTCTechnicalRider.pdf.

Thompson, Craig, and Ted Boniface. *Beyond the Curtain: How Digital Media Is Reshaping Theatre.* Stratford, ON: Avonova, 2011. http://www.avonova.ca/assets/uploads/pages/image/files/Beyond_The_Curtain.pdf.

Thompson, James. *Performance Affects: Applied Theatre and the End of Effect.* Houndmills, UK: Palgrave Macmillan, 2009.

Thomson, Kristin, Kristen Purcell, and Lee Rainie. *Arts Organizations and Digital Technologies.* Washington, DC: Pew Research Center, 2013.

Tolson, Andrew. *The Limits of Masculinity.* London: Tavistock, 1977.

Trapnell, Paul, and Lisa Sinclair. "Texting Frequency and The Moral Shallowing Hypothesis." Paper presented at the 13th Annual Meeting of the Society for Personality and Social Psychology (SPSP), San Diego, CA, 26–8 January 2012.

Turkle, Sherry. *Alone Together: Why We Expect More from Technology.* New York: Basic Books, 2011.

Turner, Victor. *From Ritual to Theater.* New York: Performing Arts Journal Publications, 1982.

Twenge, Jean M. *Generation Me: Why Today's Young Americans Are More Confident, Assertive, Entitled – and More Miserable Than Ever Before.* New York: Free Press, 2006.

Twenge, Jean M., and W. Keith Campbell. *The Narcissism Epidemic: Living in the Age of Entitlement.* New York: Free Press/Simon & Schuster, 2009.

Twenge, Jean M., Sara Konrath, Joshua D. Foster, W. Keith Campbell, and Brad J. Bushman. "Egos Inflating Over Time: A Cross-Temporal Meta-Analysis of the Narcissistic Personality Inventory." *Journal of Personality* 76, no. 4 (2008): 875–902.

Ubersfeld, Anne. "The Pleasure of the Spectator." *Modern Drama* 25, no. 1 (1982): 27–39.

Väyrynen, Tarja. "Keeping the Trauma of War Open in the Male Body: Resisting the Hegemonic Forms of Masculinity and National Identity in Visual Arts." *Journal of Gender Studies* 22, no. 2 (2013): 137–51.

Weiten, Wayne. *Psychology: Themes and Variations.* 5th ed. Belmont, CA: Wadsworth Thompson Learning, 2001.

Wellings, Kaye, Julia Field, Anne M. Johnson, and Jane Wadsworth. *Sexual Behavior in Britain: The National Survey of Sexual Attitudes and Lifestyles.* London: Penguin Books, 1994.

Westlake, E.J. "Friend Me If You Facebook: Generation Y and Performative Surveillance." *TDR: The Drama Review* 52, no. 4 (2008): 21–40.

Williams, Raymond. *The Long Revolution.* Harmondsworth, UK: Penguin, 1965.

Wong, Adrienne. "Artist Statement." Unpublished grant proposal, Canada, 2012.

Young, S. Mark, and Drew Pinsky. "Narcissism and Celebrity." *Journal of Research in Personality* 40 (2006): 463–71.

Zabin, Laurie S., Marilyn B. Hirsch, Edward A. Smith, and Janet B. Hardy. "Adolescent Sexual Attitudes and Behavior: Are They Consistent?" *Family Planning Perspectives* 16, no. 4 (1984): 181–5b.

Zola, Emile. "Naturalism on the Stage." In *Dramatic Theory and Criticism: Greeks to Grotowski,* edited by Bernard Dukore and translated by Belle M. Sherman, 692–719. New York: Holt Rinehart & Winston, 1974.

Contributors

Catherine Banks's plays include *It Is Solved By Walking, Bone Cage, Three Storey, Ocean View,* and *Bitter Rose. Bitter Rose* aired on Bravo! Canada. *Bone Cage* won the Governor General's Award for Literature (English) Drama 2008, and *It Is Solved By Walking* won the Governor General's Award in 2012. *It Is Solved by Walking* has been translated into Catalan by Tant per Tant and was one of three Canadian plays that toured Catalonia in November 2012. She is currently completing *Miss N Me,* a play about a rural hairdresser who drives to New York City to meet her idol Missy Elliot, and her adaptation of Ernest Buckler's remarkable novel *The Mountain and the Valley* for the stage. Scirocco Drama published *Bitter Rose* with *Three Storey, Ocean View* in the fall of 2014. Banks was awarded Nova Scotia's Established Artist Award for her body of work (2008) and the Queen's Jubilee Medal in 2012.

Alan Dilworth is known for his award-winning direction of contemporary tragedies and reinvented classics. His body of work explores questions of justice and what it means to be human. He has brought over 30 new Canadian plays to the stage, including his own SummerWorks Jury Prize–winning *The Unforgetting,* Erin Shields's SummerWorks Jury Prize and Governor General's Award–winning *If We Were Birds,* Andrew Kushnir's verbatim opuses Toronto Theatre Critics Award–winning *The Middle Place* and *Small Axe,* Pamela Sinha's multiple Dora Award–winning *Crash* and *Happy Place,* and the acclaimed Stratford Shakespeare Festival production of Kate Hennig's *The Last Wife.* These along with his work on Edward Bond's epic masterpieces *The Bundle* and *Human Cannon* have established Alan as a director of sometimes harrowing but always humanizing productions, known for their spare stage imagery and "operatic minimalism." In 2013, he was awarded the inaugural Christopher Plummer Fellowship Award of Excellence for his contribution to work on classical text. Alan is a resident director and Drummond-Dorrance Fellow at Soulpepper Theatre Company (*Eurydice, Twelve Angry Men, Happy Place, La Ronde*). He is a co-founder and co-artistic director of Sheep No Wool (Edward Bond Festival, *Montparnasse, Passion Play*). Alan conducts ongoing research in the performance of poetic texts with a focus on Bond, Greek tragedy, and verbatim text. He has an MFA in Directing from York University and degrees in International Relations and Education.

Barry Freeman is Assistant Professor in Theatre and Performance Studies at the University of Toronto Scarborough and the Centre for Drama, Theatre and Performance Studies. Barry is an Executive Editor of *Theatre Research in Canada* and an Associate Editor of *Canadian Theatre Review*. His research involves contemporary Canadian theatre, ethics, globalization, and interculturalism and has been published in *Theatre Research in Canada, Canadian Theatre Review, alt.theatre, Research in Drama Education*, and *Performing Ethos*. In 2011, Barry was awarded the Richard Plant Prize for outstanding scholarly essay in English by the Canadian Association for Theatre Research for the article "Navigating the *Prague-Toronto-Manitoulin Theatre Project*: A Postmodern Ethnographic Approach to Collaborative Intercultural Theatre." His current book project, *Staging Strangers: Theatre and Global Ethics*, examines ethical aspects of contemporary Canadian intercultural theatre.

Kathleen Gallagher is a Distinguished Professor at the University of Toronto. Dr Gallagher's award-winning books include *Why Theatre Matters: Urban Youth, Engagement, and a Pedagogy of the Real* (University of Toronto Press, 2014); *The Theatre of Urban: Youth and Schooling in Dangerous Times* (University of Toronto Press, 2007); and *Drama Education in the Lives of Girls: Imagining Possibilities* (University of Toronto Press, 2000). Her edited collections include *Drama and Theatre in Urban Contexts* (with Jonothan Neelands, Routledge, 2013); *How Theatre Educates: Convergences and Counterpoints with Artists, Scholars, and Advocates* (with David Booth, University of Toronto Press, 2003); and *The Methodological Dilemma: Creative, Critical and Collaborative Approaches to Qualitative Research* (Routledge, 2008). Dr Gallagher has published many articles on theatre, youth, pedagogy, methodology, and gender and travels widely giving international addresses and workshops for drama practitioners. Her new Social Sciences and Humanities Research Council–funded project is a collaborative ethnography with India, Greece, England, and Taiwan, titled *Youth, Theatre, Radical Hope and the Ethical Imaginary: An Intercultural Investigation of Drama Pedagogy, Performance and Civic Engagement.*

Nicholas Hanson is Associate Professor and Chair at the University of Lethbridge, teaching courses in Theatre for Young Audiences, improvisation, and arts administration. His recent articles have appeared in *Canadian Theatre Review, The Lion & Unicorn*, and the *New Canadian Realisms* anthology. Nicholas recently completed a four-year term as the Artistic Director of Lethbridge-based New West Theatre, the largest professional Albertan theatre company outside of Calgary and Edmonton.

Dustin Scott Harvey's work has grown to encompass a myriad of people and places come, gone, and soon to be. Through the exploration of site and exploitation of media art, Dustin creates meaningful moments that offer new ways of being together while shedding crooked light on how it is we've grown apart. His recent work is about a beauty found in the connections between strangers. These projects include theatrical walks with the help of iPods, live film events, site-specific performances, viewer-responsive audio installations, and immersive text message experiences. Each production is about creating powerful, shared experiences that are thoughtful, intimate, and temporary. Based in Dartmouth, Nova Scotia, his productions have been produced in Denmark, Wales, Ireland, Montreal, Toronto, St John's, Calgary, Victoria, and throughout Halifax. His works include *Departure, Folkloremobile, Farewell, The Common, (We) Are Here, Another City, Best Wishes, Cowboy Show,* and *Winding Up Godot.* His writings about performance have been published in Canadian Theatre Review (issues 126, 134, 159). He has a BA in Theatre Studies from Acadia University in Wolfville, Nova Scotia, and a postgraduate diploma in Acting from the London Academy of Music and Dramatic Art in London, England.

Naila Keleta-Mae is Assistant Professor of Theatre and Performance at the University of Waterloo, where she researches critical race, gender, and performance studies. Her scholarship covers a range of subject matters: from Beyoncé to Canadian federal politics to Amiri Baraka. Dr Keleta-Mae has been awarded the Lois Claxton Social Sciences and Humanities Award from the University of Waterloo, the New Scholars Prize by the International Federation for Theatre Research, the Mary McEwan Award for feminist scholarship from York University, the Abella

Scholarship for Studies in Equity from York University, and a Canada Graduate Scholarship from SSHRC. Dr Keleta-Mae is also a poet, recording artist, playwright, and director who has performed in Canada, France, South Africa, and the United States of America. She has released two full-length albums, been produced by bcurrent, Black Theatre Workshop, and University of Waterloo Drama, and been published by the *Toronto Star*, Playwrights Canada Press, Fernwood Publishing, and Frontenac House Publishing Ltd.

Andrew Kushnir is a Toronto-based playwright, director, actor, and community arts worker. He is creative director of Project: Humanity (PH), an organization raising awareness of social issues through the arts. His produced plays include *Captain Princess, foto, The Middle Place, Small Axe, The Gay Heritage Project* (with collaborators Damien Atkins and Paul Dunn), and *Wormwood. The Middle Place* has toured Toronto high schools, was produced for general audiences by Theatre Passe Muraille and Canadian Stage, and has toured nationally by PH to the Great Canadian Theatre Company and the Belfry Theatre. It received two SummerWorks Festival Jury Prizes and the 2011 Toronto Theatre Critics Award for Best Production of a Play, and it earned Andrew a Dora nomination for Outstanding New Play. He is playwright in residence at the Tarragon Theatre. Andrew is a Loran Scholar, a graduate of the BFA (Acting) program at the University of Alberta, and a 2013 recipient of the university's Alumni Horizon Award. He is currently developing a new verbatim project, *The Teacher*, in collaboration with Kathleen Gallagher.

Laura Levin is Associate Professor of Theatre at York University and Editor-in-Chief of the *Canadian Theatre Review*. She is author of *Performing Ground: Space, Camouflage, and the Art of Blending In*, a book on the relationship between body and environment in contemporary performance (winner of the Canadian Association for Theatre Research's [CATR's] Ann Saddlemyer Award). She is the editor of *Conversations Across Borders* (Seagull) and *Theatre in Toronto* (Playwrights Canada), as well as several journal issues on topics ranging from performance art to performance and public space. She has published a number of essays on contemporary theatre and performance art with a focus on performing gender and sexuality, site-specific and urban performance, and disciplinary histories of performance. Her publication "Can the City Write: Letting Space Speak After Poststructuralism" was awarded CATR's 2010 Richard Plant Award. She is Director of the Performance Studies (Canada)

Project, a SSHRC-funded research study on the development of the field of Performance Studies in Canada and Director of the MA/PhD in Theatre & Performance Studies at York.

Edward (Ted) Little teaches socially engaged and activist theatre at Concordia University, where he is Chair of the Department of Theatre. He is Associate Artistic Director of Teesri Duniya Theatre and was editor-in-chief of *alt.theatre: cultural diversity and the stage* from 2002 to 2012. Between 2007 and 2012 he was co-investigator and leader of the Performance Working Group for *Life Stories of Montrealers Displaced by War, Genocide, and Other Human Rights Violations*. His current projects include an interdisciplinary, SSHRC-funded Insight Development web and book project with Elizabeth Miller and Steven High. The website, Going Public with Oral History, Documentary Media, and Theatre, features short interviews with socially engaged practitioners from around the world reflecting on the process, politics, art, and significance of "going public" in an era of multimedia authorship. The companion book is scheduled for publication in 2016. Other publications include *Remembering Mass Violence: Oral History, New Media, and Performance*, co-edited with Steven High and Thi Ry Duong (University of Toronto Press, 2013); and "Partners in Conversation: A Reflection on the Ethics and Emergent Practice of Oral History Performance" (co-authored with Steven High), in *History, Memory, Performance*, edited by David Dean, Yana Meerzon, and Kathryn Prince (Palgrave Macmillan, 2014).

Ann-Marie MacDonald is an author, playwright, and actor. Best known for her plays, *Goodnight Desdemona (Good Morning Juliet)* and *Belle Moral: A Natural History*, and her novels, *Fall On Your Knees* and *The Way the Crow Flies*, she also enjoys a career on stage, most recently in Tarragon Theatre's production of "More Fine Girls." Her work as a screen actor has earned her a Gemini Award and a Genie Nomination. MacDonald's writing has been honoured with numerous awards including the Chalmers, the Dora Mavor Moore, the Governor General's, and the Commonwealth Prize. She hosted CBC Television's *Life and Times* for seven seasons and currently hosts the flagship documentary series *Doc Zone*. Her latest novel is *Adult Onset*.

Jackie Maxwell began her work as Artistic Director of the Shaw Festival in 2002. Her select Shaw Festival credits include *Major Barbara; Ragtime; Come Back, Little Sheba; Age of Arousal; An Ideal Husband; The Entertainer;*

Mrs. Warren's Profession; The Stepmother; Saint Joan; The Magic Fire; Gypsy; Bus Stop; Pygmalion; Rutherford and Son; Three Sisters; The Coronation Voyage; Merrily We Roll Along; Candida; and *Picnic.* She has worked extensively across Canada as a director and dramaturge for companies such as Tarragon Theatre, Canadian Stage Company, Mirvish Productions, Centaur Theatre, Theatre Calgary, and the Charlottetown Festival, and she was Artistic Director of Factory Theatre from 1986 to 1994. Recently, she directed *Good People* at Arena Stage in Washington, DC, having made her United States directorial debut in 2007 at the Chicago Shakespeare Theatre with the acclaimed production of *Saint Joan.* Jackie is also a well-respected teacher for institutions such as the Banff Centre for the Arts, National Theatre School, and the Centre for Drama, Theatre and Performance Studies at the University of Toronto. She is the recipient of a Queen Elizabeth II Diamond Jubilee Medal, an honorary Doctor of Laws (Queen's University), an honorary Doctor of Humanities (University of Windsor), and a Gascon-Thomas Award (National Theatre School).

James McKinnon is Programme Director of the Victoria University of Wellington Theatre Programme. His research focuses on adaptation, particularly contemporary appropriations of canonical classics, as well as the pedagogical applications of adaptation-based dramaturgy. His work has appeared in recent issues of *Theatre Research in Canada, Journal of Perspectives in Applied Academic Practice, Canadian Theatre Review, Teaching Learning Inquiry,* and the recent anthology *Adapting Chekhov: The Text and Its Mutations.* At VUW, he teaches courses in dramaturgy, modern and postmodern drama, and dramatic theory and criticism, and has directed two original theatre productions, *Shit Show* (inspired by Alfred Jarry's *Ubu Roi*) and *Mystery Play*, derived from the English liturgical plays and other sources. Current and forthcoming projects include a multimedia, practice-based inquiry into the legacies of Futurism, and an investigation of the influence of devising on tertiary drama and theatre programs.

John Mighton is a mathematician, playwright, and bestselling author of *The End of Ignorance: Multiplying Our Human Potential.* He is currently a Fellow of the Fields Institute for Research in Mathematical Sciences and has also taught mathematics and math education at the University of Toronto and lectured in philosophy at McMaster University, where he received a master's in Philosophy. John is the founder of JUMP Math, a charity whose mission is to improve the teaching of mathematics. The

JUMP program is used as classroom resource for math by over 100 000 students in Canada and the United States. John recently published an article in *Scientific American Mind* on the principles of teaching used in JUMP. John's plays, which include *Half Life*, *The Little Years*, and *Possible Worlds*, have been produced around the world and have received a number of national awards including two Governor General's Awards and the Siminovitch Prize. John was named an Officer of the Order of Canada for his work as a writer and social entrepreneur.

Playwright, poet, essayist, and teacher **Daniel David Moses** is a Delaware from the Six Nations lands in southern Ontario, Canada. He holds an Honours BA in General Fine Arts from York University and an MFA in Creative Writing from the University of British Columbia. His plays include his first, *Coyote City*, a nominee for the 1991 Governor General's Literary Award for Drama; *Almighty Voice and His Wife*, included in the *Norton Anthology of Drama* (2nd ed., vol. 2); and *Kyotopolis*. He is also the author of *A Small Essay on the Largeness of Light and Other Poems* (Exile Editions, 2012), and co-editor of *An Anthology of Canadian Native Literature in English* (Oxford University Press), the 4th and 20th Anniversary Edition of which appeared in 2013. Other recent publications include *River Range*, a CD of a suite of poems with music by David Deleary, and, as editor, *The Exile Book of Native Canadian Fiction and Drama*, an anthology, both published by Exile Editions in 2010. His honours include a James Buller Memorial Award (for the play *The Indian Medicine Shows*), the Harbourfront Festival Prize, and a Chalmers Fellowship. He teaches playwriting in the School of Drama and Music at Queen's University as an Associate Professor.

Julie Salverson writes plays, essays, and opera and has published extensively about the artist as witness, historical memory, ethics, and the imagination. She gives workshops and presentations for diverse groups using creative arts methods to share stories, analyse community issues, and address difficult dynamics. She edited *Community Engaged Theatre* (2011) and *Popular Political Theatre and Performance* (2010), published by Playwrights Canada Press. Her feature "They Never Told Us These Things" appeared in *Maisonneuve Magazine* (Summer 2011). She was a 2009 runner-up for the CBC Literary Awards (creative nonfiction) and in 2008 received honourable mention from *The Malahat Review* (with Peter van Wyck). *Shelter*, her cartoon chamber opera about the atomic bomb (libretto) premiered with Edmonton Opera in November 2012 and played in Toronto in June 2014 (Tapestry New Opera/Edmonton Opera). Julie works with War Horse Awareness Foundation in Alberta exploring arts/equine programs with front-line service providers. She is Associate Professor of Drama at Queen's University and Adjunct Professor at the Royal Military College of Canada. She is completing the book *Lines of Flight: An Atomic Memoir.*

Julie Tepperman is an actor, playwright, educator, and co-artistic director (with Aaron Willis) of Convergence Theatre, creators of the hit plays *YICHUD (Seclusion)*, *The Gladstone Variations*, and *AutoShow*, and co-producers of the Canadian premiere of Sarah Ruhl's three-part epic *Passion Play*, winner of a Dora Award for Outstanding Performance by an Ensemble. Julie has acted on stages across Toronto and was a company member with the Stratford Festival for two seasons. Julie's playwriting credits include *YICHUD (Seclusion)*, published by Playwrights Canada Press; *I Grow Old* (as part of *The Gladstone Variations*), with four Dora nominations and listed number 2 in *NOW Magazine*'s "Top Ten Toronto Productions of the Decade"); *ROSY* (as part of *AutoShow*); and a reimagining of the August Strindberg play *The Father* (Winnipeg Jewish Theatre/Manitoba Theatre Centre's Master Playwright's Festival). Julie was playwright in residence at Theatre Passe Muraille in 2010–11 with the support of the Canada Council. She is currently developing an opera for teens with the support of Tapestry New Opera and co-creating *Brantwood*, a site-specific musical extravaganza, through Sheridan's Canadian Musical Theatre Project. Julie is a graduate of George Brown Theatre School and the Stratford Festival's Birmingham Conservatory for Classical Theatre Training.

Judith Thompson is the author of the plays *The Crackwalker, White Biting Dog, I Am Yours, Lion in the Streets, Sled, Perfect Pie, Habitat, Capture Me, Enoch Arden, Such Creatures,* and *Palace of the End.* She is currently developing and acting in the one-woman play *Watching Glory Die* with Ken Gass and the Canadian Repertory Theatre Company in Toronto and at work on a commission for the Stratford Shakespeare Festival. Entitled *The Thrill,* the play had its world premiere August 2013. Judith is also currently at work on a play entitled *Who Killed Snow White* with Nightwood Theatre. She has written two feature films, *Lost and Delirious* and *Perfect Pie,* as well as multiple television movies and radio drama. A highly esteemed Canadian playwright, she is the recipient of two Governor General's Literary

Awards and an Officer in the Order of Canada. In 2007, she was awarded
the prestigious Walter Carsen Prize for Excellence in the Performing
Arts, and in 2008, she was awarded the Susan Smith Blackburn Award
and the Dora Mavor Moore Outstanding New Play Award for *Palace of
the End*. Judith is the founding artistic director of R.A.R.E Theatre Company, whose recent production of the play *RARE* – created and directed
by Judith Thompson in collaboration with nine performers with Down
Syndrome – was a hit and Patrons' Pick at the 2012 Toronto Fringe Festival and enjoyed an extended run when remounted at the Young Centre
for the Performing Arts. Judith is currently Professor of Drama at the
University of Guelph and lives with her husband and five children in
Toronto.

Aaron Willis is an actor, director, educator, and co-founding artistic director of Convergence Theatre (with Julie Tepperman). Directing credits
include *The Thing Between Us* (mcguffin company), *The Crucible* (Theatre
Erindale/UTM), *Danny and the Deep Blue Sea* (Baro Theatre), *Passion Play*
(Convergence/Outside the March/Sheep No Wool), *Miss Caledonia* (Tarragon Theatre), *When The Ice Breaks* (Down n Out Productions/Campbell
House Museum), *Other People* (Mutual Friends Co-op), *YICHUD (Seclusion)* (Theatre Passe Muraille/Convergence Theatre), *The Gladstone Variations – The Tearful Bride* (Convergence Theatre; Dora nomination), and
AutoShow (Convergence Theatre/Toronto Fringe 2006). Acting credits
include *Murderers Confess at Christmastime* (Outside the March/Sum-
merWorks 2013), *YICHUD (Seclusion)* (Theatre Passe Muraille/Conver-
gence), *The Incredible Speediness of Jamie Cavanaugh* (Roseneath Theatre),
Zadie's Shoes (GCTC), *Abattoir* (Kaeja d'Dance/Harbourfront Centre),
The Russian Play (Factory Theatre), *Wrecked* (Roseneath; Dora nomination – Best Performance TYA), *The Merchant of Venice* (Shakespeare in
the Rough), *(nod)* (Theatre Gargantua), *Waiting for Lefty* and *Awake and
Sing* (The Co.), and *Well* (Tarragon Theatre). Film/TV credits include
Reign and *Flashpoint*. Aaron served as Assistant Director on *EVITA* (2010)
and *Much Ado About Nothing* (2012) at the Stratford Festival's Michael
Langham Workshop for Classical Theatre Direction. He has a Honours
BA in Drama from the University of Alberta and is a graduate of George
Brown Theatre School. Upcoming: Aaron will be making his directorial
debut at Soulpepper Theatre in the spring of 2016 with *The Testament of
Mary*. Aaron is the recipient of a Metcalf Foundation Performing Arts
Internship, which has him working as a producer at Canadian Stage for
the 2015–16 season.

Index

Page numbers in *italics* refer to photographs

37, 38, 44–5; Soulpepper Theatre,
251. *See also* theatre companies
Passion Play (Ruhl), 10, *11*, 196–200,
201, 206
Paulus, Diane, 190
PeerGrouP, Netherlands, 24
Peltier, Josh, *28*, 34n6
Perfect Pie (Judith Thompson), 255
Performance Affects (James Thompson),
72
performance culture: about, 9, 15;
continuum of cultural behaviours,
162; disciplinary boundaries, 170,
172–4; and everyday life, 165,
167–72; impression management,
169, 171; as interdisciplinary, 163,
164–7; and masculinity, 145–6;
and politics, 161, 168–9; and self-
disclosure, 167–72; Situationists,
38–9, 46; and social media, 168;
ubiquity of, 15, 167–72. *See also*
everyday life; social media
performance studies: about, 15;
add-on to other departments,
162–4, 172–4, 174n10, 177n48;
continuum of cultural behaviours,
162; creative process, 166;
disciplinary boundaries, 15, 163,
164–7, 172–4, 174n10; financial
issues, 167; graduate programs, 162,
174n10; and masculinity, 145–6;
and performance culture, 172–4;
site-specific performance, 162; site-
specific venues, 165
Performing Autobiography
(Stephenson), 10
perpetual performance, 130–1, 141n9
Le Petit Coin Intact (Ndejuru), 56–7
physical disabilities, people with,
251–2, *252*, *254*
physics. *See* math and science
place, connection to: about, 13,
42–3; *THE COMMON*, 39–42,
40; in *FAREWELL*, 42–4, 47–8,

48n4; impact of theatre on, 36;
LANDLINE, 44–6, *47*, 48n6,
165–6; and outmigration, 13,
35, 43–4; psychogeography,
38–42; as purpose for theatre,
36–7, 40; Situationists, 38–9,
46; spectator-chosen places, 45;
and touring companies, 42, 207;
transformation of connections, 36.
See also *The Global Savages*; site-
specific theatre
playhouses. *See* sites for theatre
playwrights: attentive listening
by, 14, 112–16, 233; audience
feedback forms for, 257; creative
process of, 112–16, 232–4,
247–8, 256; and gender in Shaw
Festival programming, 120–3; and
human howl of assertion, 8, 255;
inspiration from actors, 256
pleasure from theatre: *AWTY*
audience reception research,
217–26; Brecht on, 217
Plowman, Robert, 39–42
PODPLAYS, 44
poetic language of theatre, 99, 103–5,
107. *See also* image work, Latham's
political theatre: affect and shock
to thought, 76–80; and affective
encounters, 67–8; affective vs.
political theatre, 68; and empathy,
72–3; presence vs. meaning culture
and political action, 77–8. *See also*
Montreal Life Stories; social change
politics and performance culture,
168–9
Ponzetti, Jim, 217
popular culture: comparison of
theatre with film/TV, 79–80,
244, 262–3; as competition with
theatre, 182–3; and masculinity,
143, 146; and military, 148–9;
and performance culture,
167–72; reality television, 181;

12345678910111213141516171819202122232425

director, 14, 119–28; musical theatre, 121, 125; and sexuality, 126; *The Stepmother*, 122–3
Sheep No Wool, 10
shelter youth. *See* vulnerable youth, ethnographic theatre project
Shirinian, Lorne, 55
Shultz, Albert, 251
Sick (Judith Thompson), 249, 255
Simon, Herb, 238
Simon Fraser University, 174n10
Sinclair, Christine, 169
Singer, Peter, 247
Singh, J.P., 22
Sinha, Pamela, 239
Sirens: Elektra in Bosnia (Judith Thompson), 252–3, 255
sites for theatre: about, 5, 164–5; in academic programs, 164–5; and fire, 31; non-venued companies, 204; preference for local sites, 5, 9, 10; social ambiance, 184, 190–1
site-specific theatre: about, 42–3; and audience engagement, 264; audio tours, 41–2, 44, 45–6, *47*; THE COMMON, 39–42, *40*; FAREWELL, 42–4, 47–8, 48n4; and *The Global Savages*, 22, *28*, 29–30, *30*; LANDLINE, 165–6; parks, 10, 37, 39–42, *40*, 196, *201*; *Passion Play*, 10, *11*; and performance culture, 162, 165–6; PODPLAYS, 44; Secret Theâtre's sites, 37, 43; TPM Theatre Beyond Walls season, 165–7; urban vs. rural spaces, 26, 43; variety of sites, 10, 37, 191, 196, 200
Situationists, 38–9, 46
Skloot, Robert, 107
slavery, 129, 132–7. See also *Angélique*
Sleep No More (Punchdrunk), 191
Slemon, Stephen, 4
slow time. *See* time and theatre
"A Small Essay on the Largeness of Light" (Moses), 16, 267–8

Smith, Ashley, 254–5
social change: actions by Facebook groups, 171–2; affect and shock to thought, 76–80; and affective vs. intellectual engagement, 68, 77–8, 125–6, 238; Brecht on, 21, 222–3; and Canadian military, 148; contestations of dominant narratives, 90; critical distance, 222–3; learning theory, 223–5; Lehmann's ethico-political, 32; making the invisible visible, 245, 251; Montreal Life Stories, 52–3; political vs. affective theatre, 67–8, 77–8; potential vs. actual, 125; role playing, 225; testing the social imagination, 25–7, 32–4; theatre's portrayal of issues on human scale, 89–90. *See also* affective encounters and theatre; empathy and identification; humanizing power of theatre; political theatre
social class. *See* class, social
social encounter. *See* community and theatre; intimacy and theatre
social learning theory, 223
social media: adding value through enrichment, 186; and belonging, 262; as dialogic communication, 185; and human need for pattern, 262; live reviews of performances, 183, 185–6; marketing with, 185–6; and performance culture, 15, 168–72; research on millennials, 181; teammates in, 171–2. *See also* performance culture; technological age
Social Works (Jackson), 8
Sontag, Susan, 80–1
Soulpepper Theatre Company: *Angels in America*, 126; BORNE, 251, *252*, *254*; *Death of a Salesman*, 126; *Kim's Convenience*, 190; partnerships, 251;

312   Index

Index

Rare, 243, 249–51, 255; revenue,
205
sound theatre, 57–8
Sowerby, Githa, 122
space, social. *See* community and
theatre; intimacy and theatre
spaces for theatre productions. *See*
sites for theatre
spectators. *See* audience
spinal injuries, people with, 251–2,
252, 254, 255
Stanislavski, Constantin, 102–4
Stephenson, Jenn, 10
The Stepmother (Sowerby), 122–3
Stevens, Wallace, 113
stillness and theatre, 86, 89
Stoppard, Tom, 124
stories and storytellers. *See* narrative
Stories Scorched from the Desert Sun
(Attarian and Van Fossen), 58–9
Stratford Festival, 5, 186, 189, 202
Stubington, Cathy, 50–1
students, elementary and secondary.
See education of children and youth
Suburban Beast, 172
Surminski, Brenda, 248–9

Taipei, Taiwan, 68
Tannahill, Jordan, 172
Tarragon Theatre, 190, 234, 250–1
technological age: audit culture
and theatre, 14, 78, 155–6; and
Brechtian defamiliarization, 22–3;
democratizing effects, 172; human
need for humanizing activities,
86–7, 106, 198; human need for
pattern, 258–62, 264; human need
for presence, 80, 183; and lack
of authentic connection, 36, 106;
and meaning in language, 107–9;
measurement and the arts, 236;
non-linear narratives, 258–60; and
performance culture, 167–72;
resurgence of narrative, 260, 261;

sense of isolation, 36, 106, 156, 198;
and slow time experiences, 86–7;
social interactions in, 183; statistics
on texting, 183; technology as
competition for theatre, 208;
theatre as antidote for, 13–14,
106–9, 111, 155; video war games,
113–16. *See also* consumerism; mass
communications; performance
culture; popular culture; social
media
technology and theatre: audio
headsets, 39, 41–2, 44–6, *47;*
cellphones, 45–6; to create intimate
connections, 46; digital vs. obsolete
technology, 38; photography, 43;
spectator participation, 43–7;
subversion of barriers to authentic
connection, 38; video chats, 45–6,
165–6
teens. *See* youth
television and film: comparison with
theatre, 79–80, 88, 244, 262–3;
and development of empathy, 240;
documentary film vs. verbatim
theatre, 93–6; film's impact on
theatre, 262; reality television, 181;
resurgence of long narrative, 259;
visual dating of film, 244
Tepperman, Julie, 10, *11,* 15,
196–212, 292. *See also* Convergence
Theatre
Terschelling Island, *30,* 31
theatre, defence of. *See* Why theatre
now?
theatre and ethnographic studies. *See*
Montreal Life Stories; vulnerable
youth, ethnographic theatre
project
theatre and other media:
comparison of verbatim theatre
with documentary film, 93–6;
comparison with film/TV, 79–80,
244, 262–3; comparison with

as safe access to, 89. *See also*
disabilities, actors with; Montreal
Life Stories; violence and trauma
vulnerable youth, ethnographic
theatre project: about, 68–70;
affect and shock to thought, 76–80;
affect theory, 72–7; international
project, 68, 69; interviews after
performances, 72–6, 78–9, 90–2;
political action, 78–9; research,
69, 72–9; respect for diversity,
70; shelter youth experiences,
69, 73–6, 94–6; social stigma and
marginalization, 76, 84–5, 90–2,
94–6; verbatim theatre, 70, 76;
workshops, 70–1; youth creativity,
71. See also *The Middle Place*

Walker, Kevin, *84*
walks, theatrical, 39–42, *40*
Walling, Savannah, 50–1
war: adaptation of *Electra* on Bosnian
massacres, 252–3; male warriors,
146; simulated combat situations
and theatrical affect, 61; stress and
extreme alertness, 61; video war
games, 113–16. *See also* military;
Montreal Life Stories; violence and
trauma
War in the Mind (film), 150
Westlake, E.J., 171
Westwood, Marvin, 150
Why theatre now?: about, 3–4,
6–7, 13, 16, 126–7; to allow
authentic human connection, 37;
to awaken the audience, 245–7;
to be a bulwark against despair,
211; because human life matters,
244–5, 250–1, 255; because it does
not date, 244; to belong, 44, 188,
262; to change stereotypes, 153–4;
to change the way people relate,
35; to connect to place and others,
36–7, 44; to contest dominant

narratives, 14, 90, 129, 131–4,
136, 137, 140; for development of
empathy, 182–3; for education and
community development, 213–14,
217–19, 225–6; to examine
roles as social actors, 90, 131; to
experience common meaning or
spirit, 266–8; to experience now,
244; to experience pattern, 260–2,
264; to experience presence and
focus, 44, 244; to experience
shared intentionality, 49–50, 53,
60–1; to experience spiritual
awakening, 247; to experience
witnessing, 90, 137–9, 150–4, 255,
257; to feel emotion, 144, 156–7;
to humanize, 84–8; to make the
invisible visible, 245, 251; to make
the world whole, 258–9; to model
new ways, 22, 33–4; to reconstitute
life for our reflection, 126–7;
to repair the world, 210–11; to
rethink assumptions, 124–5; to
search for truth, 90, 239–40; to
transcend self, 35–6, 49–50; to
witness a human howl of assertion,
255
Wikwemikong Unceded Indian
Reserve, 23–4
Wilde, Oscar, 124
Wilde-Peltier, Jessica, *28*
Williams, Kenneth, 217
Williams, Raymond, 50
Willis, Aaron, 15, 196–212, 293. *See
also* Convergence Theatre
Winterlab, Victoria, 37
women. *See* females and feminism
Women and War project, 252
wonder and awe. *See* transcendence
and theatre
Wong, Adrienne, 44–6, 48n6
Workman, Hawksley, 190
workshops and cooperation,
70–1, 126

316   Index